The Indian Contingent

The Indian Contingent

The Forgotten Muslim Soldiers of Dunkirk

Ghee Bowman

First published 2020

The History Press
97 St George's Place, Cheltenham,
Gloucestershire, GL50 3QB
www.thehistorypress.co.uk

British Library Cataloguing in Publication Data.
A catalogue record for this book is available from the British Library.

ISBN 978 0 7509 9379 1

Typesetting and origination by The History Press
Printed and bound in Great Britain by TJ International Ltd

For Rebecca

In my mind, I ultimately see you now as an eternal
    wanderer of English verse,
the eardstapa, far beyond all exile and mortality,
forever alive and forever at peace, striding those woods,
your countenance shining with a soft ethereal light.

From 'In Memoriam: Muslim Peace Memorial, Woking, 2018' by Omer Tarin.

Written and read in July 2018 to honour a great-uncle, Sepoy Sikandar Khan of 82nd Punjabis who died in Britain and is commemorated at the Muslim Peace Memorial Garden at Horsell Common in Woking.

Contents

Illustrations

Note on terms used

Indian soldiers' names were not always written down in full, nor accurately transliterated. There were many variations of the common name 'Muhammad', for example. Generally I have followed the variant used in any given document, so you will find Mohd, Muhammad, Mohammed used here. Soldiers are identified by the rank they held at the time, even if they rose to higher rank later (as many of them did).

These men were part of a special force attached to the BEF that was called 'Force K6'. After their landing in Britain they were more often known as the 'Indian Contingent'. I have used both terms.

The RIASC was part of what was generally known by Britishers as the 'Indian Army', the soldiers coming from India and all its officers (until 1919 at least) from the UK. This is a somewhat contested term – it was not a national army in the sense that Bose's Indian National Army was, so some writers of South Asian heritage prefer to call it the British Indian Army, or even simply the British Army. In general, though, I have stuck with tradition and referred to the Indian Army and the British Army as separate entities. Even when they were attached to the BEF in France or British infantry divisions in the UK, K6 never stopped being part of the Indian Army.

The war in which they fought has been referred to by some critics as the 'imperial' war, and it certainly had many imperial dimensions, but I have used the more common and widely recognised term 'Second World War'.

'India' refers to the pre-Partition territory, which includes the modern states of Pakistan and Bangladesh. I have used place names from that time: Bombay rather than Mumbai, for example.

Maps

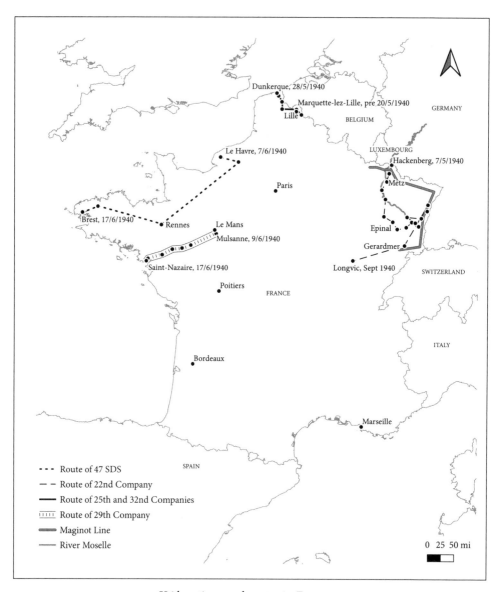

K6 locations and routes in France

K6 locations in Britain

Royal Indian Army Service Corps ranks in 1939

Rank	Abbreviation	British Army equivalent
Commissioned Officers		
Lieutenant Colonel	Lt Col.	
Major		
Captain		
Lieutenant	Lt	
2nd Lieutenant	2/lt	
Viceroy's Commissioned Officers (VCOs)		
Risaldar Major or Subedar Major		
Risaldar or Subedar		
Jemadar	Jem	
Warrant Officers		
Sub-Conductor	Sub-cdr	Warrant Officer
Non-Commissioned Officers (NCOs)		
Dafadar	Daf	Sergeant
Quartermaster Dafadar	QMD	Quartermaster Sergeant
Naik	Nk	Corporal
Lance Naik	L/nk	Lance Corporal
Enlisted men		
Driver		Private (RIASC)
Sepoy		Private (infantry)
Sowar		Private (cavalry)
Followers and tradesmen		
Maulvi, clerk		
Blacksmith, carpenter, cook		
Saddler, hammerman, tailor, barber, bellows boy, bootmaker, farrier, groom, mess servant		
Dhobi, water carrier		
Sweeper		

Glossary and abbreviations

angrezi	British or English (Urdu)
ARD	Advanced Remount Depot
ATC	Animal Transport Company
atta	wholemeal wheat flour
BBC	British Broadcasting Corporation
BEF	British Expeditionary Force
bhisti	water carrier (Urdu)
CSDIC	Combined Services Detailed Interrogation Centre
durbar	regular meeting of Indian Army unit to ask questions and air grievances
ECO	Emergency Commissioned Officer
EIC	East India Company
gora/gore	white person/people (Urdu)
GTR	Grand Trunk Road
HQ	headquarters
IAVC	Indian Army Veterinary Corps
ICF	Indian Comforts Fund
ICO	Indian Commissioned Officer
iftar	breaking the fast during the month of Ramadan
IGH	Indian General Hospital
INA	Indian National Army
izzat	honour (Urdu)
kanal	measure of land, eight to an acre
lascar	sailor from Asia in British merchant navy (Urdu)
K6	A force of four companies of RIASC mules and drivers attached to the BEF
KCO	King's Commissioned Officer
mabap	parents, mother and father (Urdu)
maulvi	imam or chaplain

MBE	Member of the British Empire
MP	Member of Parliament
MT	motor transport
NCO	non-commissioned officer
NWFP	North West Frontier Province
Oflag	German POW camp for officers (*Offizierlager*)
pagri	turban (Urdu)
POW	prisoner of war
PT	physical training
QMD	Quartermaster Dafadar
RAF	Royal Air Force
RASC	Royal Army Service Corps (British)
RAVC	Royal Army Veterinary Corps
RE	Royal Engineers
RIASC	Royal Indian Army Service Corps
SDS	Supply Depot Section
Stalag	German POW camp (*Stammlager*)
syed	descendant of the Prophet Muhammad
TB	tuberculosis
VAS	veterinary assistant surgeon
VCO	Viceroy's Commissioned Officer
WO	War Office
WVS	Women's Voluntary Service
YMCA	Young Men's Christian Association
ZFI	Zentrale Freies Indien (Free India Centre)

Foreword

This book is a labour of love. On the trail of the Indian Contingent, Ghee Bowman has travelled thousands of miles across Britain, Europe, India and Pakistan. He has tracked down lost family archives and photographs from private albums, and conducted interviews with the descendants of soldiers who thought their family histories had been rendered irrelevant to the greater story of Britain's involvement in the Second World War. He has also written a riveting and moving account of these men's lives, which has enabled him to get much closer than any previous writer to understanding the Indian soldier's experience in Europe in the 1940s. Apart from the character Kip in Michael Ondaatje's novel *The English Patient*, and a handful of historical studies which have simply acknowledged the presence of Indians in Europe, there has been very little integration of this experience into the story of the British Home Front in the Second World War, fictional or otherwise. This book changes all that and is therefore, in short, groundbreaking.

There is plenty of gripping military history here – no one should ever have to ask again if there were really Indians at Dunkirk, and their evacuation is immaculately researched. The same is true of the gruelling march of 22nd Company, who were trapped in France, and the later escapes by some of the men from the German prisoner-of-war camps, on foot to Switzerland and beyond. But for me, the most striking episodes of the book are about human relationships. By understanding soldiers lives as messy, complicated and, above all, human, Ghee avoids the trap of describing the men he writes about as simplistic collective groups. Although they were predominantly Muslim and from present-day Pakistan, they were many other things besides. The thing which comes across most clearly is the men's distinctive individuality, and the variety of experiences that they had while in Britain. The men of Force K6 included poets and musicians, cooks and carpenters and a veterinarian. They were also writers, cinema-lovers, boyfriends and parents.

Most striking, and cheering to read, are the stories of friendship and everyday encounters with local people, often in small towns and rural locations in Britain including Crickhowell in Wales, St Austell in Cornwall, Colchester in Essex and Lairg in the Scottish Highlands. The interviews Ghee has conducted with the men's families and the people they met and lived alongside give his book a much richer texture than much military history.

Another point I would like to stress is just how tricky it is to do this kind of research. Turning up in Pakistan to do historical research requires serious commitment and patience. There was no ready store of neat archives waiting for Ghee; he has had to dig around in many places and speak to hundreds of people, carefully listening to what they wanted and needed to say, and he has pieced all this together into this colourful jigsaw.

There is a strongly humane and universalist impulse running through the book, alongside a desire to re-remember more effectively – to open up the possibility of seeing the war in a different way and to move beyond simplistic memorialising, as Ghee has put it – and a conviction in the power of public history to challenge and transform racism and stereotypes. It is strange to think that this story of the Indian Contingent was once well known in Britain, that many British people had seen and welcomed Indian soldiers during the Second World War, and that newsreels and magazines had frequently projected their image. This public memory then lapsed, and was overwritten by more exclusivist versions of an island alone in wartime. This book, then, is an act of recovery. It tells us a great deal about what we might have lost over the years to the process of slimming down and simplifying some elements of war history.

This book deserves a wide readership and to be in the vanguard of shaping new histories of the Second World War. There have been many new attempts to globalise war history in recent years, by returning to histories of experiences across Asia and Africa, and Ghee's book brings us right to the shores of Britain itself. I hope Ghee's work will inform films, documentaries, TV productions, memorialisation, museums and school textbooks for many years to come. There has never been a better time to turn to these forgotten histories. These seem to me to be exactly the sort of stories that Britain needs, that people want to know, and that give us a chance to move forward in the twenty-first century.

Yasmin Khan, 2020

Prologue

On the beach

Remember that old Indian soldier
When the war that he fought has been won.[1]

Bray Dunes, Tuesday 28 May 1940. The northernmost point of France, just a few miles from Belgium and fifty miles from the south-east corner of England. This pretty seaside resort, with its restaurants, striped canopies and miles of golden sands has been transformed by an accident of history into a Dantean vision of hell. A vast plume of black smoke rises from the burning oil refinery in the harbour to the left, the smell is everywhere. In front, the sea is littered with wrecks and burning ships, while small boats nip back and forth to the sands. On the beach, tired, despondent Tommies in their khaki battledress and tin helmets line up patiently to board a boat that will take them to home, a square meal and a quiet bed. Overhead is the occasional Messerschmitt or Focke-Wulf, or worst of all, a Stuka, with its deafening, frightful 'Jericho Trumpet' siren, fitted deliberately to cause panic, diving down nearly vertically to drop its 250kg bomb on the dunes. And behind, a very few miles behind, the might of the German army is closing in, harassing the French and British rearguard, besieging the city of Lille, advancing in a seemingly endless victorious wave through Belgium and northern France.

This is the Battle of Dunkirk, the third day of Operation Dynamo, the 'Nine Days Wonder' that will see 338,000 Allied troops evacuated from under the noses of the Germans. Eighteen thousand men will be evacuated on this day, 6,000 from the beaches to the east of the town, 12,000 from the harbour. The myth of Dunkirk has many elements, one of which is that most of the men were taken from the beaches by small craft manned by civilians. In fact, the vast majority were taken from the harbour, via the two *jetées* or moles that stick out into the channel to protect the harbour entrance. Even the very name of the battle is mythical: the beaches actually belong to the suburbs of Malo-les-Bains, Leffrinckoucke, Zuydcoote and La Panne, across the border in Belgium. And the town itself is spelt 'Dunkerque' in French: 'Dunkirk' is an English spelling.

On the 28th, the coastal steamer *Abukir* was the last British ship to evacuate soldiers and civilians from the Belgian port of Ostende, twenty-five miles up the coast. As it left the harbour it was torpedoed by a German E-boat, and most of those on board, including a party of Belgian nuns, were killed. The day before had been the last day of the stand of the British and French garrison down the coast at Calais: they surrendered at dawn and marched off into captivity. The 28th was to see a massacre of French and British troops in a barn at Wormhoudt. This was a bloody time in the history of the département du Nord, a time that lingers in the collective memory of France, Britain and Germany.

Among the men evacuated from the beaches that night were 300 who looked very different from their boatmates. Dressed in khaki, yes, but a long, shirt-like *kurtah* rather than a short battledress blouse. Some wore the standard tin helmets on their head, some wore forage caps and some wore a *pagri* or turban. All had nut-brown faces, most had moustaches. All but four of them were Muslims. They carried no weapons, for they had been issued with none when they left far-off Punjab six months previously. These were the men of 25th Animal Transport Company of the Royal Indian Army Service Corps, who had travelled 7,000 miles with their mules to help the British Army. They were part of the so-called 'Force K6', also known as the 'Indian Contingent'. They marched along the beach on the afternoon of 28 May, sepoys and drivers, naiks and dafadars, blacksmiths and carpenters and cooks, and one imam.

One of them was Jemadar Nizam Din, who would stay with them all the way through until their return to India in February 1944, rising through the ranks until he obtained a commission as a lieutenant. His image and his voice are preserved for ever in a ciné clip at the Imperial War Museum, filmed on the day he reached India again after more than four years away from home. Bellows boy Mehtab Khan was there on 28 May, a man whose job was to blow air to superheat the fire that forged shoes for the mules. Besides his job, he had a talent for hockey that he would put into use playing against a youth club in Devon a year later. And

24-year-old Muhammad Sarwar of Shahpur was there; he died in hospital in 1941 and is buried in a cemetery in the Welsh garrison town of Brecon, with a view of the hills to the south. At their head was the magnificent figure of Major Mohammed Akbar Khan, at that time the senior-most Indian in the Indian Army. A veteran of the First World War who had joined the army as a humble sepoy, he towered over his soldiers, being six foot two inches tall and broad to boot. He had been one of the first Indians to be made an officer in 1919, and he would go on to be the senior officer in the new Pakistan Army in 1947, eventually dying in 1986 in his house Lal Kothi in Karachi, surrounded by his loving family.

The men of 25th Company had spent all of 1940 so far in northern France, in the village of Marquette-lez-Lille, just north of the city of Lille. There they were part of the small British Expeditionary Force (BEF), which was tasked with holding a fifteen-mile frontage of the Allied line. Despite the severe winter – one of the coldest of the twentieth century – they had lived happily around the Dillies Farm on the Canal de Roubaix, home of the mayor and his wife. They had exercised and fed their 384 mules, loaded their GS Mark VII carts with barbed wire and steel stanchions and sacks of cement for the British infantry and engineers around them. They had met the local French inhabitants and charmed them with their weekly gymkhanas, where they performed tricks on muleback and danced bhangra to the music of the *chimta* and the *dhol*. Major Akbar noted dryly in his memoir later that they 'drew hundreds of French crowds … from far and wide', and went on to write: 'The number of spectators grew enormously, especially when the spring season came. This was the phony war we were fighting.'[2]

All of that changed on 10 May, when the Germans attacked France and the Low Countries. The BEF advanced into Belgium to meet them at the river Dyle, east of Brussels. The 25th Company were left behind, without clear orders. But five days later the British Army retreated towards France: the Germans had progressed so quickly, and burst through the Ardennes forest, where nobody had expected them. Within the space of two weeks, from being part of a well-ordered, disciplined, multi-national army, the sepoys of 25th Company were part of a chaotic retreat to the coast. Communications were inefficient, with no decent radio network operating. Fifth Columnists, parachutists and spies were suspected everywhere, although there is hard evidence of only a few. The civilian population was on the move, in large numbers, blocking the roads and slowing down military traffic. And the Luftwaffe was everywhere, bombing and strafing and causing panic. The German policy of blitzkrieg depended as much on damaging morale as it did on actual military strength or tactics.

The next two weeks were some of the most dramatic in these soldiers' lives. After a time waiting, unsure of what to do, they headed for the coast, harried by German aircraft and nearly encircled by tanks. With the area containing the BEF tightening like a trap, hundreds of thousands of French and British troops withdrew to Dunkirk, the last port open to Allied ships. The 25th Company managed to get to the beach and were taken off on 29 May. In a front-page article in the *Lincolnshire Echo* with the headline 'BEF Men Come Home in Thousands: Most May Get Away', an unnamed journalist reporting from Dover wrote: 'I saw four bareheaded Indians. A movement control officer said he believed that all the personnel of the Indian Mule Contingent had now arrived in England safely.'[3] This was far from the truth: in fact only two companies had got away. The other 1,000 men were still in France, and their journeys were unfinished.

The four-year story of the men of 25th Company and their comrades is one of the great untold stories of the war. Their friendships and the racism they encountered, their struggles to find the right kind of food, the mosques they attended and improvised, the women they loved and the babies they left behind were all part of a unique experience of soldiering. They included in their number the only units of the Indian Army ever sent to Britain, and therefore mirrored the experiences of hundreds of thousands of British soldiers who had travelled in the opposite direction. They spent time in some obscure corners of the British Isles – Kinlochleven, Steep Holm, Meavy Bridge and Nantmor – and formed strong bonds with farmers and children and women throughout. The men of 22nd Company, however, didn't make it to the UK until the very end of the war, having been captured in France in June 1940 and spending nearly five years in prisoner-of-war (POW) camps. They left behind fifty-eight of their friends in cemeteries in Britain, France and Germany, men who were bombed by the Luftwaffe, suffered from accidents or died from tuberculosis. Their stories shall be told in this book.

The exploits of these extraordinary Punjabis have never been collected or told until now. Christopher Nolan, who made the 2017 smash-hit film *Dunkirk,* along with every other filmmaker or writer who has dealt with Dunkirk, left them out. Although they were well known in Britain in the 1940s – featuring in cinema newsreels, newspapers and magazines, on the BBC and even in a poster about Waterloo Station – they were forgotten afterwards, and have languished in the backwaters of collective memory since then. The very presence of Indians at Dunkirk, Monte Cassino and other battles was denied on British TV in the late 1990s. This book aims to reclaim them from the backwater and reinstate them in the mainstream: part of the current of recognition of Commonwealth and global contributions to the Second World War.

1

Seven thousand miles to help

A tree whose girth fills one's embrace sprang from a downy sprout;
A terrace nine stories high arose from a layer of dirt;
A journey of a thousand leagues began with a single step.[1]

Sixteen-year-old Aurangzeb, from the quiet Punjabi village of Rajoha, did not realise that his life would change forever during the monsoon season of 1939. The youngest of four brothers, he had been named after the great Mughal emperor, his name meaning 'Ornament of the Throne' – perhaps his parents had high hopes for his future. As in so many Punjabi families, all four brothers went into the army, one of them reaching the grand old age of 82 after his retirement. At the start of September 1939, keen to see the world and to start earning a wage, Aurangzeb heard that the Royal Indian Army Service Corps (RIASC) was recruiting, as India had just declared war. He travelled 200 miles to the city of Lahore and signed up as a bellows boy – part of a team making shoes for horses and mules. Just a few weeks later he was in Europe. According to family tradition, this bellows boy used to write poetry in Urdu or Punjabi in his breaks from shoeing and would send the poems back to Punjab, where they were kept by family members.[2]

In March 1942, a telegram arrived in Rajoha from Army HQ, informing the family that Aurangzeb had died in Wales, many thousands of miles away. He was only 18 years old. The hospital records show that he died of tuberculosis, a common complaint among the men of K6, and he was buried three days later in Brecon.[3] Forty years afterwards, in 1982, his nephew was in Britain on duty with the Pakistan Navy and tried to find his grave. He searched in vain in London, not realising that the site was actually 170 miles away to the west, so he finally gave up in sorrow and took a photo of himself outside a cemetery in London. In 2018, I showed Aurangzeb's relatives a photograph of the cemetery in Brecon, with irises growing around his grave, and a cluster of red poppies placed by the local British Legion. They were visibly moved by the picture and were reassured to know that the Commonwealth War Graves Commission look after his grave with respect. The poetry-writing 18-year-old bellows boy is remembered to this day in a quiet village in Pakistan and a garrison town in Wales.

The process that brought Aurangzeb to Wales started on 3 September 1939. Prime Minister Neville Chamberlain's much-quoted speech that took Britain into the war was heard not just in Glasgow and Godalming, but in Dar es Salaam and in Dunedin, in Labrador and in Lahore. From the outset, this was an imperial war: the countries of the British Empire were just as involved as those of the British Isles. Some parts of the Empire were given a choice and joined in without hesitation. Such was the case with the Dominions – the white settler colonies which governed themselves within the Commonwealth – South Africa, Canada, New Zealand and Australia. The subject colonies in Africa, the West Indies and the Pacific, meanwhile, were given no choice – they entered the war when Britain did. The same was true for India.

In undivided British India – the territories that would later become India, Pakistan and Bangladesh – opinion was split. Mahatma Gandhi, the spiritual leader of many Indian nationalists, expressed sympathy for the Allies in general and the Poles under attack, but non-violence remained his core belief.[4] On 14 September, the Congress Party, which had led the nationalist movement since the 1920s under its leader Jawaharlal Nehru, issued a manifesto which declared: 'If the war is to defend the status quo – imperialist possessions, colonies, vested interests and privileges – then India can have nothing to do with it. If, however, the issue is democracy and a world order based on democracy then India is intensely interested in it.'[5] Congress was against Fascism, but also against the imperialism that the British Raj represented and it would only support the British war effort if the end of that Raj was unambiguously in view. The previous president of the Congress Party, Subhas Chandra Bose, a balding and bespectacled Bengali who still had influence and followers, took a much harder line and pressed for active civil disobedience against British rule as a route to independence.

At the other end of the spectrum was Sir Sikandar Hayat Khan, the prime minister of Punjab, the northern province that was home to most of the men of Force K6. He was a staunch Empire loyalist, known as the 'soldier premier' who made sure that his sons enlisted in the army.[6] In Punjab, Hayat Khan's Unionist Party had won most Muslim votes at the recent elections. Elsewhere in the country it was Muhammad Ali Jinnah's Muslim League which was most popular among Indian Muslims. At this stage Jinnah was cautiously supportive of the British war effort, for he saw within it an opportunity for advancement of the political ideals of the League. India's Muslims were a minority, keen to assert their rights and to be seen as equal to Hindus. Jinnah's hope was that by active participation in the war effort, the Muslim route to equality in politics could be assured. The Indian people at large, meanwhile, may not have known where Poland was, and may not have cared very much at that stage, but by the time of the termination of hostilities six long years later, they had come to know the names of many obscure corners of the world – Keren, Monte Cassino, El Alamein and Imphal among them – where the men of the Indian Army had fought and died.

As governments and people around the Empire decided their response, the British and French army planners set to work. When Poland fell it was still a small war fought on European soil and showed no sign of turning into a conflict that would involve every continent and almost every country of the world. In many ways, the planners thought, this was to be a rerun of the Great War a generation before. In place of the continuous line of trenches stretching from the English Channel to the Alps, the French had constructed a concrete hedge all along their border with Germany – the Maginot Line. Opposite it, along the Rhine and the border with the region of Lorraine, stood the German equivalent, the Siegfried Line. These two opposing barriers were designed to be impregnable, but the gap between the end of the Maginot Line and the Channel was the weak spot, undefended by any permanent forts, for it ran along the border of neutral Belgium. The Allied planners predicted the Germans would flout Belgian neutrality, as they had in 1914, and throw a right hook through the Low Countries. Therefore, as well as the French armies along their northern border, the British would take station there. The Allied strategy revolved around holding the Germans with the combination of the Maginot Line and a strong force in the north, thus keeping France inviolable while the Allies built up their reserves.

The French were defending their *patrie* – their homeland – although one fifth of the French Army were from colonies in North and West Africa, Madagascar and Indo-China.[7] The men of the BEF, meanwhile, were not defending their homes but standing at a distance, holding a section of the line around Lille, away from the German border.

* * * * *

Such an army would need a lot of feeding. Napoleon Bonaparte famously said that an army 'marches on its stomach', and over the centuries a lot of effort has been expended in order to keep that stomach full of bread, and the corresponding rifle full of bullets. By 1939, supply was recognised as the core business of war. German Field Marshal Erwin Rommel said, 'the battle is fought and decided by the quartermasters before the shooting begins.'[8] The ratio of combat soldiers to non-combatants could be surprisingly high – one writer put it at 1:12 for the US Army.[9] Each front-line hero needed many more heroes of the rear echelon to support him, and those heroes are always overlooked by historians.[10] The BEF's supplies would come by rail, not from the nearest ports at Calais and Dunkirk, but hundreds of miles from Cherbourg, Nantes and St Nazaire.[11] The city of Le Mans in north-west France became a crucial staging area, and the headquarters for the lines of communication. All these places would become significant to the Punjabi sepoys of Force K6.

Transporting the supplies of food, fuel and ammunition would be undertaken by trains and lorries; at least that was the British plan. In contrast with the Great War, where animal transport was used extensively on the Western Front, the idea was that the BEF would be fully mechanised with 'not a horse in the force'.[12] The question became how to transport the supplies the last mile for delivery to the front-line troops, especially if conditions were muddy, frozen or densely wooded. This is where the mules came in. Animal transport, in fact, turned out to be a decisive feature of the Second World War, belying the blitzkrieg image of fighter planes and tanks. Over the course of the war, the humble mule, hybrid offspring of male donkey and female horse, was a crucial element in delivering supplies. This was a surprise to some:

Few people at this stage would have guessed that once again that sturdy, strong, rather lovable yet surly animal of uncertain moods, the mule, was to provide the backbone of the pack transport units, which were to make it possible for the army to advance in the steaming jungles of Burma and on the snow-clad hills of Italy.[13]

The British Army was not the only one to make use of such animals. The Germans had only sixteen out of 103 divisions fully motorised in 1939.[14] Their infantry marched on foot through France and into Russia, and most supplies were carried on horse-drawn wagons. The Soviets similarly relied on animals, and it was only the United States that got close to fielding a fully motorised army.[15] The technology was far more mixed than the commonly used photographs would show us: the Maginot Line was accompanied by the mule, the Panzer by the *panje* cart.

In France in 1939 the British transport need was identified by one officer: 'when the thaw comes, lorries will be too heavy. I'm going to get some mules.'[16] Thus, as early as 31 August, before war was declared, General Sydney Muspratt of the India Office in London passed on a 'tentative enquiry' to India about '2000 trained pack mules about 13.1 to 13.5 hands [high] with pack saddles but without personnel'.[17] A handwritten note in the file a few days later added that the figure of 2,000 was 'the first instalment', with a built-in assumption of casualties of one third. The expectation and all the planning was for a long and bloody stay in northern France. At this stage the request was still for animals only, but as the autumn progressed the War Office realised that animal-handling skills did not exist in the British Army; there was only a single company in the British Royal Army Service Corps (RASC) trained to work with mules, with only twenty-five animals and a small nucleus of men.[18] In this way was the plan for Force K6 born.[19]

The orders to prepare and assemble the force went out from Indian Army Headquarters to garrisons across Punjab on 16 November.[20] In the main army base at Rawalpindi, at the entrance to the Khyber Pass at Landikotal and at Ambala, eighty miles from Simla on the vast North Indian plains, the companies of the RIASC checked their equipment and vaccinated their men against tetanus and the animals against glanders – a bacterial disease of the lungs that can cause death within days. The core of the force was four animal transport companies – 22nd, 25th, 29th and 32nd – with around 300 men and as many mules in each company. As the force was designed to be self-contained, there was also a reinforcement unit to fill the human gaps created by illness or casualties and an advanced remount depot (ARD), which provided the same service for animals. The 47 Supply Depot Section (SDS) under Major John Finlay would supply food, fodder and other necessities to the men and animals, an Indian General Hospital (IGH) looked after the sick men, and the Headquarters (HQ) were in overall command. Right from the start, the vision was for a force that would be both militarily effective and a propaganda tool, a chance to show the world the best of the Indian Army. Muspratt at the India Office knew that these sepoys would be under the media microscope as soon as they arrived in Europe, so their uniforms, their conduct and their military effectiveness would be taken as examples of the greater whole. Men were therefore transferred from other mule companies to bring the four companies up to strength. For ease of administration and rations, it was decided that all personnel should be Muslims from Punjab and the North West Frontier – 'Punjabi Mohammedans' in the parlance of the army. The hustle and bustle of the Punjab military cantonments took on an extra layer of busy-ness as carts were dismantled for the rail journey and forms filled in for direct payment of wages to families.[21]

Each animal transport company was reinforced into a structure laid out in a 'Special War Establishment' document. The commanders knew that the companies would be spread out and operating independently, so every company contained a mix of skills, each man with a clear delineation of tasks and responsibilities such that the whole was a multi-skilled team living and working together in harmony. Most of the men were enrolled as part of the army; a few were there as followers or tradesmen, such as bellows boy Aurangzeb and mess servant Buland Khan. About 60 per cent of the men of each company were ranked as drivers. This was a highly skilled job, requiring a working knowledge of mules and how to get the best from them, combined with an understanding of loading and handling for both draught (using carts) and pack formation (with loads directly on the mules' backs). Crucially, they needed to be able to carry out these duties in a variety of terrains and weather conditions. The basic

The basic unit of K6 in France: a cart, two mules and a driver. 32nd Company at Bourghelles, 10 February 1940.

unit of the force as originally constituted was therefore a driver, two mules and a GS Mark VII cart, capable of carrying a load up to 800lbs (362kg) on road or track.[22] Six such cart teams made up a section, commanded by a lance naik – a non-commissioned officer (NCO) with one stripe, the equivalent of a lance corporal in the British Army. Four of these seven-man sections were grouped together into a half-troop, commanded by a naik (corporal), and two such half-troops made a complete troop of sixty men, with ninety-six mules, and a jemadar and dafadar (sergeant) in charge.[23] Each company consisted of four troops, plus around seventy specialist tradesmen, 'the non-combatants who made the Indian Army function', whose jobs revolved around the care and maintenance of the men, the animals and their equipment.[24]

As well as the three blacksmiths, three hammermen and four bellows boys in each company, there were also nine farriers, whose job was to fit shoes on the animals and look after hooves. Twelve grooms were present in each company, to care for the officers' steeds, and to act as servant or batman for that officer. There were also four men with veterinary roles, attached members of the Indian Army Veterinary Corps (IAVC), who were kept busy, to judge from the frequent reports of ringworm, strangles and other maladies. The eight saddlers and two carpenters worked hard maintaining and repairing all the equipment necessary for carrying loads, and the company quartermaster (a white British warrant officer) was extremely busy with supplies for animal, man and machine. This role was something of a bridge between white officers and Indian men – sub-conductor William Bosworth was described by an Indian colleague thus: 'He spoke Urdu fluently like natives would and swore in Punjabi at his seniors, who would not understand. He was a good instructor, teaching me tricks of the trade.'[25]

Additionally, four cooks acted as *halal* butchers and prepared their meat, *dhal* and chapattis. These men and their work were to become favourite subjects for photographers in Europe. A tailor or *darzi* and two bootmakers looked after the soldiers' clothes and footwear, while a dhobi washed their clothes. Another subject favoured by photographers was the hair cutting and shaving performed by the two barbers. Four *bhistis* brought water for the men, and also for the animals when needed, and may have reminded British onlookers of Gunga Din, the water carrier created by Kipling in his 1890 poem and reinvented in a 1930s Hollywood movie.[26] There were three medical staff in each company, part of the Indian Army Medical Corps attached to the RIASC. A single clerk had to keep up with the correspondence and paperwork, and four sweepers cleaned up the rubbish. A key role in each company was the maulvi or prayer-leader, sometimes referred to as a 'religious advisor'.[27] Each company therefore resembled a Punjabi village transplanted into French territory (minus women and children), self-sufficient in every physical, medical and spiritual need. Living together in close proximity all the time meant that wherever in the world they were posted, they took a little bit of Punjab with them.

Alongside the traditional officer ranks of lieutenant, captain and major was another stratum of command unique to the Indian Army – the VCO or Viceroy's Commissioned Officer. Each of the four troops of sixty men was commanded by a jemadar, a role that in a British unit would have been taken by a 2nd lieutenant. There was a risaldar in each company, and a risaldar major attached to the Force HQ. These VCOs were vital go-betweens for the men and the officers, acting as something like cultural interpreters. Jemadar Nasir Ahmad of the 47 SDS was a prime example – smart and suave and well-educated, he spoke fluent English with barely an accent.[28] The K6 commander told an officers' conference in 1941: 'VCOs must pull their weight. It is their duty to keep a finger on the pulse of personnel under their command, to explain to them the difference between customs in this country and in India.'[29]

Without the forty-eight VCOs, K6 would have been unmanageable, with little understanding by the officers of the grievances or state of mind of the men, whilst the men would have lacked the insight into motivations that the VCOs were able to interpret for them. Yet the VCOs were seen as less important than the British warrant officers, or as a newly commissioned British officer put it, 'these gentlemen, often described as the backbone of the Indian Army, were in a way comparable to NCOs in the British Army, except that they were half-officers, being entitled to salutes from Indian Other Ranks, but not from British Other Ranks.'[30] The racial attitudes that underpinned the Indian Army are evident in this in-between status.

Two weeks after their arrival in France, a British newsreel film crew visited 32nd Company in their positions at Orchies, south of Lille and just a few miles from the Belgian border. In the unedited footage a sepoy smiles at the camera, another eats from a small bowl of curry using chapattis, and then a colleague makes a humorous remark about the camera and all the men smile.[31] Straight after that, another man walks through the shot, holding a brush over his shoulder and a bag in his left hand. This shadowy figure was a sweeper, possibly Paltoo by name, the lowest of the low in the K6 hierarchy, whose job was to sweep up and dispose of all the camp waste, in particular the human and animal excrement.[32] At this stage there were around forty such men in the whole force, mostly Hindus, Sikhs and Christians, some of the tiny percentage who were not Muslims. Theirs was a skilled and specialised job. The great Punjabi writer Mulk Raj Anand wrote his first novel about a sweeper called Bakha who 'surveyed the courtyard with the pertinacity of his sweeper's instinct'.[33] This is not a depiction of a stupid or ignorant man, rather somebody who takes pride in his work. Force K6's commander wrote in 1942, when there was a shortage of such men, that a sweeper was 'an essential sanitary tradesman. If his work is not done then the health of the unit will suffer'.[34] However much they may have been perceived as inferior, these 'untouchable' men were every bit as involved in the life of the company as anyone else.

At the other end of the chain of command from the humble sweeper stood their commanding officer, Lt Col. Hills. Reginald William Welfare Hills was the very model of an Indian Army lieutenant colonel. Like so many K6 officers, he was a veteran of the Great War, having served in the ranks, been wounded and gassed twice and awarded the Military Cross in 1918.[35] He married in 1919 and joined the Indian Army in 1921, a common progression for British officers without a great deal of money, as the prospects were better in India. He rose steadily up the ranks of the RIASC, and in 1939 at the age of 45 he was promoted to lieutenant colonel to take command of Force K6. He was a serious man, a committed and hardworking officer. He was also a bit of an adventurer, taking an 'educational' car journey across Asia in 1935 with his wife Sylvia, visiting Damascus, Lebanon and Athens, then 'by steamship from Athens to Istamboul and from the latter place to Buda-pest by railway'.[36] He had a love of the written word, for his war diary entries, letters and reports are long and detailed, but generally reflect his 'official' voice, with only a rare glimpse of the man himself. His reports were not always appreciated by his superiors. A note in the India Office file remarks on his detailed September 1940 report, saying, 'there is little of real interest in this report, which is largely padding'.[37] Leaving that aside, Hills was a man of many skills, able to deal with the top brass and the media, as well as the sepoys and officers under his command. In fact, it seems that he had a genuinely caring attitude towards the men and was tuned into their welfare. Following the first deaths of his men in Britain he took great pains to ensure the men were commemorated in the appropriate Islamic way. His attitude was also touched with the paternalism of the British Indian Army. A common expression for the role of the officer was *mabap*, the Urdu word for mother and father. Thus in April 1941, when expecting the arrival of reinforcements, he wrote: 'thank goodness WO

[War Office] have agreed to my new children coming.'[38] Old-fashioned, paternalistic, intolerant of error he may have been, but Colonel Hills was also caring and sensitive towards the men under his command.

Having taken command of this new force, Hills flew from India to London on 11 December to receive detailed orders in person.[39] Meanwhile the various units loaded onto trains across Punjab and set off for Bombay in the first days of December. The 32nd Company took two long trains to carry them from Landi Kotal near Peshawar. Each train had twenty-nine carriages, twenty for the animals, five for baggage and one for cooking, with all the people riding in just three carriages.[40] Despite the best planning, the journey was not without incident. One soldier had to have a tooth extracted, and Cook Baluch Khan jammed his finger in a window and was evacuated off the train.[41] A story that was widely reported later was of two sweepers who had alighted to buy cigarettes at a station, only to watch their train steaming away southwards. Keen not to lose their comrades or be abandoned, they hailed a taxi and caught up with the train at the next station.[42] Descending from the hills of northern Punjab to the city of Lahore, the trains took them via New Delhi, then south through the fertile plains of north India. They arrived at Bombay on 8 and 9 December, into the hustle and bustle of a major seaport, where they unloaded and transferred on to the four waiting ships at Alexandra docks.

* * * * *

As the convoy steamed out of Bombay at eight in the morning on 10 December, we can wonder what the men were thinking. For the twenty white British officers on board this would have been a familiar voyage, but most of the Punjabi soldiers had not seen the sea before, let alone the wide Indian Ocean. Some, like Major Mohammed Akbar Khan, were veterans of the Great War and would have regaled their comrades with stories of sailing to war in 1914. At this stage they did not know their destination – it could have been south then east to Singapore or west to the Suez Canal and Egypt. They were probably worried about the German U-boats that were already ravaging shipping in the Atlantic.

In order to avoid giving away their position to the enemy, rubbish could only be thrown overboard thrice a day at stated times.[43] These precautions were probably justified: only three weeks before, the German pocket battleship *Graf Spee* had sunk the British tanker *Africa Shell* in the southern Indian Ocean, and Allied navies were on high alert.[44] So their little convoy was escorted by HMAS *Hobart* and two armed merchant cruisers.[45] The convoy consisted of four troopships owned by the British India Steam Navigation Company – *Rohna*, *Tairea*, *Rajula* and *Talamba* – along with another British troopship and two French ships bound for Djibouti. The vessels were packed full. The *Talamba* carried 500 mules, with 403 Indian soldiers squeezed below on the troop deck; the VCOs and clerks and the white British soldiers were in second-class cabins while the eight white British officers travelled first class.[46]

The first section of the voyage was across the Indian Ocean to the British-owned port of Aden at the southernmost tip of Arabia, where they would turn north and steam up towards Suez. This stage proved to be slow and calm – there was a following wind and a smooth sea, so little air circulated below decks.[47] Some of the men were seasick. A Punjabi sepoy on a later voyage remembered the agony:

> From Karachi, we embarked straight on a big ship. That, too, was awful. I cannot tell you how awful. The ship was like a steel coffin, hot and suffocating and very dirty. When the ship left Karachi, all of us who were down in the ship, were very sick, vomiting. And we became frightened that we had caught a bad disease like cholera or something. But the officer-*sahibs* and the *Angrezi* [English] sailors told us not to worry, it was normal, all the people who went on a ship for the first time, experienced such sickness due to the movement of the sea. But how were we to know? No-one had warned us. We were mostly soldiers from the mountains and inland villages and we had not even seen the sea before![48]

The men slept on deck and delighted in watching flying fish, telling stories and speculating on where they might be headed. They soon slipped into a routine, bringing up the animals on deck for fresh air while mucking out their stalls, and keeping fit with games and physical training.[49] There was a daily boat drill, training in gas masks and a programme of lectures. On the *Talamba*, Captain Thompson taught message writing and map reading, skills that would prove essential during their time in France and

Britain, and Major Gillmore introduced the French language.[50] On 16 December they picked up a new escort as they passed Mayyum island at the entrance to the Red Sea and turned to starboard.[51] The Red Sea proved to be even hotter than the ocean for the first two days, but then the temperature fell. On 20 December they dropped anchor at the south end of the Suez Canal and some of the men tried fishing with hooks baited with *atta* (wholemeal wheat flour), without success.

At an hour after noon that day they entered the Suez Canal, passing the memorial to Indian soldiers of the Great War, with 'two fine carved tigers at its base … [soldiers] were in high spirits and cheered as we passed', according to a report in an Indian newspaper.[52] At midnight they reached Port Said, the northern end of the canal and the south-east corner of the Mediterranean. As Muslims sailing past a Muslim country, the men were disappointed that most of them were not given shore leave, and they may have also been hoping that Egypt was their destination.[53] A few VCOs went ashore and reported that the streets 'were like the best streets in Indian cities'. The rest of the men had to be content with the boats alongside offering 'sweet-meats, scent, fruit and leather-work. Prices were extremely high and we did not buy much except oranges.'[54]

The next day they sailed into the Mediterranean, by which time most of them must have guessed their destination. At this early stage of the war the Mediterranean was largely peaceful: Italy was still neutral, there was no Axis control of any of the shores, and only a single U-boat had penetrated the Straits of Gibraltar. As the convoy progressed westwards, the weather changed to something more northern, cold and rough, causing a lot of seasickness.[55] Raghu Karnad wrote of a similar voyage from Bombay in 1943, where his Great-Uncle Bobby

slipped down to the lower decks, where the men of the ranks were stacked like cargo to the roof. It was hot as a circle of hell, and to make things worse, blackout rules required that the portholes stay closed throughout the night … The soldiers retreated to their bunks, homesick or seasick, to drip tears and vomit onto the floor. It mixed and coursed through the vessel, stroking the decks and slipping under the collars of the steel joinery. The prow of the ship counted out a white rosary against the black water.[56]

The conditions meant that for three days no training was carried out. On Christmas Day, that most European of festivals, unknown to many of these Muslim Indians, there was a lecture on protection from poison gas for VCOs and NCOs on the *Talamba*.[57] They steamed on westwards; they had passed Malta on the 23rd and reached Marseilles on the afternoon of the 26th. Captain Parsons of the Medical Corps wrote that 'the mistral was blowing hard off shore and 27 December 1939 was one of the coldest days I have experienced'.[58] Many of the men must have breathed a sigh of relief as they looked over the rail at the French mainland and the bustling port, one of the oldest in France. What was in store for them in this cold, far-off land? Perhaps they felt like Sepoy Lalu, the hero of Anand's novel *Across the Black Waters* at the same place in 1914, excited about Europe: 'the glamorous land of his dreams, where the Sahibs came from, where people wore coats and pantaloons and led active, fashionable lives'.[59]

The first stage of their odyssey was complete. They had been at sea for seventeen days and covered more than 4,000 miles: they were in Europe.

2

From the five rivers

The big river of Jhelum;
I feel forlorn, O dear;
take leave and come back soon.[1]

It was a sunny afternoon on 11 May 1944 in Epinal, a pretty French town in the valley of the river Moselle. This was the home of printmaker Jean-Charles Pellerin, famed for his nineteenth-century *Images d'épinal*: bright, naive prints that are proverbial for depicting only that which is optimistic. At half-past three the town was going about its business, four years after the German occupation had begun. André Lietard, aged 21, was visiting his sister Madame Morin, who ran a jewellery shop near the busy railway station. Unexpectedly, sixty-eight B24 'Liberator' bombers of the American 8th Air Force – the so-called Mighty Eighth – appeared out of the blue spring sky, 16,500 feet up.[2] The citizens of Epinal – *Spinaliens* – expecting the planes to pass over en route to Germany, were surprised to see lines of bombs dropping beneath them. Over the course of the next fifteen minutes the Americans dropped 168 tons of high explosive on the town.[3] The raid was part of the preparation for D-Day, the Allied invasion of Europe which came just twenty-six days later, and the fliers were aiming for the strategically important railway station and marshalling yards in the centre of the town. The plan to bomb such targets in France was controversial among the Allied planners, as it was predicted to 'cause heavy loss of life among workers … and so lose the Allies goodwill'.[4] But the US Air Force (USAAF) was doing its best to disrupt German preparations and communications before D-Day, and if French citizens got killed along the way, *c'est la guerre.*

When the Americans came back twelve days later, a raid of similar intensity caused only eighteen casualties, including six deaths.[5] But this first raid of 11 May was devastating. An early list of deaths contains seventy-two names, including André Lietard, many children and whole families, such as the Laurents of Rue du Maroc.[6] According to one report, more than 200 civilians were killed, and 500 wounded. The official American report said that opposition was 'slight' but eight B24s were missing, and described the results as 'fair to good' but noted that the bombs were 'spread widely'.[7] These American bombs could not distinguish French from German, friend from foe. Nor were they all aimed with precision.

Half a mile up the hill from Epinal railway station, on the west side of the town, was an old barracks. This building had been vacant until the start of 1944, when the Germans turned it into a POW camp specifically for Indian prisoners. On the day of the raid it contained 3,191 Indian POWs.[8] They were doing what POWs do: reading, chatting, playing football. Twenty-six bombs fell on the camp: on the guardhouse, the wall and the barbed wire. Dafadar Bhagat Ram wrote to the Red Cross that 'bombs were coming like a stream and prisoners could find no way to hide themselves and were running like sheep from one corner to another'. He continued: 'I request you that a similar bombardment will not occur again.' The guards panicked and ordered the prisoners out of the camp. While some prisoners escaped, sixty-four Indian POWs died that day, killed by 'friendly fire' from American bombs or shot by German guards. Most of them are buried in the national cemetery on the other side of the valley.[9] Among them was Driver Muhabbat Shah of 22nd Animal Transport Company of the RIASC. What had brought him from his home in Punjab to this picturesque town in the Vosges?

Muhabbat Shah was born in 1911 in a village called Syed Kasran, in Rawalpindi district in northern Punjab. His mother was called Gulab Khatun, and his father was Karam Husain Shah. His name (which means Love) reveals that he was a syed, a descendant of the Prophet Muhammad, and therefore worthy of respect from the people around him, and he was from a Shia Muslim family. Like so many K6 sepoys, all that we know about him is in a few official records, supplemented by an interview with his nephew in 2018. Before joining the army, he studied to fourth grade at school, unusual at a time when only one Punjabi male in ten was literate.[10] But his life choices were limited: join the army, or work in the fields with his father and brothers, for this was an agricultural time and place, with over 85 per cent of the Punjabi population living in villages.

Coming home on leave from Pindi (as Rawalpindi was known), Muhabbat Shah would take the historic Grand Trunk Road, still known as the GTR. Cutting through Punjab on its 1,700-mile route from Kabul to Bengal, the GTR was a major artery that had carried the people of India for thousands of years. He would pass Rawat fort, the site of a battle in 1546, taking a turn off to the south-west onto a dirt road, leaving the metalled road behind, heading towards Chakwal. After twenty-five miles, he would turn off again and bump along country tracks past acacia and eucalyptus trees, with kites circling above. The pace slowed, for now Muhabbat had reached 'the hinterland of Punjab, where distances are measured in footsteps and at the speed of bullock-carts'.[11] Soon he would be back home.

* * * * *

Agriculture was (and is) the mainstay of the villagers of Sayed Kasran, although men and women often had other pursuits alongside.[12] During the hot season, which runs from April to June, temperatures can reach forty-nine degrees Celsius, but night temperatures in January can drop close to freezing. Rainfall, as in much of South Asia, is highly seasonal, coming mostly in the monsoon from July to September, and if the rains do not come when expected, it can lead to distress and hardship. A favoured way to water the crops is still the *rehat* or Persian wheel: an ox turning a chain of buckets. Fields are flat, to allow for irrigation when water is available, and surrounded by a low ridge of soil. The soil is sandy but quite fertile, and land is measured in *kanals*, about eight to an acre.

How strange it must have felt for Muhabbat Shah in Europe, with the extreme cold, the rain throughout the year, and fields on sloping hillsides. Unlike in France, the climate of Rawalpindi meant that two harvests could be gained in one year in Sayed Kasran: maize planted in summer, and wheat planted in January. Wheat was ground into *atta* flour to make chapattis, so Muhabbat Shah would have been interested to see the same grain growing in northern France. With transport slow and difficult, if not impossible in the monsoon, the Shah family and their neighbours ate what they could grow, thus a large variety of fruit and vegetables were planted. Flowers grew widely, including some that he might see later in Europe, like the pink dianthus and the toxic delphinium, even the hollyhock, often seen as a symbol of village gardens in Britain. The young Muhabbat would have been used to seeing animals around – cattle and buffalo, mules carrying loads to market, goats and fat-tailed sheep, chicken underfoot and the occasional camel. As firewood was not in plentiful supply, cattle manure was shaped into *thapi* or dung cakes, dried on walls and used for fuel.

Agriculture, then as now, was by no means a passport to wealth, indeed being free of debt in the interwar period was 'no mean achievement'.[13] The 1908 *Imperial Gazetteer* calculated that it took four and a half rupees per month to feed a family, plus another one and a half rupees for 'furniture, clothing and other necessaries'.[14] Such seemingly small sums may have evaded a farming family struggling to win a living from a few *kanals* of land. As the old Punjabi riddle has it, *Chitti kukri chitte pair, Chal meri kukri shehr-o-shehr* (Little white hen with little white feet, Run little hen: every town, every street): the answer is a silver rupee, always escaping from our hands.[15]

While the life of the village revolved around agriculture and the preparation of food, the social life happened around the well in the daytime, the *chaupal* or guesthouse and the mosque. As the vast majority of the people of Rawalpindi district were Muslim at the time Muhabbat was born, the boy probably grew up not knowing many Hindus or Sikhs. As a member of a Shia family, he was in the minority in Punjab, but most of the houses around him were inhabited by other Shia families. His house was probably made of mudbricks, as were most Punjabi village houses at that time, consisting of a courtyard, where meals were cooked, and one or two rooms. Houses were used differently from in Europe, the climate meant that 'the house is used for storage, as a kitchen, as a place in which women sleep, and as a place in which men and women have sexual relations', while people often slept outside the house on a charpoy, a wooden frame criss-crossed with string.[16] Rising from his charpoy, the young Muhabbat may have started his day a little like this scene from the great Punjabi love story *Hir and Ranjha*:

As he set out, the skirt of night was lifted and the yellow dawn appeared. The sparrow chirped and the starling began to sing. The men took their oxen out to plough, and the girls brought their milking stools and cleaned their milk cans. The women of the household began to grind corn, while others kneaded flour with their hands. The noise of the grinding stone was heard in every courtyard.[17]

When the work was done, in the dark evenings the family would gather together to chat and tell stories, while the men smoked a *huka* (waterpipe) or *bidis* (Indian cigarettes) and drank sweet spiced tea. If they were lucky, the villagers would have a *borh* or banyan tree to sit beneath. This extraordinary arboreal monarch grows wide rather than tall. When it feels a little unstable, it drops down a creeper from a branch, which then takes root, thickens and becomes a new trunk. Thus over the decades a banyan may develop many trunks to support a wide canopy, and so one tree resembles a little wood all by itself. Wherever they sat, the villagers told stories – of farmers, rajas and rats, of lovers like Hir and Ranjha, in the 'fabulous manner of the Punjabi storyteller'.[18] The young Muhabbat may have seen a touring theatre company perform 'rude plays called *swangs*', but it is highly unlikely he saw a film until he reached a town like Pindi. Indian cinema was becoming established in the interwar period but was generally restricted to the towns and cities. Some of the older boys may have seen the great local wrestler Gama, the *Rustami-i-Zaman* or world champion, who in 1910 was on his way to London to take on all comers. For games, Muhabbat and his friends played *gulli-danda*, where a small stick is hit with a larger stick, while more sedate pursuits like *chaupar* or *pacheesi* suited the evening or the older villagers.

In another village, near Mirpur, a future K6 soldier grew up with a pond that acted as a reservoir:

Boys learned swimming and girls washed clothes sitting on an old root of the tree emerging above the water level. The piece of soap sometimes would slip out of their hands and boys would dive in to find and give it back to the girls for a smile. Buffalos enjoyed sitting in the water. They would let the boys have a ride for a good rub of their backs and back of ears.

The village was surrounded by fields of wheat, maize, millet and other cereals depending on rain at the right time. There was no ground for us to play in. During moonlit nights we played Kabaddi (a sort of rugby, tag or the British Bulldog) in a small part of an old flattened graveyard.[19]

Life for boys like Muhabbat Shah was quiet, rural and without a great deal of money, but it was also a carefree life.

Fifty miles north of Sayed Kasran was the city of Rawalpindi itself. A bullock cart transporting sugar cane might take two days to get there, but a tonga (one-horse cart) was the chief means of transport for people and could get you there in a day or less. Driving such a cart would have been good training for his job as a mule driver for the young Muhabbat Shah. Pindi was a major centre of life and trade for Punjabis and *gore* (white people) alike, with a population approaching 100,000. It was connected to the rest of India and the world beyond by the GTR and an efficient railway service. Its military garrison was the largest and most important in all of India, with four regiments of cavalry and infantry based there, along with artillery and engineers. As a home to many Europeans, it also contained a park with ducks, partridges, even a fox and jackal, and was known for its cleanliness and its smart shops selling imported clothing and food, and even alcohol. For the locals, it was a vital centre, with a bustling marketplace where large landowners and those with just a few *kanals* brought what they had grown themselves to sell to both locals and *gore*. This was the sort of market that could still be found in France and in some parts of Britain, where the producer sat behind a pile of tomatoes, onions and carrots from their own soil, or brought a goat and three chickens to sell. In Pindi larger farmers transported grain and sugar cane by cart or on camelback, and porters were always in demand. Everything you needed for life could be bought for a few paise or an anna: plates and cups, medicines, or a bazaar letter writer would write to the government for you. All human life was here, and when the purchases were finished, you could relax with a chai or kulfi (ice cream), or play *pacheesi*, before visiting the Hindu temple, Christchurch in the military cantonment or the beautiful Merkazi Jamia Mosque.[20]

＊ ＊ ＊ ＊ ＊

Located right in the north-west corner of India, Punjab was of central importance to the British Raj. Its name means 'five rivers', derived from the Persian words *panj*, five, and *ab*, water. From west to east, the five rivers are the Jhelum, Chenab, Ravi, Beas and Sutlej, the Ravi being the river of monsters, and the Chenab the river for lovers, according to tradition.[21] All five rivers drain into the Indus, which in turn enters the sea near Karachi. The district of Rawalpindi, together with its neighbouring districts of Chakwal, Jhelum and Campbellpur, was part of the Pothwar plateau, home to the bulk of the K6 men. The word *pothwar* means land of the poppies, and the dialect – Pothwari – has been described as a 'fountain-head of songs, poetry and tales from the earliest times'.[22] The massive escarpment of the Great Salt Range divides the Pothwari plateau from lower Punjab, and at its foot is found the Khewra salt mine, discovered by the armies of Alexander the Great after their horses refused to eat the salty vegetation there. In 1911, the year of Muhabbat's birth, over half of the 25 million Punjabis were Muslim, a third were Hindu and an eighth were Sikh.[23] Indeed, Sikhism was born there, its spiritual centre is at Amritsar, and most Sikhs outside Punjab are descended from people who migrated from there. The importance of Punjab to the British Empire for the ninety years from 1857 to Partition cannot be overstated: it was both the breadbasket and the sword arm or 'garrison state' of British India.[24]

The British Indian Army was the second element that forged Muhabbat Shah's identity, as it had done for hundreds of thousands of other Punjabis. Military culture is distinct from civilian culture, and the Indian Army was a strange mix of British and Indian. Before 1857 it was the East India Company (EIC) that controlled the British armed forces in India; this was essentially a large private army. After the 'Mutiny' of 1857, when large sections of the army, supported by civilian rebellions, rose up against the EIC, the British took over direct rule of both the country and the army: the British Raj had come into being. For the next ninety years the Indian Army held a 'central but deeply ambiguous place' in the Empire as a whole, soaking up half of the government's revenue.[25] It provided a valuable force for conflicts around the Indian Ocean, such as the 1868 expedition to Abyssinia and the invasion of Burma in 1885. It kept the Indian people under control, as backup to the police. And it provided employment for hundreds of young British men recently out of Sandhurst, who became its officers. During the Great War the Indian Army proved its worth again and again, in the trenches in France and at Gallipoli, in the Middle East and in the East African campaign. Over 1.5 million served, and 34,000 died.[26] In the aftermath of that awful conflict, the ambiguity of the Indian Army in Punjab was underscored at Amritsar in April 1919, when at least 400 peaceful protestors and pilgrims were massacred in Jalianwala Bagh.[27] The rifles that killed them were fired by Indians and Nepali Gurkhas, but the orders were given by a British officer.

Motives for joining the army were complex, but the main driving force was economic. In 1921, when Muhabbat Shah was 10, a sepoy's basic pay of sixteen rupees per month was enough for the soldier to save and send some home to his family.[28] On top of their basic monthly pay, sepoys could earn one-off payments and pensions that would supplement the family income from farming and other sources.[29] An individual soldier rarely kept all his pay: a large proportion was sent home to support other family members. On top of the financial motivation to join the army there was a broader concept of *izzat* or honour: becoming a soldier was a manly thing to do, something that was expected in some parts of Punjabi society. The Indian Army of the Second World War is often described as the 'largest volunteer army in history', fighting in almost all the main conflicts where the British fought.[30] It grew from a 'hopelessly unprepared' force of 200,000 in 1939, to a maximum of 2.6 million men – and 11,500 women – by the end of the war.[31] Even Winston Churchill (who held some anti-Indian views) appreciated the contribution of the Indian armed forces, although Britons have largely forgotten it in the twenty-first century.[32]

One fundamental concept underlying the pre-war Indian Army was the Martial Race Theory. This said that the army should be based on certain groups or 'races' from Indian society, such as Sikhs, Gurkhas and Punjabi Muslims. The men of these groups were inherently masculine and martial: possibly small in stature, but warlike and obedient. Like other 'race' theories of the late nineteenth and early twentieth centuries, it was based on a combination of physical measurement, observation of traditions and an idea of fundamental qualities derived from 'colonial pseudo-scientific discourse'.[33] Established by Field Marshal Roberts of Kandahar in the wake of the 1857 uprising, however, there was another criterion at work in this idea of martial races – the groups deemed as 'martial' were those that had supported the British. There was therefore an 'implicit blacklist of castes that led the uprising', so these 'races' were not so much martial as loyal.[34]

There were undoubtedly military traditions among certain groups, including Sikhs and Pathans, and also the *kshatriya* order of Hinduism, but traditions are not determiners. The British took these traditions, added loyalty, and turned 'what had been a matter of practical choice into a dogma proclaimed with theological rancour'.[35] So the men who made up nearly all of Force K6 are presented as 'the square-shouldered athletic Mussulman of the Punjab'.[36] Most modern writers reject this theory as inherently racist and illogical. As a retired Pakistani major general told me, 'any race given the right cause ... will fight. Who expected the Vietnamese [to fight so well against the French and Americans]?'[37] In fact the Second World War saw the ending of the Martial Race Theory, with the commander-in-chief of the Indian Army, Claude Auchinleck, responding to criticism in India and insisting on recruiting from all areas.[38] In time of emergency, the Empire had no choice but to draw from wherever it could persuade men to enlist.

One result of this Martial Race Theory was targeted, localised recruitment. The British establishment expended considerable time, effort and money in those areas and among those people deemed to be warlike. The Pothwari plateau was one such area. The army issued recruitment handbooks specific to each geographical area and 'race', so Punjab was covered by two: one for Sikhs and one for Muslims. Joining the army was a preferred option for young men – in a land of uncertain rainfall, the failure of a wheat harvest could lead to a harvest of army recruits instead.

The army became a family tradition, as it is in other parts of the world, and part of the reason for volunteering was often this inherited sense of loyalty to the ruler. Muhabbat Shah's nephew Nazar Hussain had four uncles serving in the Second World War, all of whom became prisoners, one in Burma, one in Singapore and one in Egypt, as well as Muhabbat himself in France.[39] Apart from Muhabbat Shah, all eventually came back alive. In a Punjabi *mahiya* (poem) of the early twentieth century, a mother says to her son:

> The moon is never afraid of eclipse;
> Stalwart youths like you are never afraid of guns.[40]

The note of resignation in her voice is clear, and justified – 24,500 Indian sons did not return home at the end of the Second World War.[41]

In the period between the two world wars, the Indian Army continued to evolve. The RIASC were frequently called upon for service on the North West Frontier, that area so loved by writers of *Boys' Own* stories. This was the border with Afghanistan, where Pashtun 'tribes' were unwilling to live under British rule and rebelled frequently. It is highly probable that Muhabbat Shah worked in that difficult area: many RIASC companies were deployed on the frontier. The men of the Indian Army were also accustomed to working closely with the British Army, for each infantry brigade was composed of one battalion of white British soldiers and two of Indian or Gurkha troops.[42] In 1939, as the war began, Indian Army sepoys were deployed across the wider region: in Egypt and Palestine, in Singapore, Burma and Hong Kong, constituting the backbone of imperial forces in many parts of the Empire.

As Muhabbat Shah prepared to leave Sayed Kasran for Europe, he said to his older brother: '"Now I am going to war, Lala. I do not know whether I will return or not. I ask you to grant me forgiveness." His brother said to him, "You are like my son."'[43] Muhabbat Shah never returned to Sayed Kasran. When I showed his nephew Nazar a photograph of his grave in Epinal, the tough farmer started to recite a prayer, and then tears came to his eyes. He explained that the graves of the rest of the family are located in the local Shia communal hall and that every Thursday he prays for his deceased relatives. Now that he knows where his *chacha* Muhabbat is buried, he feels a sense of closure.

* * * * *

When Force K6 landed in Marseilles, there were two Indians among its twenty-four officers. Both were Muslim, and both would become major generals after the war, one in Pakistan, one in India. A significant change in the army had started in 1919, in the immediate aftermath of the Great War, a change that men of K6 were intimately involved in. This was the process known as 'Indianisation' – the gradual replacement of white British officers by brown Indian officers. In an army that was evolving, part of a wider society that was changing, the process of Indianisation had both a moral and a political edge. It was an essential step towards independence and had proceeded more quickly in some branches of Indian life – the civil service being ahead of the military. Indianisation was an evolution that spelt hope for young ambitious Indian men but made a lot of the older Britishers wary or afraid. It was incomplete by the time of Partition in 1947 and some white military and civil officers stayed on well past that time.

Until the end of the Great War, all the officers in the Indian Army (with the exception of some medical doctors) had been white British men. By 1918 the pressure of public opinion and the experience of the Great War had shown the government that Indian men were up to the job, so they looked around for a way to start training Indian officers in the manner that British men were trained at Sandhurst. A group of young VCOs, aged 19 to 25, were chosen to attend a training course at Daly College in Indore 'on account of their aptitude as instructors and leaders'; they were fluent in English and Urdu and had the 'ability to read indifferent handwriting as well as print'.[44] Among that very first group of thirty-nine men was Jemadar Mohammed Akbar Khan, a 22-year-old from a military family in Chakwal with experience of combat in Mesopotamia, modern-day Iraq. With him was the future commander of the Indian Army, Kodandera Madappa Cariappa (universally known as 'Kipper'), whom he would track rank for rank over the next thirty years.[45] Akbar graduated thirteenth in order of merit from the course and was assigned to his old regiment, Probyn's Horse.[46] Twenty years later, when K6 arrived at Marseilles, Akbar was there as a major in 25th Company.

Also arriving at Marseilles was a younger Muslim Indian officer: Captain Anis Ahmad Khan. This was not his first trip to Europe, for Anis had graduated from Sandhurst in 1924.[47] Sahibzada Anis Ahmad Khan was born in 1904, to a blue-blooded Indian Muslim family (*sahibzada* means 'son of a nobleman'). His father was Cambridge-educated Sahibzada Aftab Khan, vice chancellor of Aligarh Muslim University, a man whose name was 'so illustrious, so highly respected in the whole of Hindustan' that there was 'not a single door that could not be opened' by his name.[48] Sandhurst was the military heart of the Empire, where the victors of the Indian 'Mutiny' of 1857, of Omdurman and the Boxer Rebellion had been trained; over 150 Indian cadets studied there during the interwar years.[49]

Anis Ahmad Khan with his wife Razia and four of their children, Mussoorie, 1 September 1939 (Zeenut was born after the war).

Here Anis was among 18-year-old public schoolboys from Eton and Haileybury and the sons of past heroes. A 1923 photograph of his training company includes Edmund de Gonville Hosking Bromhead, whose father had won a Victoria Cross fighting the Zulus at Rorke's Drift.[50] John Masters, who went on to serve with the Indian Army, wrote of the spirit of cadets in the interwar period, of their drinking and horseplay, and says laconically, 'perhaps we were no worse than our contemporaries at Oxford or Cambridge'.[51] The overriding impression is of 18-year-old boys released from public school, zooming up to London whenever possible, working hard and playing hard.

It is doubtful whether the young Anis, scion of a respectable and academic Indian Muslim family, conformed with the off-duty expectations of the white British men around him. Another Indian Muslim cadet recalled his life at the college a little later as 'spartan', and described a sense that the Indian cadets were regarded as 'an inferior species'.[52] Whatever Anis may have felt inside, acceptance and integration or inferiority and isolation, at the surface level he did what all cadets did in order to graduate as a junior army officer: 'arrive, learn, conform, pass on'.[53] When K6 arrived in France in 1939, Anis was a captain in Muhabbat Shah's 22nd Company.

Over the next four years, more and more of the officer posts in K6 would be filled by Indians: a quarter by July 1943.[54] Indian officers and white British officers were not on equal terms, however. Indians were not paid the same as their British counterparts, nor were they permitted to serve on courts martial, and there was a general feeling that they were still on a lower level.[55] Some social clubs would not accept them as members, and Auchinleck himself bemoaned:

> The differential treatment in respect of pay and terms of service … the prejudice and lack of manners by some British officers and their wives, all went to produce a very deep and bitter feeling of racial discrimination in the minds of the most intelligent and progressive of the Indian officers.[56]

At the level of the humble sepoy like Muhabbat Shah, the discrimination was even wider, and went largely unremarked and unchallenged; it was assumed to be a natural part of the imperial order. A British private posted to India earnt 850 rupees, while an Indian sepoy received merely 285, about a third.[57] K6 of course were on Indian Army pay rates, so would also have experienced this, being paid much less than the British troops they worked with. An odd quirk of the system is that the Indian 80th Pioneer Company, recruited in Britain, were paid British rates, 'although they are not soldiers in the strict sense of the word, they are, by receiving British rates of pay, in a much better position than pukka Indian troops'.[58] Stepping off the *Rohna* three days after Christmas in 1939, Muhabbat Shah had no idea that his journey would bring him into contact with such discrimination, nor that he would lose his life in a small French town four years later from a bomb made in a factory in the USA.

3

Fony Vaar

I like the War … It is only War that gives us a normal existence. What do you do in peacetime? You stay at home; you don't know what to do with your time; you argue with your parents, and your wife – if you have one. Everyone thinks you are an insufferable egotist – and so you are.[1]

As the men of Force K6 disembarked from the *Talamba* and the *Rohna* at Marseilles on a grey December day, foremost among them was a stout soldier with a fine-looking beard and moustache greying around the edges underneath his *pagri*, and a stern look in his eye. He was a man who commanded the respect of everyone he met, a soldier in his prime, with a lifetime of military experience. This was Risaldar Major Mohammed Ashraf Khan, the senior VCO in K6, a vital go-between for Lt Col. Hills, who trusted him and his judgement of the men absolutely. His role was unique: he had an overview of all the Indian soldiers in the force, who saluted him and respected him completely, and he dispensed advice to the younger VCOs. But he also had a view upwards and sideways: he needed to be able to work with British and French officers and civilians, and he became experienced in greeting the many dignitaries who were to visit over the coming months.

He was 44 years of age, and since the time of his enlistment as a sepoy in the RIASC at the age of 17 in 1913, he had risen steadily through the ranks.[2] He had already been to Marseilles, for in the Great War he had served in all the major campaigns involving the Indian Army: in France, Egypt, Gallipoli and Mesopotamia. He appeared to have been an archetypal Punjabi Muslim: one from a noble martial race. Indeed, his grandfather served with the British under Major Abbott against the Sikh rulers in the 1840s. In fact he was not from Punjab itself, but the North West Frontier, being of the Karlal tribe of the Hazara people. His home was in the village of Dubran, a remote place that remained beyond the

Risaldar Major Ashraf Khan, 7 May 1940, in
London with a leave party.

reach of proper roads until the 1980s. To reach it from the rest of India
required taking a train to Haripur, sixty miles north of Rawalpindi. A
tonga ride to Shah Maqsood town was the next stage, followed by a ten-
mile walk across the hills to Dubran village – a half-day in itself.[3] As he
looked around the quay at Marseilles, at the cranes and workers of this,
the oldest port in France and the home of its national anthem, he must
have felt a long way from home.

The work of unloading the stores from the ships took nearly two
weeks, but the men and animals were much quicker, taking just five
hours in total.[4] Ashraf may have been surprised at the level of interest
among the locals: 'the news of the arrival of animals … spread quickly
and a large concourse of local inhabitants, military etc, gathered to watch
the disembarkation.'[5] Some of the Marseillaise population remembered
a similar occasion a generation before, when four Indian divisions
disembarked to a hero's welcome in September 1914, only to be thrown
straight into the trenches.[6] Perhaps the sepoys of 1939 thought they were

destined for the same slaughter, having heard the stories from the veterans among them, Ashraf included. Watched by newspaper correspondents and photographers from around the world, and a newsreel film crew from Pathé, the mules descended through a tunnel-like covered ramp into the light of the new country.[7] Generally the mules seemed happy to disembark after seventeen days at sea, and Hills joked later that 'only two out of more than 2,000 wished to transfer to the navy' and stay on board ship.[8] All on dry land, the men and mules marched to their camps at Chateau Reynarde and Chateau d'Espagne, just a few miles from the docks, escorted by policemen on motorcycles.

When they arrived there, the men found the two camps less than perfect. Major Seth Apcar, in charge of the Remount Depot, was characteristically frank in his war diary: 'reception arrangements generally very bad indeed'.[9] This was largely due to the poor weather – 1940 was to prove one of the worst winters of the twentieth century. At La Reynarde, the VCOs were billeted in a cottage, while the men were housed in rows of bell tents, and the ground was covered in snow.[10] By 5 January, the mule drivers' uniforms were habitually soaked with mud halfway up to their knees.[11] At night the men shivered in their tents, and the commanders were forced to give out extra blankets, as many as four per person.[12] Unsurprisingly, some men became ill, and three had to be admitted to the local British military hospital.[13] In a reversal of the usual 'Delhi-belly' cliché, Risaldar Jalal Din of 25th Company went down with dysentery.[14] This first experience of European-style accommodation was disappointing, but the men and animals survived because of their strength and hardiness. Major Finlay of the 47 SDS wrote on New Year's Eve that the 'men have worked extremely well and kept in remarkably good spirits considering their living conditions'.[15]

* * * * *

Alongside the freezing weather, France was also in the grip of the *drôle de guerre* or Phoney War, the name being Indianised as Fony Vaar.[16] Since the Germans' rapid victory over Poland in September 1939, there had been a general quiet on the Western Front. A joke in the Indian Army newspaper *Fauji Akhbar* went:

Schoolmaster: Why is it quiet on the Western Front?
Student: Because the soldiers are not allowed to speak loudly, [sir]?[17]

The feeling that this was not yet a proper war was widespread. French and German soldiers faced each other across the gap between the Maginot and the Siegfried Lines, but there was little activity or bloodshed. Both sides were preparing and building up their forces. The Germans still hoped that the British would accept peace, and the French were fixed on a plan of defence. Not everywhere was so peaceful, however. The British and French navies were heavily engaged in a sea blockade of Germany, while German U-boats and battleships were rampant in the Atlantic and elsewhere, attacking and sinking Allied merchant ships. The *Graf Spee*, which had caused such anxiety in the Indian Ocean in November, was scuttled after being damaged in the Battle of the River Plate off the coast of Argentina on 13 December.[18] The war may have seemed 'phoney' to some journalists, but the families of the sixty-one sailors of HMS *Exeter* who died in that battle had a different view.

In reality the pause on the Western Front was a time of preparation, of trying to guess the opponent's plans, of 'ominous activity – behind the curtain'.[19] The situation developed in April, when the Germans overran Denmark and attacked Norway, and there were eight Indian Army officers in the British force sent to bolster the Norwegians.[20] The slowness, the seeming gentlemanliness of that period now seems like a missed opportunity and contrasts sharply with the brutality of what was to unfold before peace in 1945; but during that first harsh winter, nobody knew what was to come.

Throughout the first few freezing weeks of 1940, the various units of Force K6 were dispersed around the country and found their feet. By the end of January, Hills was able to report that, despite the severe climate conditions, 'the Force is comfortably housed and fit'.[21] The 29th Company were the first to leave Marseilles, going by train to Le Mans, home of the famous twenty-four-hour car race, then a staging post between the BEF and their supply ports on the west coast. They quickly settled into their routine of training and exercising, but the local British commanders were unable to find enough work for them.[22] On 20 January Major Shannon recorded the lowest temperature experienced by K6 men that winter, minus seventeen degrees Celsius, but that did not prevent the men celebrating Eid Al-Adha, the Muslim festival that commemorates Abraham's willingness to sacrifice his son to God.[23] Life continued despite the extreme cold.

The 32nd Company departed from Marseilles a few days after 29th Company, and joined the British First Corps near the Belgian border at Orchies, an area that had been occupied by the Germans for much of the First World War.[24] They were 'employed to capacity' there, working with the Royal Engineers constructing defences.[25] Among their number was Lance Naik Chaudry Wali Mohammad, from Mohra Vaince village near Rawalpindi, a physical training (PT) instructor and hockey player whose son now runs a taxi company in Woking.[26] On 1 February the company were visited by the BBC. Richard Dimbleby and Z.A. Bokhari – who later founded Pakistan Radio – recorded them telling stories and singing songs, and a camera recorded that process (as well as the cooks preparing dinner) on film.[27] Unlike some of their French comrades, mule drivers had little time for leisure pursuits at this early stage. A cartoon in the *Echo du Nord* shows two French soldiers in their dormitory. One smokes a pipe while he knits, and says to his comrade, 'I'm making a pullover for my wife. She has no time, she's too busy making shells!'[28]

The 25th Company, meanwhile, were attached to Second Corps near the large city of Lille, known as the 'Manchester of France' because of its textile industry.[29] After a journey where the train carriages were like 'ice chests and their tops were covered with an inch or more snow', they reached St André station on 6 January and marched three miles to their base at Marquette-lez-Lille.[30] On 20 January they had a visit from a gas expert. The men had been trained in the use of gas masks during the long sea voyage, but this expert brought masks for the mules and spent several days fitting them on the animals.[31] Their commanding officer, Major Wainwright, drew a map which shows their situation on a bend in the river Marque, around the farm of Monsieur Dillies, who had been an artillery officer in the Great War and was now the mayor.

Major Akbar wrote that the men were very pleased to be stationed at the farm, and that they were able to convert part of a brickworks for use as a mosque. Akbar himself was billeted with the mayor and his wife, although they had difficulty finding a bed that was long enough for his six-foot frame, so one of the company carpenters was called upon to add some extra planks. When they first met, Madame Dillies asked Akbar if he had any children. He said that he had seven. She asked him how many wives he had and was surprised when he told her that he had only one, Kudsia. With little direct experience of Muslims, Europeans would fall back on clichés and what they had seen on films and read in books. In a similar way, an article in the local paper *Echo du Nord* describes a VCO with a long moustache, melancholy eyes and skin with a 'tint of liquorice'.[32]

The 22nd Company, with Captain Anis and Driver Muhabbat Shah among them, were the last to leave the south of France, staying until the start of May. They were kept very busy, chalking up 800 carts used during the month of January.[33] The Reinforcement Unit and the 47 SDS also stayed at Marseilles for the moment, while the Advanced Remount Depot moved up to Le Mans with 29th Company. With the companies dispersed over such a wide area – 600 miles from Marseilles to Lille – the units with a central responsibility faced considerable logistical challenges. Their own Indian General Hospital found their designated site at Caserne Quesne in Dieppe small and ill-equipped.[34] They managed to open on 11 January with eighteen beds, but 'that the situation was satisfactory no one but a crass optimist could believe'. The headquarters was stationed in the north, near where the action was expected to develop, and Ashraf and Hills were very busy driving from one camp to another, trying to maintain an overview, making improvements and keeping an eye on morale. This zooming around had its inevitable consequence on 17 February when the van carrying Ashraf slid into a field in bad weather.[35] Both Ashraf and the British driver were badly shaken but otherwise unhurt, and Hills remarked that the concerned response by the British drivers showed the 'esteem in which the Risaldar Major is held by British troops'.[36] The bewhiskered VCO was winning friends and respect all round.

The men of K6 were becoming poster boys in the BEF. With one eye on public opinion and the other on the history books, Hills was happy with the media coverage. The 25th and 32nd Companies hosted visits from many VIPs over their first few weeks in the north. On 15 January the Duke of Gloucester (the King's brother and a senior liaison officer with the BEF) visited both companies, 'much to the delight of Indian troops', and promised that the King's Christmas card would be issued to the men.[37] On 15 February at Wambrechies, with snow falling, a film crew and two photographers accompanied Major Akbar as he conducted Lord Gort, the BEF commander, around the 25th Company positions, introducing them to a loaded pack mule with a gas mask, which brought a smile to the politician's face.[38] This was not Gort's first visit. A few weeks before he had written to India of the force's 'first-rate quality', saying:

> The four mule transport companies that you have sent us are quite excellent and, in the short time that they have been here, have created a very good impression on all sides. In discipline and military efficiency they leave nothing to be desired; they have settled down at once to their new conditions without any fuss; and their soldierly qualities are commented upon by all who come in contact with them.[39]

The twin aims of valuable work and high profile were being fulfilled.

After the initial flurry of media interest, the coverage continued at a high rate. This may have been part of the Phoney War syndrome – with no major battles to report on, the media fell back on behind-the-lines stories. Certainly the men of K6 never again experienced the sheer volume of press attention that they did in France. Major Martin, the officer commanding 32nd Company, wrote to his sister in Burnley at the end of February that he had seen at least fifty newspapermen himself, that the 'Times, Express and Telegraph are always round' and that he'd had fifteen visitors in one morning.[40] A well-known journalist, Philip Gibbs, wrote a piece for the *Times of India* from 'somewhere in France' – censorship required that precise locations were never revealed. His article sings the praises of this 'bunch of handsome fellows' (another popular press angle) who:

> have already learned some French and can make themselves understood in cafes and estaminets, where they get coffee and sweet syrup. At night they keep warm in Nissen huts, where they have their meals of mutton or goat's flesh ... Near the lines, they have built a little mosque in a factory, where the maulvi says the prayers at sunrise and sunset.[41]

The men's experience of France would have been much harder without their *agents de liaison*. On 3 January each company was joined by a French soldier who was attached to them until they left the country months later.[42] The agents' job was to interpret language and customs, to ease egos and cut through red tape. They were fluent in French and English, and at least one of them gave French lessons to some of the men in his company and may have picked up some Urdu too.[43] These agents were an essential corner in the triangular interaction between Britain, France and India. The writer André Maurois had done such a job in the Great War and wrote about how dependent a British officer became on 'his Frenchman'.[44] The most senior was Sous-lieutenant François de Champeaux, the son of a French count and an American heiress. He stayed with the K6 HQ until they left France in June, and later in the war he became a member of the Resistance and worked with the American XV Corps after D-Day.[45] He was just one among many luminaries whose paths crossed with the boys of K6.

The job of the liaison agents was not an easy one, with distrust and even hostility from French villagers and a lack of respect from some British soldiers. Many villages found large quantities of British soldiers billeted in their houses and barns. In the village of Bourghelles, Monsieur Lefebvre of Rue Marechal Foch rented land to 32nd Company for a barracks; there was sometimes a profit to be made from the visitors.[46] Generally, relations between the Indians and the French were positive. Akbar wrote that they were invited to visit local farms, which must have been interesting for men from an agricultural area.[47] The good relations may have been partly a product of close supervision by officers and the fact that, as Muslims, none of the Indians drank alcohol – a contrast with the Tommies, famed for their love of the beer and wine served in *estaminets*. The sepoys' principal drink was tea, 'drinking [it] at all hours of the day' in the Indian manner, 'very sweet and made, if possible, with tinned milk'.[48]

Their eating habits must have looked strange to Monsieur Dillies and their other French friends, for they travelled with special rations to suit their taste buds. Their commanders knew the importance of the right food for maintaining morale and strength, and their daily ration was designed to deliver 4,500 calories. As well as ten ounces of vegetables and three and a half ounces of *dhal* (lentils) each day, it included twenty-four ounces of *atta* – enough to make about twelve chapattis, their staple food.[49] The correspondent for the *Echo du Nord* was unsure how to explain this bread to a Lillois audience, and called them '*galettes brulantes de pain sans levain*' (hot cakes made from unleavened flour), which makes them sound rather like a Breton speciality.[50] These *galettes* were used to eat '*pilaf de mouton*', for the men were allowed six ounces of meat a day, from sheep slaughtered by one of the Muslim personnel in the *halal* manner. A company of 300 men would get through six sheep each day, thus contributing to the prosperity of local sheep farmers.[51] The ration also included sugar, spices, milk and *ghi* (clarified butter), with lime juice and Marmite thrice weekly. This schedule of rations, based on what the Punjabis ate at home but with more meat and more calories, was clearly an adequate and balanced diet, comparing well with the average 3,000 calories a day that British civilians consumed during the war.[52] Additionally, the men were more than capable of finding ways to supplement their diet, making their own chutney and buying chocolate.

Although they ate very differently from their BEF comrades around them, their basic uniform and equipment was not so different. Their standard wear was a two-piece khaki battledress with the top section being a long *kurtah* or shirt rather than the British blouse, plus short trousers with puttees on the lower leg.[53] It was their headgear, however, which set them apart. As well as the standard tin helmet and forage cap, they often wore a turban or *pagri*. For Punjabi Muslims this came in two parts: a *lunghi* or cloth wound round a conical woven cap called a *kullah*, itself the marker of an Indian Muslim. The *pagri* could be taken off as a single piece, which must have been an advantage given the amount of time dedicated to winding the *lunghi*. What they did with the end of the *lunghi* was a deliberate signifier of rank. While lower ranks wore the end neatly tucked in, senior NCOs, VCOs and officers wore it spread like a peacock's tail – the tuft that was 'beloved of the rural aristocracy of the Punjab'.[54] This was a very conscious association that the army wished to create: those in command were there because they were a better class of people, from superior stock with a right to rule. Indeed, in Persia the peacock was seen as a guardian of royalty, and both the Persian shah and the Mughal emperor sat on the Peacock Throne or *Takht-i Tāvūs*. This symbolism was carried forward to Britain in the Durbar Room at

Osborne House, designed by Bhai Ram Singh, which includes a peacock. There was thus a direct symbolic connection between the turban and the monarch: the officer showed he would protect the king-emperor as a peacock protected the Mughals, tuft fanned out like the proud peacock fans his tail, displaying aggression and beauty to all.[55] At this stage the drivers of K6 were unarmed – a tradition derived from working on the North West Frontier, where rifles were often stolen by the enemy.[56] This lack of weapons would make the men very uncomfortable.

An essential factor in maintaining morale was communication with home. As they did not know their destination when they left Punjab, the men were allocated a special postal address in Delhi where the mail was held until they had reached France, and paid for by Army HQ – an unusual measure.[57] As for all troops throughout the war, mail going in both directions was censored, but unfortunately very few letters survive from the force. Only a small proportion of the men were literate in Urdu, but this increased as the war went on. Driver Jalal Din of 25th Company, for example, whose first language was the Punjabi dialect of Potohari, was not literate in Urdu, but learnt the Qur'an in his time in England and also learnt to sign his name in English and Urdu, in common with many of his companions.[58] Hills wrote in January 1940, 'practically all the personnel are literate and I think they will have no difficulty to write letters', but this was probably an exaggeration intended to fend off an unwanted offer of help.[59]

This unwanted offer came in a letter from Ikbal Ali Shah, sufi and writer, long-time UK resident and one of the leading lights in the Indian Muslim aristocracy in Britain.[60] His letter, written on behalf of a group of prominent British Muslims, promised 'help in all possible ways towards making our co-religionists happy in France', including warm clothing, Indian entertainment and help reading and writing letters.[61] Hills' reply was polite, but he clearly did not want anything that would smack of interference. He told Shah, 'all my personnel are really fit, in great spirits, and tremendously keen to give of their best to His Majesty' and listed a number of priority comforts, including ten wireless sets, twenty-three gramophones with records to accompany, and ten sets each of equipment for hockey and basketball. This initiative clearly paid off, and these leisure items were highly valued by the men. A few weeks later a Red Cross visitor to a soldier in the hospital in Dieppe remarked on the way that 'the soft strains of his native songs cheer his heart in the evenings'.[62]

The force also acquired its own designated welfare officer, responsible for organising a programme of visiting entertainers and films wherever the men were posted. This officer was Dr Chandra Dharma Sena Gooneratne, given the honorary rank of captain for the task.[63] This interesting figure was a Ceylonese Christian working for the Indian Young Men's Christian Association (YMCA), who had served in the First World War and then gained a PhD at the University of Chicago.[64] A photo from 1926 portrays the particular combination of qualities that made him the right man for his job with K6: he stands holding a smart-looking horse, in the uniform of the Chicago University Officer Training Corps, with a turban in place of a 'doughboy' hat.[65] Gooneratne's was an essential job in a time when the Allied armies increasingly emphasised welfare as a way to maintain good morale, and he was to stay with the sepoys for the duration of their time in Europe.

As Muslims, an important part of their welfare was access to a place to pray. There was at that time only one mosque in France, the impressive Moroccan-style Grande Mosquée de Paris which had stood near the Jardin des Plantes since 1926, testament to North African participation in the Great War and subsequent migration.[66] But a mosque in Islam does not need to be such a grand building. Muslims may pray wherever they gather, and this is precisely what these sepoys became used to over the next four years. Akbar reported that 25th Company in Marquette had 'turned a hall into a mosque and the REs [Royal Engineers] have installed electric light in it'.[67] Senior soldiers like Akbar and Ashraf had an important part to play in this area, in providing an example to the men as well as acting like ambassadors to the broader French and British people around them. One can imagine many theological and practical discussions between VCOs and liaison officers such as de Champeaux at HQ.

The role of religion within the force was also reflected in their special newsletter, *Wilayati Akhbar Haftawar*, launched on 20 April 1940 and running until January 1944. It came in a four-page format, written in Roman Urdu and edited by Lt Col. Ferrar, ex-Indian civil service and an accomplished linguist.[68] Ferrar was keen to receive material from the men, writing in his first editorial that 'certainly mistakes will be made by the English Editor. In this matter, the editor seeks forgiveness from readers and is also desirous of every kind of letter.'[69] In this way the men were being encouraged to use the newsletter as an outlet for their own voices. The purpose of the newsletter is clear from its contents – to inform the men about the war and to entertain them, but above all to keep up their morale and to persuade them that they were doing the right thing. It was a propaganda tool. Around a quarter of the space was taken up with photographs, and the men must have been amused to recognise their colleagues throwing snowballs or riding a camel at London Zoo. Indeed, one of the newsletter's functions was to provoke laughter and light relief in dark times. There were plenty of photos of dignitaries and VIPs, as well as images from India or illustrating Indian participation in the war. A fairly typical picture appeared on the front of the second edition, showing Princess Elizabeth on her fourteenth birthday, in riding gear in Windsor Great Park, with the caption describing her as 'a jolly, intelligent and soft-hearted princess. May God make her life long.'[70]

In an early edition, the imam of Woking Mosque, Abdul Majid, wrote that 'Islam factually and principally is a religion of love, calm and peace' but that:

we see from our experience that sometimes such situations are created in the world in which it is necessary to combat oppression and violation with armed force. Some people think that we should not use force even to establish justice against cruelty and violence. These people are just building castles in the air ... This kind of uncomfortable situation cannot just be handled by words or negotiations.[71]

He finished by quoting from sura 23 (al Mu'minun) in the Qur'an: 'Repel the evil deed with what is better.'[72] Anxiety was high within the Empire about the possibility of German recruitment of Muslims for a holy war against French and British Empires. In the Great War, the Germans had tried to subvert Muslims in the trenches, with some success.[73] Muslim POWs had received good treatment in the so-called *Halbmondlager* (half-moon camp) at Wünsdorf, south of Berlin, the site of the first mosque in Germany.[74] In 1939 German propaganda was stepped up again, and

Goebbels' Reichsministerium für Volksaufklärung und Propaganda was a world leader in the arts of manipulation. There were regular radio broadcasts from Berlin to India, using Indians resident in Europe who took an anti-Empire stance. On 29 December 1939, just three days after K6's ships berthed at Marseilles, a German broadcast referred to K6 as '*Englands Schlachtkälber*' or England's calves for the slaughter.[75] In April, Akbar broadcast from London to India (the first of many such transmissions) referring to Lord Haw-Haw, the notorious British traitor on the radio programme *Germany Calling*, who had been 'spreading very wrong news about the men'.[76] Taken all together, the German action represented a considerable campaign against public opinion in India as well as the men in France, and the India Office in London was anxious to use the newsletter and other means to counter it.

* * * * *

Spectators at the 25th Company gymkhana, 21 April 1940, Marquette-lez-Lille.

As the months in France rolled on, and winter turned to spring, the men built strong relationships with the people around them. The 25th Company held a gymkhana at Marquette in April, as they had been doing for several weeks. The occasion was Eid Milad, the birthday of the Prophet Muhammad. Photos show the men clustered round a radio, listening to the BBC broadcasting the Punjabi songs that they had themselves recorded a few weeks before. Later on, the men demonstrated some wonderful trick-riding skills on the back of mules. There was also a performance of what was probably the first example of bhangra dancing in Europe. Six sepoys, each wearing a long *kurtah*, with a cloth on their heads, are shown dancing a traditional dance with their arms out wide.[77] Another photo shows the musicians – one with a *chimta* or tongs, a metal percussion instrument based on the tool used by a blacksmith. Next to him sits a drummer, playing a *dhol*, a drum with a bass sound coming from the right hand and a higher tone from the left, that 'remains mum when told to speak [but] screams upon being beaten'.[78] The final photo shows a mixed group of Indian and French spectators, relaxed, smiling and clapping, children sitting on the soldiers' laps. Just nineteen days before the German blitzkrieg, 25th Company had succeeded in winning over the 'hearts and minds' of the local children.

A few days later, the men finally got some leave, and a group of fifteen went to London, led by Ashraf and Akbar. They were met by a large crowd, who 'watched the Indians leave Victoria station and set out at a brisk march for the headquarters of the Moslem Society of Great Britain, in Eccleston Square, where they will stay'.[79] This was their first encounter with English crowds, but it would certainly not be their last. Over the next few days they visited Harrod's, met VIPs at India House and the Overseas League, and were entertained by Jocelyn Lucas, MP for Portsmouth South.[80] On Tuesday 7 May they were in Westminster, wearing their best walking-out uniforms and medal ribbons, where they encountered an old gentleman wearing a trilby hat and carrying a stick, out for a walk with his small dog. He stopped for a chat and was snapped by the photographer.[81] Perhaps he was intrigued by their 'picturesque' appearance. Maybe he had seen photos of them in France and wanted to find out more. Or maybe he was one of the tens of thousands of British citizens who had been in India, in the army or the civil service or in business and wanted to reminisce and

Leave party at Woking Mosque, 10 May 1940. Major Akbar is in the centre, in uniform, bareheaded. He has written in the names of many of the soldiers.

practise his Urdu. On Friday 10th, the *Times of India* reported on a big reception at the East India Association, chaired by the new secretary of state for India, Leo Amery, and attended by lords and dukes and other dignitaries from Britain and India.[82] On that day they visited the Woking Mosque for the first time, and were getting ready for a BBC recording the next day when they heard the news: Germany had invaded France and the Low Countries. The *sitzkrieg* had become a blitzkrieg and all leave was cancelled. Akbar and Ashraf hurried back to France.

4

Blitzkrieg

The blow in the west has fallen. At dawn today the Germans marched into Holland, Belgium, Luxembourg. It is Hitler's bid for victory now or never.[1]

The speed of the German advance surprised everyone. As in 1914, Belgian neutrality was breached by the German attack, so the BEF and the French First Army advanced as planned into Belgium to meet them in a line along the Dyle Canal, around the university town of Louvain. The main German thrust came in an unexpected direction, however, through the Ardennes forest to the river Meuse, which was crossed successfully on 15 May 1940. This was the point when the battle was won and lost, just five days after the start of the campaign, and the American reporter William Shirer, who was based in Berlin, wrote, 'almost all my friends have given up hope.'[2] The next day the BEF was ordered to retreat from the Dyle Line – unaware of the old Punjabi proverb '*Agge daur te pichhe chaur*': when you go ahead fast you lose what has been gained.[3] The victorious General Guderian's Panzer tanks reached Brussels on the 17th and by 19 May they had tasted the salt waters of the English Channel, cutting off most of the BEF and hundreds of thousands of French troops with them. As the BEF and French withdrew, they were everywhere surrounded by streams of refugees, an older generation who remembered four years of German occupation twenty-five years before. From the 25th Company's camp at Marquette, Major Akbar watched their passing:

A constant flow of cars, carts, lorries, people on foot … They were moving in a solid block, over-riding the pavements, jammed tightly across the width of the road from house to the other house … It was like some fabulous, gargantuan, malevolent monster. This body moved perhaps at less than 1½ miles per hour, but it did move. No one knew its destination.

It swept everything before it. The pedestrians ran among the cars calling for lifts, holding up their bleeding feet. The scene was terrible. Everybody was in haste and trying to get through – but where are you going?[4]

On 19 May came an order for the evacuation of supply and support troops, referred to by a senior British officer as the 'useless mouths who ate up provisions without contributing to the fight'.[5] That category included the muleteers of the RIASC. The 32nd Company were the first to leave, marching from their bases near Douai, south of Lille. As they squeezed along the narrowing corridor that reached to the sea, the Punjabi farmers were disturbed to see the animals that had been left behind: 'Cattle graze in the pastures, pigs squeal about the barnyards. All are thirsty for the farmhouses are deserted. The cows have not been milked for some days and their udders are painfully swollen.'[6]

Their route took them through the town of Cassel, which was heavily bombed. A British armoured regiment reported 'very heavy bombing of convoy of Mule transport on Southern entrance to village. Several Indian drivers and their mules were killed.'[7] This was almost certainly the occasion when Groom Akbar Khan from Rawalpindi died – his grave lies in the village of Wormhoudt, along with many others from the BEF.[8] This air attack may also be the source of a later report in the German propaganda magazine *Signal*. A journalist accompanied a Luftwaffe plane attacking many targets, including what he calls a 'horse-drawn Artillery column', and an illustration shows British soldiers with helmets fleeing in panic, along with a couple of men wearing turbans.[9] Unfortunately the war diary of 32nd Company has not survived, so the details of Groom Akbar's death are not known, and the only source for 32nd Company's route is a report that Hills wrote in July.[10]

Hockey player Chaudry Wali Mohammad vividly remembered bomb blasts, explosions and constant gunfire: 'the German planes were like terrible birds flying overhead and firing on us … I did not sleep for fifteen days.'[11] The 32nd Company were ordered to abandon their equipment and animals at Bergues, just eight miles from the beaches.[12] Having brought the mules all the way from Punjab, this was hard for the men. Driver Sher Mohd was given responsibility for the 'treasure chest', which contained the unit's store of cash and the men's medals, as well as the little ammunition they had for their revolvers.[13] They reached Dunkirk on 23 May, and Chaudry later recalled:

> We didn't think we would come out of there alive … Everything was on fire. The whole of Dunkirk was alight. There were so many fires it was like daylight … The ship we were supposed to board was sunk. We got down to the beach and found the ship had sunk, so then we had to run back to the woods.[14]

They finally embarked on 25 May and ended that day in the British Army base at Aldershot in Hampshire.[15] There is an interesting by-tale of their journey. Captain John Ashdown, their second-in-command, later told his family that he was ordered to abandon not only the mules and equipment, but the men as well. He refused, was court-martialled but released. This story is fairly well known and has been quoted by recent journalists, partly because Ashdown was the father of the British politician Paddy Ashdown.[16] Unfortunately there is nothing in the archives that bears out this story, either in London or Delhi.

On 12 May Force K6 had received its first and single largest loss of life for the whole war. Fifteen men were sent from the Reinforcement Unit to join 22nd Company, working with 51st Highland Division.[17] A low-flying German aircraft attacked the train and dropped four bombs. Four RIASC men were killed and two were wounded. The dead men were buried at the large British Great War cemetery at Terlincthun, near Calais. Hills' report on the incident said that 'since that date other casualties have occurred and are to be expected'.[18] This was a real war, and death was part of the equation.

The 25th Company were somewhat later escaping to the coast than 32nd Company.[19] There was an initial flurry of activity on 10 May, while the rest of the BEF left their carefully prepared defence lines and advanced into Belgium. The next ten days were spent looking after their animals and waiting at their camp at the Dillies' farm while history was made all around them. Hurricanes of the RAF's 87 Squadron came and went from the airfield next door, and German aircraft bombed regularly.[20] On 15 May Akbar returned from England, and the following day Captain Thompson, who had been covering Akbar's two troops, left to return to the Reinforcement Unit. On 19 May, the day that Guderian's reconnaissance units reached the English Channel near Abbeville, six Messerschmitts flew over the camp and bombed the airfield. Three men, including Warrant Officer Sardar Ali, one of the company's star hockey players, experienced a near miss when a bomb dropped and splashed them with mud. Miraculously this was the closest that any men of 25th Company came to death during that fateful month. Finally, on the evening of 20 May, they received their marching orders from Major Barrington, in command of the Cypriot mule company. They loaded their carts with all the equipment, food and forage they could carry, leaving behind some hay, straw and live sheep, and set off westwards by night along the Belgian border, reaching their destination at Forêt de Nieppe in the middle of the night, having marched thirty-five miles. From there they continued northwards towards the coast, 'fighting their way home to Blighty', as Churchill put it.[21] The confusion continued, however – with no reliable radio or telephone, their officers had repeatedly to seek out staff officers to receive clear information and orders, while being bombed by the Luftwaffe 'like a rat in a cage with a cat inside it'.[22] In the early hours of 22 May they halted near Cassel at a place called Winnezeele, where Major Wainwright reported 'men tired but cheerful' and there they had a 'good night's rest'.[23]

One of the men enjoying that respite was Jemadar Nizam Din. This gap-toothed, craggy-faced VCO was a soldier with long experience on the North West Frontier, and would turn out to be one of the few men to stay with Force K6 until their return to India in 1944. By then he had risen through the ranks and was a lieutenant. Such were the opportunities the war afforded – for a man from Rawalakot in Kashmir this would have been unthinkable before 1939.[24] But Nizam Din worked hard and displayed great qualities – he was recommended for a Mention in Dispatches for 'setting an outstanding example' in the period before Dunkirk. Major Wainwright's recommendation continues: 'He showed leadership and devotion to duty of a very high order and was untiring in his efforts to maintain the morale and discipline of the Indian ranks. He was always ready to accept any mission however arduous or dangerous.'[25] He had acted with coolness in organising and leading the men in very trying circumstances. The fact that 25th Company (and the other units) stayed together so well was largely due to VCOs like Nizam Din.

During the stay at Winnezeele they took the opportunity to send Akbar with their lorries back to the farm at Marquette, where they picked up some useful supplies, including a number of sheep. A platoon of the Worcestershire Regiment found them a few days later:

> When we arrived at Cassel we found the RIASC muleteers just moving out to Dunkerque and the Chateau grounds we took over from them had been bombed or shelled and 18 horses and mules killed. The English NCO in charge also handed over a meal they had cooked of chicken and bread and butter which was very acceptable as we had not had anything to eat, except a few biscuits, for two days.[26]

It was not until Sunday 26th that Major Wainwright, having driven seventy-one miles around the tightening triangular pocket that contained the BEF and the French First Army, finally received clear orders to march to the coast. The mules were to be set free, and all equipment to be left behind, except their personal equipment and six days' rations. They marched at half-past ten, 300 Indians including Akbar, and twenty-three Britishers, including the RASC drivers. Along with them was their *agent de liaison*, a new man called Caspar, who would have had mixed feelings about leaving his country at its time of need. On the night of the 27th, according to their war diary:

> Dunkerque was now in ruins, burning furiously and being bombed incessantly. Captain Cole returned to unit by midnight 27/28 with orders to march immediately to Bray Dunes via Teteghem and Zuydcoote.
> 2300 Company marched.
> 0200 Coy passed Teteghem & met staff officer at junction of road Dunkerque–Fournes who ordered unit to jettison packs and blankets. Men donned greatcoats but lost the remainder of their kit. The unit was directed towards Fournes & finally on to sand dunes near Fort des Dunes. No one could be found to issue orders & CO decided to halt until daylight to avoid losing contact.[27]

And so, in the small hours of 28 May, they reached that fateful beach, still together, still a unit, with all their men intact, but with only the clothes they stood up in.

As dawn broke at Fort des Dunes, Wainwright set off for information, and Akbar found that 'the situation all along the beaches of Dunkirk was pathetic. One saw our defeated army in thousands in utter confusion. It was a most depressing sight to see thousands of unarmed soldiers miserably wet, hungry and thirsty and in despair.'[28] For experienced professional officers like Akbar, Cole and Wainwright this must have been an awful sight, and one that ran the risk of taking away the men's faith in the Raj.[29] The war diary records: '0800 About 2000 British troops were wandering about in vicinity of Casino & beaches. Later this number increased to over 10,000 ... Driver Green RASC was reported missing.'[30]

Fort des Dunes was a major French fortification four miles east of the town of Dunkirk and would prove to be one of the last French forts to surrender, on 3 June. Although it may have seemed to Wainwright and Akbar that discipline was breaking down, in fact the chain of command was intact, the narrowing perimeter was being held by British and French troops, and the evacuation was being carefully managed by the Royal Navy. As the day wore on, it became clear that boarding a ship would take time, and the men moved gradually nearer to the beach itself, having been bombed by the Luftwaffe again. At six o'clock Wainwright and Akbar were told to march to the East Mole, a *jetée* or breakwater nearly a mile long, made of open concrete piles with a wooden walkway, not intended as a place for mooring. With so much of the harbour out of action, the beachmasters were forced to improvise, and this mole and its western counterpart would prove crucial in getting away so many soldiers.[31] It also figured prominently in Christopher Nolan's 2017 film *Dunkirk*.[32] The march to the mole was led by Akbar, as Cole and Wainwright were searching for a lorry to carry the sick men. One can only imagine how the 25th Company's march looked to the Tommies and the French civilians around them: 300 mule drivers, grooms and farriers, carrying their maulvi and the other sick men, in an orderly column through the jumble of vehicles and abandoned equipment along the sands in the gathering twilight, en route from the Pothwar plateau to Salisbury Plain.

The march continued in the evening light, but as they neared the mole, they were forced to split up due to pressure of numbers. The war diary does not mention the long wait, but the fact that it took them eight hours to cover about five miles shows the slowness of the process. Luckily rain fell in the afternoon and evening, which combined with RAF sorties to mean that the beaches were relatively unharassed by German aircraft that day. All of 25th Company managed to get on a variety of boats, and by three in the morning they were all off the mole, 300 of over 47,000 troops transported across the channel that day.[33] By the middle of the morning they were in England, at Dover station, where they were greeted by Women's Voluntary Service (WVS) workers with tea and biscuits. The sepoys asked the women:

> to lend them their empty brass trays and copper buckets... [and] started playing folk lore tunes on these utensils. Our entire party joined in singing and dancing. Even the lady workers and many British spectators joined in the dance ... it went on with great enthusiasm till the guard gave the warning whistle.[34]

They were taken to a variety of military camps across the south of England, including North Camp near Aldershot, where they were welcomed by 'Muslim Woking Mission worker, British Muslims and Indian Muslims led by KS Mahmud ... with gifts for the men'. They were home, or rather, they were in their new home.

* * * * *

The Dunkirk myth that sprang up after the evacuation has different forms. The French version is characterised by the idea that their soldiers were used as human shields. The senior British naval officer on the beaches said that the French felt they 'are defending Dunkirk for us to evacuate, which is largely true'.[35] There is an armada of writing in English on the 'nine days' wonder of May–June 1940'.[36] The single word 'Dunkirk', with its anglicised spelling, is used to stand for the whole story of the BEF and the Battle of France. The filmmaker Nolan, who was born in 1970, remarked that Dunkirk was a 'story I grew up with in its mythic, almost fairy-tale form'.[37] The elements of that myth include the tropes of sand, small ships and Stukas that inhabit every anglophone film representation of Operation Dynamo. The only French film version of the story does not even use the name 'Dunkirk', preferring the neighbouring suburb of Zuydcoote, and presents a challenge to those familiar tropes, with soldiers being shown as more disciplined, with their equipment and an officer at their head, and even some love interest in the town.[38] For people in South Asia, the name 'Dunkirk' is not generally recognised, and the fact that 615 Indians were present on the beaches in the summer of 1940 is a surprise.

However Dunkirk is seen now, it was not the end of the Battle of France. Apart from the millions of French troops ready to fight, there were still around 140,000 British troops in France (including over 1,000 men of K6) and no plans to evacuate them. For political as much as for military reasons, Churchill and his war cabinet decided to reinforce these men and create a second BEF, under General Alan Brooke (later Lord Alanbrooke). A plan was formulated to make a stand in Brittany, centred around Rennes, with both ends of the line anchored on the coast.[39] Alanbrooke was not convinced this plan had much chance of succeeding, and said to Churchill on the phone: 'I had been sent to France to make the French feel that we were supporting them. I replied that it was impossible to make a corpse feel, and that the French Army was, to all intents and purposes, dead.'[40] Just a few days later, the new French premier, Marshal Pétain, broadcast to the nation, ordering the troops to cease fighting, and one of Alanbrooke's French liaison officers 'burst into my room and collapsed in a chair shaken from head to foot with sobs of tears'. France was in a 'whirlpool of … catastrophe', and the second BEF now had to be evacuated. Operation Aerial was the codename.

As part of Aerial, the Indian General Hospital was the next part of K6 to be evacuated. On 10 June the seventy-two staff and patients were loaded onto cattle trucks and taken by train to La Baule, just outside St Nazaire, a port city at the mouth of the river Loire.[41] The men of the hospital waited there a few days and then marched to the port on 16 June. With enemy bombers overhead, they were forced to take cover 'flat against a wall' before continuing their march and boarding MS *Sobieski*, a Polish cruise ship of the Gdynia-America line. As they left, the ship was attacked by German planes, but was not damaged, docking at Falmouth on 18 June. The men of the hospital unloaded and were put on trains to Leeds. Along with 32nd Company and 25th Company, a third component of Force K6 was now safe.

The 47 Supply Depot Section had been based at Marseilles until 9 May.[42] Their commanding officer was the dark-haired, moustachioed, serious-looking 45-year-old Major John Finlay, who had postponed his retirement to join K6 in 1939.[43] He had an excellent working relationship with his unit, and he always spoke well of his men in his diaries. The SDS supplied the suppliers: they ran a large store of food, forage and materials that they sent on to each company when needed. They were also responsible for the crucial flow of live sheep and were therefore required to keep good relations with local farmers. This small unit included thirty-one non-combatants in its total of forty-three men, with job titles that included issuer, checker, clerk and paulin maker.[44] These were clerical, technical men with specialised trades carrying out an essential service for the men and animals of the Punjab, helping to bridge the gap with home.

The day before the Germans attacked, the men travelled from the south coast to the north coast of France, while a special goods train carried 350 tons of supplies. At Le Havre the next day they opened their store in the docks at 'Magazine Généraux', attached to a British supply depot, and recommenced supplying hay, sheep and spices. They stayed there for the next eleven days, with periods of intense air raids and intervals of relative peace in a kind of stop–start existence, until they were ordered across the river Seine on 22 May, only to be ordered back the next day – such was the confusion behind the lines. The only incident on that slow journey was when 'a Frenchman on a motorcycle travelling at speed ran head on into the leading lorry damaging himself and his vehicle considerably'.[45] They resumed their supplying operations at Le Havre, with 'visits by enemy aircraft now a daily occurrence' at dusk, and one air raid that completely destroyed the houses opposite their billet, as well as all the forage. On 7 June, two days after the Germans renewed their attack on the French Army, the men of 47 SDS were ordered to evacuate to the west, leaving all their supplies behind. They spent a large part of that day sitting in a train at the station, waiting to depart, while 'nervousness increased'. They left the next day, travelling through air raids at Rouen and unloading at Saint-Thégonnec, south of Roscoff. There they were 'well housed in huts. No air raids. Life in the country very pleasant after Le Havre', until they were driven to Brest, the country's second military port, to embark on a ship that would take them to England.[46]

RMS *Strathaird* was a P&O cruise liner that regularly sailed the mail route from London to Australia via Suez and Bombay, and its crew of 490 included many Indian lascars.[47] These were sailors in the British merchant navy from east of the Cape of Good Hope, mainly India. They worked longer hours than their European counterparts, slept in worse conditions, ate a cheaper diet and were generally exploited.[48] Labour Party politician Nye Bevan described them as 'cheap human fodder'. Their combined labour was 'indispensable to British trade in a global economy' and amounted to 50,000 men, about a quarter of the merchant navy.[49] So when the men of 47 SDS walked up the gangways of the *Strathaird* on 17 June, they were 'very happy' as the 'Indian crew – many of whom were Punjabis – greeted and treated them royally'.[50] Finlay goes on to record that there was 'Indian food in quantities', so the crossing to Plymouth must have seemed like something of a home away from home.

The *Strathaird* sailed out of Brest with '6,000 troops, hundreds of civilians, 200 children and the gold from British banks in Paris' and arrived in Devon on 18 June.[51] The men stepped on English soil for the first time the next day (two hours before their comrades of 29th Company arrived at the same port), and Finlay enthused about their reception: 'Arrangements beyond praise. Tea, food, cigarettes, everything. Even beautiful weather and a band! … no Indians have ever landed in the headquarters of the Commonwealth with a warmer welcome.'[52] They were accommodated at Marsh Mills, at the head of the estuary of the river Plym, where they were 'very happy' and were soon to be joined by 700 of their countrymen.

Those 700 men were from 29th Mule Company, Reinforcement Unit, the Advanced Remount Depot and the HQ, all based around Le Mans.[53] As the small column of the ARD passed through one town, a 'party of British officers hearing rumble along street at night think the Germans have come' – the sense of panic was always just around the corner. Information during the march was in short supply. François de Champeaux, the aristocratic anglophone *officier de liaison* attached to Hills' HQ was dispatched to Paris on 3 June for information, returning three days later with more questions than answers. In the words of historian Marc Bloch (himself forced to surrender at Rennes a few days later), 'from the beginning to the end of the war, the metronome at headquarters was always set at too slow a beat.'[54] On 9 June Hills was ordered by British General de Fonblanque to proceed westwards by train. Hills, knowing that there were more British and Canadian divisions arriving, argued instead that they should march to Nantes on foot, and undertook to be 'entirely responsible for the march'. Indian-born de Fonblanque agreed, so on 10 June the column of Indian troops set off from Mulsanne on minor roads, with mules and carts and all their kit. That night they marched twenty-five miles to the village of Malicorne on the river Sarthe, and the 'headlights of refugee cars lit up column on the move', and a further sixteen miles to Chateau le Grip, where de Champeaux managed to secure them good accommodation at a low price. On Tuesday 11th they marched eighteen miles to Thorigné d'Anjou, which was a 'poor camp site, crowded and very little cover. All animals taken to graze at side of roads twice daily as no provision of fodder on operation march.'

On the next day they rested, sharing out grain for the animals and cigarettes and food for the men. One of 29th Company's horses was sick and had to be destroyed, and the men managed to sell the skin for fifty francs: some normality was maintained. Colonel Hills, meanwhile, was always trying to find meaningful work for men and animals, and made enquiries about using mules for forestry work – this on the same day that 51st Highland Division were forced to surrender near Le Havre. Through all the documents from this time hovers an aura of unreality – that these men had no idea of the scale of the defeat that was unfolding, nor of its pace.

The following day they heard that Paris had been evacuated by the French Army – the Germans marched in later that day – and that night the column had a 'pleasant march' of seventeen miles to Chateau Ancenis du Bois. Hills was informed in great secrecy that the BEF HQ would leave France, and that night the column marched another twenty-five miles to Héric, with Jemadar Fazal Dad of 29th Company 'again [losing] his way'. There they received orders that must have sounded insane on first hearing: they were to abandon but not destroy their animals, carts and equipment and proceed by lorry to St Nazaire. Major Gillmore of the Reinforcement Unit was at first suspicious of the messenger bringing this order, as there was much talk of spies and Fifth Columnists at the time, so he conferred 'as to the genuineness of this order and whether the bona fides of the messenger were trustworthy'.

Once the officers were sure that the order was from British commanders, Hills ordered everything 'to be handed over to the local civil authorities who would distribute the animals to local farmers and kit etc to refugees'. The 29th Company men left their mules 'with great reluctance' and prepared to depart with 'one ground sheet and two blankets only per man and three days rations'. They probably squirrelled away some valuables in their pockets – money and a photo from home – and Nur Muhammad, the Reinforcement Unit's maulvi would have taken great care to ensure his Qur'an was wrapped and stored in a safe place. Thus ended their epic march through the French countryside in the worst summer that country had seen. Their 120-mile journey was one of many, unknown to the history books, and was carried in their memories as a momentous stage in their great odyssey. Major Shannon of 29th Company wrote, 'it is noteworthy to record that at end of seven days march of approx. 120 miles, only one man of the unit was evacuated as sick.'

The next day all 700 men were loaded onto lorries and driven twenty-five miles to a suburb of St Nazaire called Montoir, where, ever aware of the threat from the air, they left their vehicles in three minutes flat. On Monday 17 June they marched together to the docks, where they found thousands of troops waiting to embark. Hills was 'determined that I would rather sail in the last ship than have units split up', so was pleased when they were all assigned to sail on SS *Floristan*. Air raids continued all day, and as 29th Company were boarding that evening:

> Just as head of unit was embarking, verbal message given … by captain of ship on quay side that fifty enemy aircraft were approaching. All men were ordered by naval authorities to dump their bedding rolls on side of quay and embark as quickly as possible. Men were despatched in batches of twenty at a time to ship's two gangways. All men were embarked very quickly together with approximately 35% of bedding rolls, which were thrown up by Agent de Liaison Sgt Chef AR Debon, who having completed his duty with the unit remained on quayside to see unit off. This Sgt Chef did excellent work single handed in throwing as many men's kits as possible aboard.[55]

Robert Debon had marched with the men every step from Le Mans. This was his duty as a French soldier, but many other soldiers had left their duty that summer, morale shattered. We can picture him on the quayside, throwing a bedroll, then another one, then another, until a hundred have been tossed up to the eager Indian hands catching and stowing in a human chain aboard, while matelots, squaddies, air force 'erks' and civilians look on with interest. As a French soldier, Debon's duty now was to stay in his country – even though he knew that Pétain had ordered the army to stop fighting the previous day – but he must have felt a pang of regret as he watched the *Floristan* steam away into the Atlantic, Gauloises cigarette in his mouth. Two years later Debon wrote from occupied France, saying that he 'hopes that the allies will soon come to the aid of France where all good Frenchmen will do all in their power to help'.[56] That this strong bond formed in just five months speaks of the charisma of the men of K6 and the openness and friendliness of their cultural and linguistic interpreter.

Floristan was stuffed to the gunwales, with about 3,500 troops and some British civilians, but all of the K6 men were 'in good spirit and although very tired, were behaving admirably under strain'. Nerves were stretched as they moved away from the quayside. They were attacked three times as they departed, and when a Junkers 88 bomber came at them the next day, it was shot down by soldiers using Bren guns, to much cheering and shouting.[57] The *Floristan* was lucky: that day saw the sinking of RMS *Lancastria* in the same harbour, the worst maritime disaster in British history, with the loss of around 3,500 lives. Corporal Donald Draycott of the RAF 'took my tin helmet off, my uniform, my boots, clutched my paybook and my French francs and jumped feet first over the side'.[58] He lived to tell the tale, and reported that, 'fifty yards away from me, men were singing "Roll out the Barrel".'[59]

Floristan sailed in a convoy of twenty ships, arriving at Plymouth Sound on Wednesday 19 June, where the men spent 'a peaceful warm night on board'. They were delighted to eat fresh rations, as they had been living on 'bread and biscuits, butter, marmalade, Bully Beef and tinned fish since 16th'. On the morning of 20 June, they marched off the ship, with a 'Royal Marine band in attendance on wharf'. They found the 47 SDS waiting for them at Marsh Mills camp, where they spent the next ten days under canvas, washing, exchanging their French francs for British shillings, eating and smoking. The relief must have been palpable, and there is an interesting postscript to this chapter. A young RASC officer called Philip Malins was also in Plymouth, recently evacuated from Dunkirk. He saw the men at Marsh Mills, and it was 'the wonderful bearing of the Force K6 personnel there which caused me to apply for the Indian Army', which he subsequently did in 1942.[60] Back from France, from the second round of mayhem and slaughter, the men of Force K6 were acting as ambassadors again.

Across the UK that summer, soldiers were recovering, sleeping long hours, eating their fill and telling their stories in pubs. Alanbrooke's diaries record a real fear that the Germans would invade and that the army would have to fight them across southern England.[61] But the mood in the country was curiously upbeat. The defeat could seem like a sort of victory, as the majority of the BEF had come home safely, albeit without most of its equipment. There was also a strong sense that the country was now alone against the Nazi hordes. That feeling had two alternative expressions as seen in cartoons from the time. The more famous cartoon, published in the *Evening Standard* on 18 June is by David Low and shows a Tommy standing defiant by the stormy sea, rifle in hand and fist raised towards the bombers overhead. 'Very well, alone' is the caption.[62] In a later cartoon in *Punch*, Fougasse (Kenneth Bird) portrayed two soldiers sitting near the sea on a sunny day.[63] One smokes a pipe and the other reads a newspaper – they could almost be on holiday. The first one remarks, 'So our poor old empire is alone in the world', and his mate replies, 'Aye we are – the whole five hundred million of us'. Fougasse was a veteran of the Great War and had seen the value of Empire soldiers at Gallipoli. He knew that 'alone' meant 'with the Empire', including India. Low was himself from New Zealand, so perhaps he had the Empire in mind in his more famous stormy cartoon. A successful cartoon can articulate a moment, summarise a feeling, capture the national zeitgeist. It is hard to know whether Low or Fougasse captured the mood best. There is a strong feeling of defiance in both cartoons, but in Fougasse there is also a confidence, a sense of calmness. For Fougasse, the sense of aloneness was an inclusive sense – there was a wider 'we'. The BEF had included men from the white Dominions, and the men of K6 were there to represent the Jewel in the Crown. They would do that for the next forty-three months in the very home of that crown: Great Britain.

5

Mules by the Maginot and the march up the Moselle

Hail, Moselle, great bearer of fruits and men.
Noble patricians honour you, youth practised in war.[1]

While most of the men of K6 were finding their feet in the new world of England, one unit was still in France: 22nd Mule Company. Among their number, alongside Muhabbat Shah, were some key figures of Force K6: jokers, escapers, collaborators and diehards. One notable character was Dafadar Abuzar of Hathiya Pain village in Jhelum, a few miles away from the Grand Trunk Road. From a classic Punjabi Muslim martial background, this man sounds like 'Mr Average', being described later as medium height, medium build, with a 'wheat complexion, slightly bald in front, space between two front teeth'.[2] His later career in the war was anything but average, however. He was born in 1912, so was 28 in the summer of 1940. He had been educated to middle-school level in his village and was clearly very bright. At the age of 11 he moved away from his village to the town of Sialkot, to live with his cousin, who was in the RIASC. This cousin was a great influence on the young Abuzar, for when he was 18 he also joined the RIASC at Lahore. He progressed swiftly through the ranks, served in Waziristan, and by 1939 was an ambitious young troop dafadar with 22nd Company. In a troop of fifty-eight men and a similar number of mules, the dafadar was second-in-command to the jemadar (in this case Jehan Dad) and was therefore a figure of some authority. As the war progressed, Abuzar would take advantage of opportunities to advance up the ladder of promotion, sometimes by moving sideways.

One person who thought very highly of Abuzar at that stage was Sub-Conductor Tom Hexley. Apart from being something of an adventurer, Hexley is also very important to this story as a chronicler and archivist.

His detailed report is the main source of information on much of 22nd Company's progress. Additionally, his sister Irene kept an album full of photos, telegrams and press cuttings tracing his progress from India to France to England, back to India and then finally to Scotland. Hexley was from Birmingham; his great-grandfather was a clock-maker, and his son described him as a 'working-class Brummie'.[3] Like Abuzar, Tom Hexley rose up from the ranks, starting his military career in 1924 at the age of 18 in the Royal Regiment of Artillery as a gunner. The teenager took a while to settle in, for the training report from his course at Shorncliffe near Folkestone reads: 'This recruit started badly, but made very great improvement, and was finally one of the smartest in his squad. Keen and hardworking. A good shot.'[4] One can almost feel the man straining to improve. A photo from soon after that shows the young Tom, his hair combed back in a high bouffant style, his grey eyes looking slightly nervously at the camera, right arm displaying the single stripe of the lance bombardier.[5] This photograph was probably taken in November 1925, as part of the celebration for this promotion. A few months later he embarked on a journey that would profoundly affect his whole life. His regiment was posted to India in December 1925, where he learnt his soldiering and started to look about him at the world. He also received multiple promotions and got married in May 1928 to Rose Mary Bailey, from an Anglo-Indian family. Within two years there were two children, Noel and June, and by then young Tom, now an example of responsibility, had a second stripe on his arm as a bombardier.

By 1933, Tom had been in the army for ten years and had a decision to make. He brought his family back to Britain for ten months' leave, and to help him decide whether to stay in the British Army or join the Indian Army. His daughter June later wrote that 'the Raj had better prospects', and so their fate was sealed. As a supremely practical man, Hexley joined the RIASC, where he was in charge of bakers and butchers, supply columns and animals. His confidential report for 1935 (by which time he was a staff sergeant) described his 'great zeal and ability ... plenty of initiative' and concluded, 'He should go far'.[6] The officer who wrote that report had no idea just how far Hexley would go. Meanwhile Hexley was doing the things that young white men in India did, working-class and middle-class alike. His family photo album shows him visiting the Taj

Mahal and other tourist sites, going hunting – where he 'bagged a tiger and a panther' – and with his trusted horse Blackie, 'the finest horse on the frontier'.[7] Hexley was learning skills, exploring the world and having a good time too. Perhaps because of his mixed-heritage wife, Hexley seems to have got on well with Indians of humble backgrounds – there are plenty of photos of him with Indian colleagues, and one shows him 'eating curry dhall and ghi'. After several tours of duty on the frontier, Hexley was ready for dangerous service overseas, and was seconded to 22nd Company in November 1939 as sub-conductor, warrant officer responsible for the company's stores: essentially a quartermaster.[8]

When the Germans attacked on 10 May, Abuzar, Muhabbat Shah, Hexley and the rest of 22nd Company were to be found near the much-maligned Maginot Line. This extraordinary feat of engineering consisted of a series of forts, trenches and defence-in-depth that stretched along the entire Franco-German frontier from the Dreiländereck or Three Nations Corner near Basel in neutral Switzerland to the town of Schengen in neutral Luxembourg. Unfortunately, it did not stretch as far as the Channel, and thus a section of 200 miles was left unprotected. This line was constructed in the 1930s as a response to the slaughter of the Great War and the remilitarisation of Germany under Hitler. With the motto of '*on ne passe pas*' (they shall not pass), it was supposed to fulfil a 'braking function' and slow down the German advance.[9] Safe behind the Maginot Line, the French troops would 'let the enemy bleed itself white in fruitless assaults, while the Anglo-French blockade excluded the vital raw materials and slowly strangled the economy of Germany'.[10] Looking at forts like the Ouvrage Hackenberg, the men of 22nd Company would have been impressed, for it was truly a marvel of mid-twentieth-century engineering, hermetically sealed from the outside, with electrically operated 135mm heavy guns and a railway inside to carry troops from one blockhouse to another, a vast electricity generator and extensive kitchens. Unlike in the Great War, however, there was no continuous line of trenches, and forts such as Hackenberg were only part of the system.[11] Infantry and armoured divisions were stationed in front of these forts, and such units required deliveries of supplies.

From Hackenberg to the German border is a distance of around ten miles. In that corner of the Franco-German frontier, east of the river

Moselle, the BEF deployed Saarforce, named after the Saarland on the other side of the border. The idea was that an infantry brigade (later a division) would be under French command, in between the Maginot forts and the border. The majority of the BEF, much further west towards the sea, were facing Belgium, but the Saarforce were facing real Germans with real German guns, and this experience would 'blood the BEF to front line patrol activity'.[12] From 13 April the division in question was the men of the inexperienced 51st Highland Division. They found themselves in trenches among 'rolling country … peppered with huge beech woods and blossoming orchards'.[13] The farms and villages had been evacuated, so this country was at first very quiet, and only the 'singing of the ubiquitous nightingale gave evidence of life'. A peaceful scene for 22nd Company to enter, soon to become the first soldiers of the Indian Army on the front line.

Having spent longer in Marseilles than the rest of Force K6, 22nd Company arrived in the area north of Metz on 7 May and were posted to the small village of Monneren, three miles east of Hackenberg.[14] In this countryside of woods and fields, full of deer and wild boar, their job was to deliver supplies to the engineers and Highland infantry regiments in the front lines. Hills visited them and wrote of their 'good work, particularly on one occasion when ammunition was required by an outpost that was being attacked'.[15] As in the Great War, the sound of a lorry engine, and its high profile, would draw fire from the opposing trenches. Mules were quieter and far less visible, so they were used to carry barbed wire, sandbags, timber and ammunition right up to the trenches, within view of the German lines. Sapper Jack Sherratt of the Royal Engineers was attached to the Black Watch in the Grosswald forest, east of Hackenberg. Sixty years later he still had vivid memories of the scene:

> Myself and two sapper comrades were resting in our bivouac on the edge of a small clearing in the Grossenwald forest, being off duty at the time in preparation for night work.
>
> Suddenly without any warning we were confronted by a mule column of the RIASC led by an officer which had emerged silently from the forest. The Indian troops and mules were immaculate, their KD [khaki drill uniforms] was spotless and pressed, the mules shone. Quite a contrast to three scruffy

sappers. The officer who had a chest full of ribbons starting from WW1 wanted directing to the 4 Black Watch. There were no paths in the forest so we had to point in the direction of the Black Watch HQ hoping they would not finish up in the enemy lines.

They disappeared as silently as their approach. We never saw them again. I assumed that when we withdrew to the Somme area late in May they returned to the Middle East via the South of France.[16]

The silence that Sherratt observed was blown apart on 10 May when this front line became active. Three days later there was a large-scale assault by the Germans, the 'Battle for Remeling'.[17] As Sherratt says, 51st Division withdrew on 20 May, but 22nd Company stayed behind: three of the four troops were brought together near the village of Luttange, a few miles south of Hackenberg on the road to Metz.[18] On 19 May they were joined by Major Eardley of the Royal Army Veterinary Corps (RAVC), seconded to help look after the animals.[19] A few days later the whole company withdrew to Metz, and thus began their epic march up the Moselle River.[20]

* * * * *

The Moselle runs northwards for 340 miles from a mountain called Ballon d'Alsace near the Swiss border, through the Vosges mountains, across the wheat-growing plains of Lorraine to Metz, then along the Germany–Luxembourg border to the Roman city of Trier until it reaches the Rhine at Koblenz, where it empties its water into that great stream beneath a statue of Kaiser Wilhelm I. Unlike the rivers of Punjab that our men knew so well, this was a lush green river, with forests, fields and vineyards on each bank, an area famed for its wines. On 24 May 22nd Company crossed the river north of Metz and camped at the railway sidings at Woippy. For the next three weeks they remained there, working with the British supply depot, loading and unloading trains. During this period, the 'nine days' wonder' of Dunkirk started and finished, Italy entered the war and their erstwhile comrades of 51st Division surrendered at St Valéry. But the areas close to the Maginot Line were generally left by the Germans until the end; indeed the only French troops that were still fresh were to be found there, immobilised in their forts.

So 22nd Company were, for the moment, in a small oasis of calm amidst the multiple disasters of that summer. On 13 June a party of VCOs were taken to visit one of the Maginot forts, probably Hackenberg itself – the French were still confident of their ability to hold the line. That same afternoon, their commanding officer, Major Hitchcock, who had just passed a selection board for promotion to the rank of lieutenant colonel at the age of 47, received an order to evacuate Metz immediately.[21] Large quantities of stores (including sixty sheep) were loaded onto their carts and lorries, the latter driven by white British RASC drivers. Lieutenant Laslett zoomed off on his motorcycle to pick up 'odd people' who were away from the camp, including the *agent de liaison* Soldat Gluckmann-Rodanski. Hexley wrote that the latrines 'were filled in and the campsite left clean in correct Indian Army style' and then goes on to give praise: 'The cheerfulness of Sweeper Basanta and his complete and unshakable trust in the British "Badshah" at all times during the months which followed was marvellous. He carried out his usual duties at all times and, to the best of my belief, did not have an enemy in the Coy.'[22] They left as darkness fell. Captain Anis with the seven lorries went on ahead, and the rest of the company followed with their carts, travelling much more slowly. Like their comrades in the other companies before them, they marched at night.

They arrived the next day at their first stopping place, Pont-à-Mousson, having lost one driver who was knocked down by a French car, spent four hours waiting to cross the river in Metz, and nearly lost five carts which took a wrong turning and headed north in the darkness. After a short rest they continued southwards along the riverbank as 'the inhabitants of Pont-à-Mousson turned out "en masse" and many complimentary remarks were passed on the bearing and fitness of the men'. For the peasants of eastern France, bewildered by the rapid collapse of so many of their institutions, the sight of a column of mule carts driven by Indian soldiers was still a novelty, despite the troubled times. Optimists in the company would have felt reassured: the weather was fine, there was still a plentiful supply of food that was familiar for men and beasts. With the lorries driving ahead, Laslett on his motorcycle running messages and Hexley on his horse, Ginger, galloping up and down the column, they must have made quite a spectacle of old and new technology, of Europe and Asia together.

There were large numbers of refugees on the roads and in the towns, but there were also long stretches of road with very little traffic. At this stage they were still hoping to be able to get onto trains at their next stop – the town of Mirecourt, south of Nancy. Captain Anis continued with the lorries, with Laslett on his motorbike looking for a good route round Nancy. Hexley then took over the motorcycle but got separated in the darkness. He managed to find the carts again: 'by following the trail of oats shaken off the carts by the rattling over cobbled roads. (I thought of the "Babes in the Wood" at the time).' It almost sounds as if Tom Hexley is enjoying himself dashing around the French towns in the dark. He caught up with his comrades at Canal de Jonction, six miles south of Nancy, where they bivouacked for a few hours.

Next morning they marched off again to Mirecourt, where they hoped to board trains to take them west. Major Hitchcock went on ahead with Gluckmann-Rodinski and found that the French Army HQ were 'not a bit interested in our fate', as they watched the rapid advance of Guderian's Panzers, now heading back eastwards towards the Swiss frontier. Hitchcock was beginning to show signs of worry – in which direction could salvation lie for a column moving at thirty miles a day? They continued past the centre of Mirecourt, where rumours abounded of the French armies being on the run (this was the day that the great French fortress at Verdun was captured), and Laslett witnessed the railway station 'choked with refugees and the station staff at their wits ends … complete chaos'. The following day, the Luftwaffe 'carefully and methodically bombed Mirecourt railway station'. A train was no longer an option there.

The next day Hitchcock allowed the men and animals to rest, possibly because he did not know what to do. This was 16 June, the day that Pétain ordered the French Army to stop fighting and the day that Guderian reached the Swiss frontier, thus cutting off all the Maginot Line troops – and 22nd Company – from the rest of France. Hitchcock did not know that yet, and in the absence of any other information, Laslett rode off again on his motorbike and returned with news that the local French Army HQ was no better informed, with their own communications broken down.[23]

At this stage Captain Anis made a bold suggestion: they should abandon their animals and carts, and transport the men in the seven lorries due south as fast as they could, until they were out of the path of the Germans. As each lorry could carry about twenty men, this would take two trips. Many BEF soldiers did manage to evade the advancing Germans by going south, escaping via Switzerland or Spain or in one of the last boats from the west coast. Hitchcock refused, maintaining that it was against Indian Army tradition to abandon equipment, and preferring to head south-east on foot for neutral Switzerland, around 100 miles from Mirecourt. Anis' plan might have worked if they could evade the advancing Panzers, and after the war Anis was very critical of his commanding officer, saying that he lost his nerve and was no longer in control. In fact, Anis told his daughter that he considered taking over command, but the major showed him a photograph of his daughter Veronica, which melted his heart.[24]

The men marched again that evening, south-east towards the river, through 'heavy French military traffic which seemed to be travelling in all directions'. They crossed the Moselle again at Epinal, and bivouacked in a wood to the south of the town. This was the morning of Monday 17 June, the day that the last of K6 escaped St Nazaire on the *Floristan*, and Hexley wrote that the men were all now aware of 'the gravity of the situation'. In the afternoon Anis and the lorries drove off south along the river while the carts marched 'in a Vosges Mountain rainstorm'. On this day the *route nationale* was 'deserted and good progress was made'. Along the way they were very surprised to meet a group of seven men from the Royal Navy who had been involved in Operation Royal Marine, floating mines down the Rhine from Strasbourg in a partially successful attempt to disrupt German river traffic further down.[25] These were the first Britons they had seen for several days, and it was 'rather a shock', according to Hexley. The naval men were now trying to get to Switzerland on foot, so they hitched a lift. The company and their guests arrived at Remiremont in the evening, and there they learnt of Pétain's broadcast and the impending surrender of all French forces.

The whole company stayed at Remiremont for all of Tuesday 18th, the day that Churchill spoke of 'their finest hour' and the unknown French Brigadier Charles De Gaulle (soon to be leader of the Free French, later president) broadcast his 'Appeal' to France.[26] Although the men of 22nd Company must have felt they were in a strange limbo, the work of a mule driver was never over, so feeding, grooming and watering continued, and Hexley conducted a clothing and kit inspection. Hitchcock was very worried, but Laslett 'with his usual cheerfulness kept our spirits up', even after another unsuccessful motorbike trip to French HQ. French military engineers later destroyed the bridge over the Moselle and reported German reconnaissance troops arriving.

On Wednesday 19th a French artillery colonel told them that the local French forces were preparing a 'last stand' at the ski resort of Gérardmer, further up into the mountains, and advised 22nd Company to follow suit. Hitchcock stated that 'his intention was to save life if possible and wait for the French Armistice to be signed. We were all resigned to our fates.' Captain Anis twisted the knife, and 'mentioned several times that his advice at Mirecourt should have been acted upon and an effort made to evacuate the men southwards'. Meanwhile, Jemadar Jehan Dad of 'A' Troop was severely stricken with sciatica and had to travel in a stretcher in the back of a lorry under the skilled care of the medical officer, Jemadar Rana Wali Mohd Khan, so Abuzar took over the troop and 'carried out [his duties] most efficiently and cheerfully'.

As they prepared to march again that evening, German artillery started to fire at them and a cart overturned, but the only article lost was 'the hat box and headgear of Captain Anis'. Again, Hexley praises the sweepers, writing, 'my last memory of the camp is a picture of Sweeper Basanta cheerfully struggling to "fill in" the latrine site under shellfire!' Hexley and Laslett went ahead on the motorcycle, two-up, and found a campsite near Gérardmer, but there was no water supply for the mules, which was to prove a serious problem in the next few days. Next day the animals were 'continually half whinnying and braying' from thirst. Later they were fed wet grass, which went some way to easing their condition.

For the next few days the company stayed where they were, preparing physically and mentally to surrender, while the negotiations for the general Armistice started and concluded at Compiègne. After slaughtering extra sheep for a *barra khana* (feast), Laslett and Anis explained to the men what was to be expected as a 'prisoner of war': that it was an honourable imprisonment with certain specific conditions, not to be confused with going to a civil or military prison for committing a crime. Hitchcock offered the seven British RASC drivers the chance to escape if they wanted, but they all chose to stay with the company – an indication either of their attachment to the men or their wariness of moving in unknown territory. Laslett and Hexley, the two young adventurers, talked of trying to escape, possibly even by motorcycle, but decided to remain with the men 'for the morale of the Coy and Major Hitchcock'. It is notable that they were as concerned about their commanding officer's feelings as they were for the men under them. On Saturday 22nd the French signed the Armistice (although the local troops did not capitulate until the next day), which prompted Hitchcock to decide to surrender on the 25th, a choice made easier by German artillery fire from the town of Gérardmer and extreme thirst among the animals. At 10 a.m. Hitchcock and Eardley went down the hill to the town to negotiate the surrender. Hexley recorded that, on his return, Hitchcock ordered:

> that a good turn-out be made, so during the afternoon kit was cleaned. At Metz I had issued out medal ribbons to the Coy and these made a good show. Buttons, boots, belts and harness were well cleaned and at [1900] hours the Coy was ready to march. The Coy marched steadily to the gates of Gérardmer in column of route and attracted the attention of many enemy officers and men by its smart turn out.[27]

The 'smart turn out' was an object of considerable pride for the officers of the RIASC; we can be sure that the carts, men and mules were looking their best and that the officers and VCOs were mounted on horseback. Hexley was told to dismount by a German officer and his horse was taken away, probably to be used by that officer. Hexley does not record hearing the cliché 'For you the war is over', used in so many war films when a soldier is captured, and in fact for him, the war was by no means over.

At this time of confusion and high emotions, Hexley was surprised to find himself suddenly in command when the four officers (Hitchcock, Eardley, Anis and Laslett) were put in a lorry and taken away without their kit, 'presumably for interrogation'. Hexley wrote: 'From the back of the lorry Capt Laslett with his usual cheerfulness called out "OK Hexley?". I called back "OK, Sir" That was the last the Coy and myself saw of the officers. They were taken away with just what they were wearing.'

Hitchcock takes up the story of the four officers.[28] He records that they were treated in a manner that was 'courteous, strictly correct, and might even be called considerate' and then driven into the mountains, to the Col de Bonhomme, where they were left in 'the middle of a mass of French and Belgian other ranks'. At this stage, they were still considering escape, despite being 'extremely hungry and very tired after the exertions and nervous strain of the preceding ten days'. The Col de Bonhomme is just fifty-five miles from Swiss territory through wooded hills; they had a map and compass, a tin of bully beef and some biscuits and were confident they could escape. But Hitchcock records that they were concerned for the fate of the men. We can imagine that Anis still bore his resentment against Hitchcock's earlier refusal to drive south to Dijon. The next morning, 'we were roughly summoned by an Under-Officer of unpleasant appearance, and placed in charge of a lance-corporal and guard of three soldiers, mounted on cycles and all armed to the teeth including stick bombs in their boots'. As they marched they were overtaken by a car. A German officer got out and 'rapidly worked himself into such a frenzy that I seriously expected him to have a stroke. It is the only occasion on which I have seen anyone go black with rage, which he literally did'. Thereafter, the lance corporal became stricter, firing 'potshots' over their heads and 'cracking a whip'. All thoughts of escape faded: their long captivity was just beginning.

* * * * *

Hexley had been left with the men because he was a warrant officer, not a commissioned officer. It was normal practice to separate officers from other ranks for imprisonment: the Geneva Convention on the treatment of POWs accorded them different status and conditions.[29] But the status of VCOs was less clear – this was a type of rank unknown to the Germans. The India Office had predicted exactly such a situation, sending a table of Indian Army ranks to the German government in December 1939, just before K6 arrived in France.[30] This table showed a jemadar as the equivalent of a German *Leutnant* (2nd lieutenant), a risaldar was like an *Oberleutnant* (1st lieutenant) and a risaldar major like a major. A letter of June 1941, when more Indians had been taken prisoner in Crete, reinforced the point: 'these officers are Viceroy's Commissioned Officers and as such should be treated as Commissioned Officers.' In fact, this may have given the eleven VCOs of 22nd Company a higher status in captivity than they were used to in the army, for a jemadar like Jehan Dad would not usually be perceived as being of the same rank as a British 2nd lieutenant. Like all prisoners held under the Geneva Convention, VCOs continued to receive pay – a VCO receiving forty-five Reichsmarks per month.[31] The VCOs of 22nd Company were soon to be separated from the men, and treated well – a German propaganda photo shows five VCOs chatting amiably with a German officer.[32]

The differential treatment of the VCOs, officers and other ranks throws some light on German racial hierarchy. A few weeks previously, at Airaines on the Somme, a German had shot and killed Captain Charles N'Tchorere, a black officer of the Tirailleurs Sénégalais (French West African colonial troops), when he claimed the right to stay with his fellow white officers when captured.[33] He was one of many: at least 1,500 black African soldiers were murdered by the German Army that summer. Goebbels' propaganda companies sought out the African soldiers, which Nazis took as 'living proof of the bastardisation of France'.[34] On 1 July the Wehrmacht's colour magazine *Signal* ran a story of the 'first colour photos of the Great Battle in the West' showing French colonial soldiers as prisoners: 'a colourful mingling of peoples in all the shades of the earth'.[35]

The Third Reich was built around 'scientific' racism, it was a central part of its mission. Why then did the Indian POWs taken in France and later seem to evade that treatment? The answer is that Indians were seen as fellow Aryans within the Nazi racial hierarchy. Hitler believed that the origin of the German 'master race' was in north India, so Punjabis were distant cousins. Added to that was a feeling that Germans had something in common with Islam, building on the 1914 alliance with Muslim Turkey. In July 1940 the German historian and diplomat Max von Oppenheim sent a memo to the German Foreign Office recommending a policy of inciting rebellion against France and Britain in the Islamic world: this was part of what has been called 'Berlin's Muslim Moment'.[36] Later, in 1944, Himmler declared, 'what is there to separate the Muslims in Europe and around the world from us Germans? We have common aims.'[37] There was an ideological link to the German ambition to recruit Indian soldiers into its army. Even though many Muslim scholars and citizens around the world rejected Nazi racism, from the German point of view an Indian

POW was seen as being on a similar rung to a white British one. Ill-treatment was reserved for Soviet POWs and Jews and Romany Gypsies in concentration camps. Indians, it seems, were lucky.

Guderian's men captured 150,000 French soldiers in the Alsace-Lorraine area that June.[38] The 320 men of 22nd Company were but a tiny fraction of that total. As the only Indian POWs in German hands for the next year, they were pioneers of a sort. Eighteen months later Commander-in-Chief Wavell recognised their communal bravery in a special order that read:

> His Excellency the Commander-in-Chief has received a report describing the conduct of No 22 AT Company (Mule) RIASC during the period of the German operations against France, May–June 1940. Throughout this period, and subsequently as prisoners of war, the discipline and devotion to duty of all ranks was of the highest order.
>
> His Excellency considers that their behaviour under the most trying circumstances is a great credit to all ranks of the unit, and their record is one which is in keeping with the best traditions of the Indian Army.[39]

The next five years would see those traditions stretched to breaking point, as Anis, Muhabbat Shah, Basanta and Abuzar endured boredom, bombing, hunger and temptations in the *Stalags* of the German Reich.

6

Back in Blighty

O wonder!
How many goodly creatures are there here!
How beauteous mankind is! O brave new world
That has such people in it.[1]

While Hexley and Barkat Ali and the rest of 22nd Company were heading to their fate at Gérardmer, the remainder of Force K6 was heaving a collective sigh of relief to be safe in England. Sub-Conductor James English was with the Reinforcement Unit at Plymouth, and wrote to his family in Leicester on 26 June: 'I vowed I would attend a church! Any church, the first Sunday I was at home on English soil once more.'[2] English was a professional soldier with a lifetime of experience, having served in the Great War as a trooper with the Scots Greys and been wounded at Ypres.[3] He was eventually made an officer in 1941, nine days before his fifty-first birthday. Now, in June 1940, this round, moustachioed, smiling man was back in Blighty, his homeland.[4] The sepoys of K6, however, were still 7,000 miles from their homes and families in Rawalpindi and Jhelum. Many things were strange to them, from the beaches to the rivers, the food to the green rolling hills of Devon and Kent. The people they encountered were different from the Britishers they knew at home. The soldiers and *memsahibs* of Rawalpindi were replaced by ordinary white people, some of them very scared. Among them were poor folk: ragged children, recently unemployed men and women with the lost look of hunger. They saw working men and women, trudging through the streets on their way to a shop or an office, eating lunch in a Lyon's Corner House while staring bleakly out of the window. The grandeur of *gore* in Hindustan was replaced by the everyday drudgery of white people at home. Perhaps these people were no different, no better than the people of Punjab.

The thought that Britishers were not superior was only one of the strange elements of this brave new world, the unfamiliarity accentuated by the good weather and the unique circumstances of that 'Spitfire summer'. With supplies of Indian food restored, with washing and resting completed, access to regular prayers, but with a total absence of animals to care for, the sigh of relief was followed by a series of question marks. Over the next ten months uncertainty hung over these men as their role evolved and they moved around the country. They started to meet British men, women and children in large numbers, including VIPs and pressmen, they were entertained to tea and cakes, and they started to fall in love.

That summer of 1940 lives long in British popular memory. It was a moment of change, of fear, of belt-tightening and breath-taking, and is remembered as a time of standing together, although not everyone subscribed to a single national mood.[5] After the Battle of France was concluded at the end of June, the Battle of Britain began, to be followed by the Blitz on London and other cities, lasting until May 1941.[6] From September onwards there was a daily fear of invasion, and civilians became used to living in air-raid shelters. A shelter could not protect one from anxiety and depression, however, and not all the British men in K6 were happy to be home again. On 22 September the young Captain Raymond Marmaduke Thompson of the Reinforcement Unit committed suicide.[7] This sad and desperate event was not unusual in wartime. He is buried at Tidworth in Wiltshire, beneath the cherry blossom.[8]

Having seen the battlefront in France, the men of K6 were now part of the Home Front. Like so much of the British Army, they would spend most of the war in Britain itself: 'the experience of war, at least prior to D-Day, for the vast majority of people in the Forces was a period of waiting, a time of boredom with routine and frustration with authority, a time of separation from loved ones and of the absence of home comforts.'[9] This was the time when the idea of the 'People's War' emerged – that the Home Front was as important as the battlefront, that everyone must 'do their bit' for the war effort.[10] The Ministry of Information, in charge of propaganda, put it succinctly on a poster: 'If the Home Front breaks, everything breaks.'[11] Having been present at Dunkirk and St Nazaire, the Punjabi sepoys were now part of that effort and could be embraced by Britishers as part of 'us'. The new secretary of state for India, the diminutive veteran MP and linguist Leo Amery, visited 25th and 32nd Companies at Pirbright on 8 June and recorded in his diary:

> The men, all Punjabi Moslems, were a fine strong-faced lot and the Indian officers looked good men, especially a fine old Major, Akbar, with old Mesopotamian experience. The men seemed to have done splendidly under fire, though their actual casualties were not heavy, and their discipline on return was generally noted. Had tea with the officers.[12]

The military and political hierarchy approved, which was to make Hills' job easier for the next three years.

However great the approval, these men were different. The previous day, the men of 32nd Company had visited a real mosque for the first time since leaving India six months before. This was the elegant Shah Jahan Mosque in Woking, founded in 1889, the first purpose-built mosque in Britain, and the centre of Muslim activity in Britain in the interwar period.[13] Chaudry Wali Mohammad recalled that first visit years later:

> We were all very puzzled how in this foreign land there could exist a mosque particularly as no Muslims seemed to live here … Soon after sunrise the next morning [Friday 7 June 1940] we gathered together and marched to Woking. When we were a short distance away we saw this small but beautiful mosque … We offered our prayers and thanked God for the opportunity to pray here.[14]

The newsletter *Islamic Review* recorded the visit:

> the enthusiasm of the men was so great that only one idea seemed to dominate their actions and their movements – they wanted to see their Mosque and bow their heads before their Creator under proper Muslim atmosphere … The visitors were received by the English Muslim ladies, Mrs. Burrows, Mrs. Groves and Mrs. Farmer, who also went round offering to each one of them cold drinks which were most appreciated after the long walk in the hot sun.[15]

After prayers, tea was drunk and a photograph taken – the only photo on record of an entire company. The mosque became K6's official leave centre from May 1941, with parties of thirty arriving weekly and regular trips to London, Waterloo Station being just twenty-five minutes up the line. Such was the comfort in the Nissen huts that Chaudry described it as 'like a five-star hotel at that time'.[16] Its importance as a centre for spiritual and physical rest was recognised by officers and men alike, and 25th Company's Major Wainwright wrote to the imam on 1 July expressing a wish to visit the mosque, thanking him for sending a copy of the Qur'an and stating: 'My intention is to read and digest a small portion each night before going to sleep.'[17] Whether he fulfilled that promise is unknown.

* * * * *

After the first few weeks, the men found themselves increasingly distant from Woking and the south-east. They were dispersed around the country, partly out of necessity, partly out of uncertainty, and found themselves in small towns and villages, mostly away from the worst of the Blitz. At the end of June came a surprise. Three hundred and six French mules had been evacuated from Norway and arrived on the docks at Glasgow.[18] Major Akbar and Captain Cole took 200 men from 25th Company to pick them up, and then went even further north to Lairg in the Highlands, a village where they would pass many happy days later in the war. Hills visited and was not impressed with the animals, describing them as 'uneven and in really poor condition'.[19] They were, however, the first mules they had taken charge of since leaving France, and those 200 men at least were doing the work they had been trained for. Soon after, 29th Company (now including James English and his bearer Lall Khan) had work to do, being posted to join the British Army Remount Depot at Rossington Hall near Doncaster, a grand house with extensive stables, recently vacated by an order of Catholic monks.[20] Here they found horses to look after (also French), and to exercise in the parkland around the hall. They seemed to have spent an enjoyable time here, attending the town council meeting and being inspected by King George VI, the first Indian soldiers in the war to be so honoured.[21] They took baths at the local coalmine and:

soon made friends with the locals, and young boys were soon introduced to eating chapattis that had been cooked over rocks heated by an open camp fire. The soldiers were invited into the mining village and Cambridge Street was the site of at least one formal tea party, where a Yorkshire miner's family shared rations with soldiers who were thousands of miles from home.[22]

A reporter for the *Doncaster Chronicle* visited and was impressed by their makeshift place of prayer:

> There was a plain carpet on the grass, railed off with a cord, no roof, no sides, open to the sun, and it is on that carpet that these men from India assemble five times each day and make their dutiful obeisance to Allah the All-knowing. Their mullah, or religious leader, turbaned, bearded, robed and sandalled, without a word of English, was good enough to recite a few verses in Arabic from the Koran – including the Fatiha, or opening chapter, which almost corresponds to our Lord's Prayer and is recited by Moslems on all special occasions. His sonorous tones, now low, now rising to a higher level, rang out in that typical English scene, and made many of us wonder if ever the Koran had been recited in a stranger setting.[23]

This positive and welcoming experience in Yorkshire was to be replicated over and over as the sepoys explored the UK during the next three and a half years.

Soon after that, the rest of the force were reunited in the heart of England, at the pretty town of Ashbourne in Derbyshire. Their short stay in this rather special place was to prove memorable for many of them. When they arrived there in the summer of 1940, a few of the men were billeted at the home of Herbert and Gladys Foster.[24] Herbert was a nurseryman who lived at a house called the Plateau with his wife Gladys and Betty, their 3-year-old daughter. They had two acres of nursery for shrubs and trees, plus four pens for hens laying eggs. From the beginning of July they were joined by men of the HQ accountancy department, led by Captain Gian Kapur. Kapur was a Hindu shopkeeper from Lahore turned army accountant, in his mid-40s, with experience of service in the Great War.[25] As Kapur was a Hindu, he brought with him a Hindu

Kundan Lall, Herbert Foster, Betty Foster and three unidentified sepoys at the Fosters' house near Shirley, autumn 1940.

Gian Kapur and Herbert Foster.

cook, Kundan Lall. Kapur and his colleagues very quickly became part of the family – Betty has strong memories of the men outside, cooking on a primus stove, while Kapur ate with the family. The men who were working up at the 'big house' would come down to the nursery in their spare time and help Herbert with the hens and the shrubs in the nursery. Betty quickly learnt to call Kapur 'Uncle Gian' – a courtesy title common to India and rural England.

After just four months the HQ moved on to Devon. Uncle Gian did not forget the Fosters' hospitality, however, and visited them several times before his return to India in 1942. By that point he had been awarded an MBE for his work with K6.[26] After Kapur's return home, he kept in touch with the family. He wrote a letter every Christmas, and Foster wrote back. He sent presents for Betty – ornamental shoes, a bowl and a ring – which she keeps safely to this day. The letters did not stop until the 1980s, when he became ill. Gian Kapur died at Meerut in 1985, aged over 90. The depth and the long duration of the friendship between this bespectacled businessman and the farming family from the middle of England is remarkable. It may be a product simply of circumstances – a friendly man a long way from home who was missing his country and family, at the first place he stayed after a traumatic time in France, coupled with a welcoming household who saw 'things were very serious then' and that 'the Indians had come to help us'.[27] In one of his final letters to England, in December 1980, Kapur wrote, 'How I remember the night we went to Shirley pub & were challenged by the sentry. I answered "FRIENDS".'[28] That seems like a suitable way to characterise their relationship, a warm memory of a warm friendship that lasted a lifetime.

Their time at Ashbourne saw a wide variety of activity. On 8 August they too were visited by King George VI, an occasion widely reported in the press and newsreels.[29] As part of that visit, the King was presented with two chapattis to take home for his daughters, Princess Elizabeth and Princess Margaret Rose. One wonders what happened to those treats, whether they were eaten by the current Queen and her sister, given to a courtier, or perhaps preserved in the royal archives. James English invited his sister Frances to join them – she lived close by in Leicester – and a family photo has brother and sister with Lall Khan, a close relationship made even closer after the men's experiences together in France.[30] A Pathé newsreel shown in India (with commentary by Z.A. Bokhari) was shot partly during that visit.[31] In the film we see men praying in the open air, sheep wandering free in the camp, and it closes with the men waving the King and Queen on their way, to shouts of '*Allahu Akbar*'.

Press coverage continued. The *Derby Telegraph* carried a story on 22 August, just four days after the 'hardest day' of the Battle of Britain. Sandwiched between a photo of a local wedding, an advert for Lava soap ('The soap that likes hard work') and a story of the assassination of Leon Trotsky in far-off Mexico, we learn that Akbar and some of his colleagues had attended a fete at Ashbourne vicarage, which was opened by Lady Nora FitzHerbert of Tissington Hall, and that the soldiers had sold chapattis to the townsfolk.[32] The men were now fully at home in Derbyshire.

One of the friendliest articles came from the *Ashbourne News Telegraph* in September 1940, a detailed piece entitled 'Indian Camp an Ornamental Wonder'.[33] The reporter describes the decoration around their tents at Shirley camp, with turf, stones and flowers used as decorations to pick out the name or badge of each unit, or a motto in Urdu, creating an effect 'of ornamental walks rather than of a military camp'. As the reporter wanders around, the emphasis is clearly on the social life of the camp: there is an English lesson in progress, he visits the mosque tent and watches the men playing chess, table tennis and hockey, and encounters the 'inevitable camp comedian'. And of course he visits the cookhouse, and observes the preparation of 'chappatties or wheat-cakes … [which] are becoming noted among residents in the district'.

Meanwhile, real work with animals was in short supply, so the men were put to use helping local farmers with the harvest.[34] The *Daily Mirror* reported on their work on an unusual crop on 15 October, by which time Ramadan had started:

Chanting native songs, 45 Indian soldiers have been pulling flax, with 180 other soldiers at Old Hall Farm Dunstall near Burton on Trent. They have worked each day, and from 5am till 7pm have abstained from eating, drinking or smoking, because this is their month of fasting. Miss Einsten, a land girl, was the only woman working among them. She stooked.[35]

There was still time for sight-seeing, with groups of men exploring scenic Derbyshire, visiting the Midland Agricultural College and observing sheep-dog trials.[36] On 6 August a party of nine had tea with the Duke of Devonshire at Chatsworth House, one of the grandest stately homes in the country. They were moving in the highest circles of British life. Six weeks later some men of the Reinforcement Unit visited Kedleston Hall, the birthplace of Lord Curzon, the Viceroy of India who had set up the Imperial Cadet Corps, which gave honorary commissions to the sons of rajahs and thus paved the way for Indianisation. There is a certain irony in this imperial circuit of soldiers of 1940 paying homage in the house of their former ruler.

Not all the interactions were so positive. Rosemary Spencer of Ashbourne remembered an occasion when an Indian soldier went up the tower at Osmaston Park and took potshots at the people below, until Mr Potts the gardener talked him down.[37] Worse was to follow in September. Local girl Doreen Allsopp was on the bridge, watching the mules going to the water. She saw a rat run behind a mule who kicked out and caught Farrier Asghar Ali in the chest. His comrades carried him back to the camp.[38] A few days later he died, and local boy Gerry Williams recalled:

At dawn on a morning in September 1940 I was awakened by a noise outside my bedroom window. Looking outside I saw a very large parade of soldiers. Some were mounted on horses and others marching. Another group, in the middle of the parade, were hauling a gun carriage on which the coffin of Asghar Ali lay. The carriage was hauled at the front by a team of foot soldiers with ropes and restrained at the rear by another team with ropes for the descent down Derby Road hill into Ashbourne. I found the sight of the Funeral Cortège, at my young age, very moving.[39]

Asghar Ali was buried in the town cemetery, where his grave was looked after for many years by Sidney Taylor and members of the local British Legion.[40]

After just a few short weeks, a plan for K6's future had emerged, and they were ordered to the south-west of England. A letter in the local paper expressed regret at their departure:

As an old soldier of the last war who served with the Indian troops I can assure them they are worthy successors to their forebears. In striking contrast to the stern duties of their calling, their love of and kindness to the children has been most apparent and will always be remembered by them.

We have every confidence that they will acquit themselves well when the call comes and wish them all that is best, and a safe return to their homeland.[41]

The feeling was mutual. Major Finlay was one of the last to leave:

By 31 Oct the fine weather had ended. It was a dismal morning. Dawn was just breaking when the rear party crowded into the lorry that was to take them from Shirley Camp for the last time. A surprising number of womenfolk appeared from the nearby house. 'Good-bye' they shouted. 'Good-bye, good-bye' chorused the rear party in English and, as the lorry slowly drew away the grey, wet dawn was positively shattered by a full-throated and prolonged 'War Cry'. Even my sophisticated and hard-boiled soul was stirred by this last episode in a camp I shall always remember with affection.[42]

We can be sure that young Betty was there, with her mother and father, to wave them off from their short sweet stay in Derbyshire.

* * * * *

That autumn was their first in Europe, their first chance to enjoy apple harvests and spiders' webs in England. It was also their first experience of the Muslim holy month of Ramadan outside of India. The twenty-eight-day fast from daybreak till dusk must have been hard for them. On 1 November, Hills wrote: 'last day of the Ramzan, which practically all of the contingent observed, and to which they have all stood up well. Parties from units despatched to the Woking Mosque for the celebrations.'[43]

When they left Ashbourne, they found themselves spread over a wide area. The 29th and 32nd Companies were at the British Army base at Bulford on Salisbury Plain. Major Akbar joined 32nd Company there and went to visit Stonehenge, that extraordinary prehistoric site, writing a report on the visit which was broadcast to India by the BBC.[44] Akbar flips round the age-old tradition of Britons visiting ancient Indian sites, and writes fluently of the history of the monument, its probable uses, the source of the sarsen stone in Wales, and the legend of the Devil who tried to steal the stones. He also relates how they negotiated the entrance fee:

> The guard said indeed you may visit this old site but you have to pay one shilling for entrance fee per person. In the meanwhile another truck came with Indian soldiers being dropped off at this site. As the guard saw them wearing turbans his intention changed and he turned towards us smiling and said 'you may all visit this monument free of charge'. I was so surprised by this and asked why as you were asking for a fee of the entrance, the respected officer smiled and said who would dare to charge a fee from guests. Later the guard called upon his daughter and they gave us a free historic tour.

Alongside such light-hearted activities, the men were now receiving training for their new role. Hills had protested loudly and repeatedly to the War Office about their unarmed defenceless state in France, so some old Lee–Enfield rifles were found, and training undertaken.[45] From then on, all K6 drivers carried rifles, and were trained in their use. There was also a plan to switch their primary role from animal transport to motor transport, in anticipation of working as lorry drivers at railway stations, ferrying supplies from train to warehouse.[46] Around this time there was a steady flow of invitations to military and civil parades in local towns and villages (they attended sixty-one in total during their time in the UK), such as the War Weapons Week parade in Oxford at the start of December. Later, Subedar M.I.Y. Khan of Bareilly told of his friendship with a Mrs Dingle of Durrington:

> On Salisbury Plain one evening a village woman standing at her cottage door called to me 'It's my birthday; come and have a cup of tea with me.' From that day she treated me like a son, her own son was serving in the Middle East and thinking of him, she guessed I might be lonely so far from home. I often went to her house and met many friends there.[47]

The rest of the force was to be found further down the long peninsula of Devon and Cornwall. The 25th Company and the Reinforcement Unit were sent to Duporth Holiday Camp near St Austell, a camp that was to be home to many of the men over the next few years. Here they were found work on coastal defence and road construction, with detachments being sent to Bigbury, Kingsbridge and Noss Mayo in Devon.[48] Later on, part of 42nd Company was stationed at Meavy Bridge on Dartmoor.[49] Meanwhile, visits and parades continued. The men of the Reinforcement Unit went to the royal farm at Stoke Climsland in Cornwall and were 'deeply interested' in the herd of eighty pedigree Devons (a photo in the *Scottish Daily Record* shows a sepoy leading a sturdy-looking bull to pasture) but less impressed by the pigs, which are *haram* to Muslims.[50] Their hospital, now at Devonport in Plymouth, was visited by Nancy Astor, the first woman to take a seat in the House of Commons.[51] The worst ailment to affect the men that winter was influenza, with forty-six men laid low in 25th Company alone.[52] Hills was pleased to report, however, on the continuing education of the men in British ways, writing in December that 'there is modern sanitation … the Contingent is now bromo conscious', indicating that they were now using British Bromo brand toilet paper.[53]

Major Finlay and the 47 SDS were at Truro initially. In February 1941 they moved to Plymouth, their biggest city so far. Here they found accommodation near Plymouth Hoe, and Finlay reported the men were 'happy and rather surprised that there have been no air raid alarms since their arrival'.[54] This changed just two weeks later after a heavy blitz on the city, with considerable damage to their office, but no Indian casualties. They moved to Down Park House in Yelverton on the south-west side of Dartmoor, where 'morale very good. Men … are not sorry to be out in the open country.' A little later the hospital was also evacuated from Plymouth to Stowford House near Ivybridge, as a bomb had destroyed their billet.[55] Even in the rural south-west, danger was not far away. Over 1,000 civilians were killed in the Plymouth Blitz, but the units of K6 had a lucky escape. Hills and his HQ, including Uncle Gian and Kundan Lall, were now at the Crownwell Hotel on the south side of the Teign estuary in Shaldon, looking across at the seaside town of Teignmouth.

Wherever they went in these rural areas, they were usually the first Indians that the villagers had seen, and thus acted in a small way as pioneers or ambassadors for post-war migration. The invitations to parades and marches continued. The Remount Depot, also based at Duporth, rode across country to Penzance in April, in full dress uniform and *pagris*, via Helston and Marazion, and past St Michael's Mount to parade through that quintessential Cornish port. They then visited Land's End 'by charabanc where tea is given'.[56] Their trip from Sargodha was now complete; they had travelled from the north-west of India to the westernmost part of England.

One thing that they brought to the West Country was their passion for hockey. They came from a country which had whole-heartedly embraced the sport, having won gold medals at the Olympics. At the 1936 Berlin Games, 20,000 Germans and fifty Indians watched India beat Germany 8–1 in the final, and the German team were 'simply unable to keep up

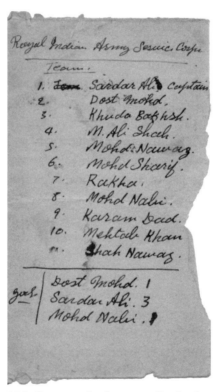

25th Company hockey team list for the game against Kingsbridge Youth Club, spring 1941.

with the Indians' astonishing energy and skill'.[57] Kenneth Hord, wartime editor of the popular *Daily Mirror*, reported of K6 enthusiastically: 'Hockey is their favourite sport and they are the best players in the world. The closest game they had last season was when they won 11–0.'[58]

In spring 1941 a team from 25th Company was challenged by Dennis Caseley, who ran a successful youth club in Kingsbridge at the southernmost part of Devon. The Indians won by four goals to zero, and Dennis' son Patrick recalls that afterwards:

> both teams trooped off to The Cosy Café for tea and I went along with my parents to join them. I remember them being calm, polite and very pleasant men and I was certainly included in their company. My Dad managed to find an envelope which he opened out and asked them to list the members of their side which one of them did. I still have that piece of paper and … a copy of the stamp and postmark which has a 1941 date.[59]

The list of names holds an interesting insight into religious and 'caste' sensitivities in the Indian Contingent. Among the Muslim names (Jemadar Sardar Ali, who scored three goals, bellows boy Mehtab Khan and so on) we find Rakha, a Hindu sweeper with 25th Company. It seems that the divisions between caste identities were suspended, at least for the ninety minutes of the game, and close physical contact was allowed, even if Rakha subsequently reverted to his 'untouchable' status. Perhaps, surrounded by white people, they were happy to suspend the interior distinctions of India and concentrate on beating the white men at their own game.

They were not the only Indians in Britain. At the outbreak of war there were somewhere between 5,000 and 10,000 Indians in the UK.[60] Indians were to be found at all levels of society, from working-class men like the lascars of North Shields and Cardiff to the intellectuals working at the BBC and the nobility passing through or in residence. A Mass-Observation respondent in Cumberland recorded 'a community of Indian pedlars housed in Workington' in June 1943.[61] One Anglo-Indian family produced Noor Inayat Khan, who became a British spy in France. Her brother Vilayet was a naval officer in a minesweeper on D-Day.[62] There is an interesting reversal here, the Indian presence in Britain reflecting the British presence in India. One created the other, and the political slogan used by descendants of migrants to the UK

– 'we are here because you were there' – has its roots in this time, before the flow of migration shifted from Britain outwards to Britain inwards. That watershed moment probably came in the late 1940s, so the men of K6 were ahead of a wave of movement from South Asia to Britain.

Among the pre-war Indian population were the men of 80th Company of the Pioneer Corps, who were used for construction work throughout the UK, including London and Ilfracombe.[63] This unit was a unique example of soldiers recruited from Indian men resident in Britain, mostly lascars, the majority being Muslims.[64] They were never a full-strength unit, peaking at 172 sepoys.[65] The story of one of their privates indicates the reason for their lack of success in recruiting, for he deserted twice, preferring to work in armaments factories, where pay and conditions were better.[66] Contact between the sepoys of K6 and other resident Indians was limited: the India Office and their own officers endeavoured to keep them away from the 'undesirable' politicals like the India League and to steer them towards those who were more supportive of British policy in India. Equally, the men were given free rein to walk outside their camps and encountered a variety of people during their leave.

These Indian residents were involved in the war effort in a wide variety of ways, including an initiative that was to prove crucial to the well-being of K6 men in the UK and Germany. This was the Indian Comforts Fund (ICF), established in December 1939 at India House on Aldwych in the heart of London.[67] Initially it was specifically designed to help the men of K6, but over the course of the war its target group expanded to include POWs, lascars, Bevin Boys (Indian mechanics training in the UK) and the Pioneer Company. Its volunteers were a mixture of Indian women resident in the UK, white women with Indian experience, and Pioneers to do the heavy lifting. With the help of their slogan, '7000 miles to help you', they managed to mobilise very large numbers of people throughout the country to donate money and to knit warm garments. Their detailed list of around 400 donors in March 1942 includes the Egyptian ambassador, the Beckenham Mothers' Union and St Mary's Girls' School in Cheshunt.

The ICF found its greatest level of public engagement through an extensive programme of garment manufacture. Wool was dispatched from its London HQ to a 'great band of unseen skilful knitters' around the country, who turned it into socks, gloves, balaclavas and other warm garments. These work parties – of which there were 1,683 at the end of 1941, totalling a staggering 60,000 knitters and using nearly 30,000 pounds of wool – ranged from small groups of women in a village to whole schools. Early in 1941 two VCOs from K6, Ahmed Nawaz and Gulzar Khan, visited a group of knitters in the village of West Woodlands near Frome with Colonel Hills, where they found 'nearly all villagers have been knitting comforts for the Contingent since Feb 40'.[68] As well as the knitting, the fund supported K6 and other Indians in the UK in a variety of ways. Books and board games were distributed, including *carrom* and *pachesi*, as well as 600 records in Urdu, Punjabi and Hindi. The ICF held a tea party at India House 'every Tuesday for men from the Indian Contingent. Our young men are helped to establish contact with their fellows from all parts of the British Commonwealth and from America.'[69] The fund also paid the bus fares of leave parties from Woking when they visited London three days each week. All of this shows a level of respect and care for the visitors: thousands of knitters all round the country, clacking away with their needles making hats and gloves to warm the Punjabis, is a potent image.

Another essential element of the men's well-being, along with the ICF and the work of Dr Gooneratne, was the regular broadcasts by the BBC. As mentioned earlier, on 1 February 1940, while they were still in France, they were interviewed and recorded by Richard Dimbleby and Z.A. Bokhari, telling a story called '*Ek tha mirasi*' ('There once was a singer') and singing a song from the ancient Hir and Ranjha story.[70] A week later, Hills wrote to Bokhari asking for a radio programme specifically for them, saying, 'they are so lonely … they are so cut off … it is essential that they should hear something over the radio in their own language'. So, starting on 14 April, the BBC broadcast a programme for the Indians every Sunday morning, including music and speech. Bokhari and others at the newly formed BBC Hindustani Service took pains to seek out music that would appeal to them, and HQ conducted a survey of the men which found that their favourites included religious music like Qawwali and Ghazals by K.L. Saigal and Sardar Akhtar, Punjabi folk songs like *mahiya,* humorous songs by Charwe and music from the film *Acchut Kanya.*[71] In due course, the relationship with the BBC diversified, with the men recording messages to family at home, as well as songs, for which they were paid £2.[72] There was also a third type of recording, whereby the sepoys addressed the British public via the Home Service. In September 1940, as part of a series about the Empire and Commonwealth entitled 'In It Together', Hills interviewed Akbar and Flight Lieutenant Jai Singh of the RAF, with the message 'The Empire as the Hope of the World'.[73] Akbar went on to become a regular for the BBC and, after the war, for the new Pakistan Radio. The BBC described him as 'excellent, a useful broadcaster when divorced from Lt Col Hills his CO'.[74] Like many of his comrades, Akbar was to develop new skills during his time in Europe.

* * * * *

Asghar Ali had been their first death in the UK, but as time went on, there were more. Casualties are expected in wartime, and Hills wrote to the Imperial War Graves Commission in July 1940, requesting that spaces be allocated in cemeteries in all the areas where they were stationed, rather than being centralised at Woking, as they had been in the Great War.[75] After Ashbourne, the next need was in Cornwall. In November 1940, a great storm blew down some trees at Duporth camp. J. Martin, the Air Raid Precautions first aider, was among those called out, and recalled years later:

> The winds were at gale force and it blew down a massive tree which landed right across the chalet in which the soldiers were sleeping … I remember the labour gang digging under the tree and chalet to get to the soldiers. I still have the picture in my mind [of] a gale force wind, a moonlight scene with scudding clouds being blown across the sky – and the weird chanting of the Indian soldiers around.[76]

Two bodies were found, of Tinsmith Ghulam Nabi and Saddler Muhammad Gul, and they were joined two days later by Warrant Officer Hashmat Ali, who died from his injuries.[77] A national newspaper deemed the funeral important enough to send a reporter:

> Home Guards, standing shoulder-to-shoulder with Indian Army transport muleteers on a bleak West Country hillside, paid tribute at the funeral of two of the Indians' comrades who had been killed accidentally.

The lids of the coffins were off, revealing the dead men, each clad in three sheets of spotless white linen. The Indian mourners stood bare-footed, softly chanting the prayers which their maulvi (Indian chaplain) intoned.

Then the coffin lids were screwed on, the Home Guards stepped forward, saluted the dead and reverently placed wreaths of English roses on the coffins of those Indian patriots who had come thousands of miles to fight for the King-Emperor.

Slowly the coffins were borne two miles to a military cemetery, and on the way the Indian bearers and escort sang of man's coming and going and of the will and goodness of Allah …

All the florists in the town combined to supply scores of wreaths for civilian friends of the men of the Indian contingent.[78]

The burials were conducted in accordance with Muslim practice: each body was washed and shrouded in three cloths, the grave was dug so that the body lay on its back, with the face turned to the right, towards Mecca, and the funeral was followed by three days of mourning.[79] Their graves are all looked after by the Commonwealth War Graves Commission, each marked by a standard headstone, with regimental badge, name, rank and regiment, service number and date of death.[80] As graves for Muslims, these also carry an inscription in Arabic, 'he is the forgiving one' at the top, and 'we belong to Allah and to him shall we return' at the bottom. The bodies of Ghulam Nabi, Muhammad Gul, and Hashmat Ali still lie in the cemetery at Charlestown.

While the search for a proper military role continued, the men could carry on with odd jobs and parades, for propaganda was war work, and Hills was happy to accede to the 'constant requests' for attendance at parades, as 'I am of opinion it is of value both to this country and to India for the Indian Army to be represented'.[81] In November, Major Wainwright visited Plymouth and Topsham looking for work, while Fawcett tried Truro.[82] They were unsuccessful at that stage, but by the end of March things were clearer, and Hills reported the experiment with 'mechanisation' had been abandoned and all units would again be working with animals, as they had trained for years to do.[83] More than that, Hills' badgering of the India Office and the War Office paid off the following month, when he learnt that reinforcements were on their way from India. Force K6 was about to rediscover its reason for being in Europe: Operation Jupiter was at hand.

7

We'll keep a welcome

We'll keep a welcome in the hillside, we'll keep a welcome in the Vales.

The famous Welsh welcome of this 1940 song was extended many times to the soldiers of Force K6.[1] On 16 October 1942, a party of twenty officers and VCOs was invited to the seaside town of Rhyl for a trip that included an overnight stay, all designed as a fundraiser for the ICF. According to Jemadar A.G. Khan, as they arrived 'the clouds scattered and the sun came up … we were able to see the whole city blooming and glowing'.[2] They were taken for tea at the house of the Lord Lieutenant of Flintshire, Admiral R.G. Rowley-Conwy, where they were, of course, photographed. Later in the day they went to a dance at Queen's Dance Hall, which continued till 1 a.m. and where:

> There were thousands of men and women wearing splendid dresses … Its galleries were full of spectators. We had never seen such a huge crowd of people. We all sat down on couches and began watching different dances. Some Indian men and women who were already there also participated in the dance. Some English girls were wearing beautiful Sarees and they performed an Indian dance. In short, all the arrangements were brilliant. Cheerfulness and diligence was everywhere.

This extravagant reception was not unusual in their time in Wales, a place where they were truly welcomed.

In the middle of April 1941, at Llangattock Park in Crickhowell, the UK-based sepoys of Force K6 were all concentrated in one place for the first time since Marseilles, strengthened by the addition of three more companies. From this point on, their work was clear, and they became increasingly skilled and confident in carrying it out. They were posted to some very remote areas of the UK, passing through the cities. They forged strong relationships with Britons everywhere they went; they worked hard and experienced drama and tragedy, including death. While the war rolled on, growing in scope and reaching out its tentacles to new frontiers, the men of K6 kept their heads down and, like so much of the British Army, focused on training. Their comrades in the Indian Army were helping to liberate Ethiopia from the Italians, then in Syria and Iraq, Egypt and Libya. After the Germans attacked the Soviet Union in the summer of 1941, the Indian Army occupied Persia, and large numbers of RIASC personnel were used transporting supplies through the mountains into Kazakhstan and the wider Soviet Union.[3] At the end of the same year, the war suddenly became bigger still, when Japan attacked the Americans at Pearl Harbor and the British in Malaya, Singapore and Burma. By the end of 1942, most of the world was involved in the conflict, and the Japanese were knocking on India's door, having driven the Allies almost completely from Burma. Joseph Stalin urged the UK and the USA to open a Second Front by attacking the Germans in Europe, a request which was to dominate Allied planning until D-Day in June 1944.

One option for the Second Front, championed by Winston Churchill, was Operation Jupiter. Churchill's idea was to take and hold German airfields in northern Norway, to 'safeguard the passage of convoys to Russia'.[4] 'If the going was good we could advance gradually southward, unrolling the Nazi map of Europe from the top,' he wrote in a memo in May 1942.[5] Unfortunately, nobody shared the prime minister's enthusiasm for this idea, Alanbrooke describing it as a 'mad plan'.[6] Ultimately, although an enormous amount of time was spent in planning and preparing for the operation, it was never put into practice. The troops used in this attack would need to be trained to work in the difficult terrain of north Norway: mountainous, snowy and very cold in winter. They would also need to use mules to transport their supplies, hence the new-found clarity of purpose for Force K6. Many in India would rather have had those experienced troops back at home, especially after the Japanese invasion of Burma – indeed a memo from India in June 1942 said: 'urgently require experienced personnel for large AT expansion here mainly for ops on Assam Frontier'.[7] But that was not to be. In fact, the very reverse had happened in the spring of 1941, when three new mule companies were sent from India to join K6.

Those three companies – 3rd, 7th and 42nd – left their bases in March, as the 'band of the Kashmir Rifles played the Company out and the unit was cheered enroute'.[8] Their journey differed from the original K6 route: the Mediterranean was now a dangerous place to sail through so they had to steam all the way round Africa. They left Bombay on 5 April on board the *Empress of Japan* and stopped at Cape Town, St Helena, Freetown and Gibraltar, arriving on the river Clyde on 15 May.[9] They disembarked the next day and thus became the very first units of the Indian Army to be specifically posted to the UK. They continued southwards by train, arriving at Crickhowell on 17 May, where Hills welcomed them with a speech claiming that 'The Contingent considers itself second only to His Majesty the King Emperor's Household Troops' and warning them that 'you will find life and work strange to commence with'.[10] Among the men of 3rd Company was a 20-year-old lance naik clerk from Mirpur in Kashmir, Yaqub Mirza by name. He remembered their arrival beside the river Usk:

> During the sea voyage of forty-two days, lice had bred on our bodies and heads. We were clean shaven and put into quarantine. Next day we were given a shower bath, steaming hot with repellent smelling disinfectant, all naked like monkeys, together in one big tent. The bugler with a white beard wept. It was a shameless parade for us all.[11]

Things improved soon when they were issued with new uniforms and received a welcome parcel of toothpaste and sweets from the ICF. They were visited by Z.A. Bokhari from the BBC for Eid, who recorded the singing of Qawwali for subsequent broadcast. The next Sunday, after church, some local people came across the river to meet them, and Yaqub Mirza recalled:

> There were some young girls too amongst them. Their legs below their skirts were very attractive. I asked one in particular if she could speak English. She replied with a smile, 'Yes, I can. Can you?' I replied, 'Yes, I think I can. Your bare legs must be cold.' 'No! I am wearing tights – look.' She told others about me. I became famous.

The pretty market town of Crickhowell lies six miles west of Abergavenny, on the road to Brecon and Aberystwyth, taking its name from the Iron Age hillfort above it – *Crug Hywel* being the Welsh for 'Hywel's Hill'. With the Black Mountains to the north and the Llangattock Mynd to the south, it is surrounded by upland. Across the river Usk to the south lies Llangattock Park, once the home of the Duke of Beaufort, now a campsite. This was to be home for the boys of Force K6, and in fact one of the places where most of them spent the longest time. It was a warm, friendly and welcoming town, with a slight feeling of detachment from the rest of the world, where they formed some strong bonds and where they are still remembered today, but it is also the location for the only recorded instance of racism towards them, as recounted later on. By the time they moved there, they had been re-equipped with a variety of horses and mules, including the French ones which had come via Norway and Glasgow, some sourced locally in the UK, and some from the USA and Canada.[12] Having left their carts in France, they were now operating as pack units, whereby the loads were put directly on the animals' backs, using a special saddle. They had also been joined by two companies of British mule drivers from the RASC, whom it was their responsibility to train – Hills' command was expanding.[13] Now the training of men and animals of K6 went into top gear, with 3rd Company reporting at the end of May 'process of hardening men continues. Route march twelve miles, combined with dispersion and [anti-gas] training. Weather very wet.' A few weeks later the weather had changed, but the training continued: 'First exercise on pack carried out – loads 160lbs – one man leading one horse. Day hot but thunderstorm in evening.'[14] The men and the animals were becoming hardened and disciplined, in preparation for meeting their comrades in the British infantry.

Their intended role in Norway was first-line transport: carrying food, ammunition and other supplies to the troops closest to the enemy. The fundamental idea of pack transport was that the mule driver should hold the head of the animal and not assist with the loading – that task would be carried out by an RIASC comrade or a British soldier.[15] This required close coordination and liaison, so they trained for long periods side-by-side with British infantry. Their destinations were therefore determined by the location of the infantry regiments they were working with – they were posted around the country to some of the coldest, wildest and wettest parts, places that many Britishers would never visit outside of sunny weather.

Most of their time in Wales was spent with men from the north-east of England: 70th Brigade, consisting of the Durham Light Infantry and the Tyneside Scottish Regiment. This brigade, whose badge featured a polar bear, had been posted to Iceland as part of Operation Fork, the UK occupation of that northerly island state. Six members of K6 had joined them there, to attend a winter warfare course in January 1942.[16] Risaldar Inayat Shah subsequently gave lectures on his experience, reporting 'Weather very cold and heavy snow all day'.[17] If anyone doubted the ability of Punjabis to work in extremes of cold, Inayat Shah was ready to disprove them. Later in Scotland the men worked with 52nd Lowland Division, all Scotsmen, and they built good relationships. When they parted company with 52nd Division in 1944, the men of K6 were presented with decorated shields 'to commemorate their association with the Division in Scotland'.[18] In the end, these brigades were preparing for an assault that never happened. The men of K6 never saw the fjords of Norway, but we can be sure that their hard training proved useful after their return to India, for their work with infantry brigades in Burma.

With animals to look after, there was always plenty of work to do, and there was never a day completely idle. Even at Eid, even on Christmas Day, the mules had to be fed, watered and exercised. An animal transport company of 320 men and its mules is a complex structure that combines careful planning and inspired improvisation when needed. On arrival at a new campsite, for example, the process was clearly laid down.[19] After taking the loads off the mules, some men watered the animals while the others pitched tents and started cooking. The animals were then tethered and fed, and only then would the men get to eat. After repairs and checking animals, the men might have some time for relaxing, smoking, chatting and praying.

The centrality of the camp routine was demonstrated by an article written by Lance Naik Nadir Husain of the newly arrived 7th Company. Husain, like so many of his comrades, was used to military life on the North West Frontier and sought to indicate the differences with camp life in Britain. He pointed towards terrain: 'The land in England is soft and covered with green grass and full of shady trees. The land in North West province is hard and stony where few small bushes and no trees are found.'[20] He listed differences of trees and water: 'There is lots of rainfall in England and the land remains wet all the year.' Kitchens in the UK had chimneys, which was better for the men working there. Manure was sold in both areas, but toilets were different. And the work of the dhobi or laundryman was harder as 'there is no problem in drying clothes under the sun in North West province. In England the sun is only seen sometimes so they have other arrangements to dry their clothes.' Nadir Husain and his colleagues were acutely aware of what was around them, and the contrasts with home.

While in Britain, the men became used to working with packhorses as well as mules. An article in the popular weekly magazine *Picture Post* described the process of training the horses, presenting an extraordinary combination of people from East and West who meet around the quadrupeds. The first section opened in Melton Mowbray where: 'a string of fresh clipped horses, head to tail, swings round the corner, led by a blonde in jodhpurs and velvet hunting cap'.[21] We then meet a 'freckled redhead', along with 'one-time typists, secretaries, shop assistants, dancers'. The basic training of the horses was being carried out by English girls who, we are told, need 'courage, strength and patience' for the task. The photos in the second part of the article were taken around Crickhowell and featured locations by the Usk bridge, for a shot of swimming horses, and on top of Llangattock Mynd.[22] The story followed the packhorses as they worked with RIASC drivers in the hills. Disaster struck:

> on one occasion, towards the end of a forty-eight-hour exercise in the Welsh mountains, a very tired pair of horses, leading a section, sank up to their shoulders in a peat bog. Every effort was made to extricate them, but without result. The rest of the section decided to abandon the horses to the care of their driver and return the following morning with a fresh team to pull them out. Later in the night, the Indian driver, feeling chilly, and sure that the two miserable horses felt the cold, lit a fire. At once, the terrified horses, with a snort, a kick and a bound, shot out of the bog and galloped away.[23]

Thankfully, for this nation of animal-lovers, there was a happy ending.

The daily routine for man and beast was strict, with a clear sequence for loading, unloading, feeding and so forth laid out in the RIASC training manual.[24] Mules were required to be watered at least three times a day, fed thrice and groomed twice. They should drink at least six gallons a day, permitted to drink as long as they like but 'mules are fastidious drinkers and will refuse water that a horse or pony will drink readily'. As they have small stomachs, they should be fed little and often, their ration including barley, lentils, chaff and rock salt.[25] In a company with hundreds of mules, this added up to a considerable amount of fodder, both in weight and in bulk, which of course had to be delivered to the unit. The always professional Major Finlay wrote about the 47 SDS: 'This unit has to maintain about 2600 men and over 3000 animals. The average weight of one animal's ration is 20lbs a day and loosely baled hay bulks greatly. Demands for labour have inevitably been considerable.'[26] After feeding, the mules were groomed twice a day. This started with five minutes spent on inspecting and cleaning the hooves with a pick, followed by five minutes of 'slapping with hollowed hand', which 'starts circulation, brings dust up to the surface and loosens scurf'.[27] Then follows half an hour of grooming with a body brush and curry comb, five minutes each on tail, eyes and ears, nostrils and dock. A further five minutes of hand massage is the finishing touch, which would be followed by a check from an NCO or officer. This all adds up to an enormous amount of work, especially as some drivers had responsibility for more than one animal. With such a routine, the men of Force K6 were hard workers indeed.

Another important aspect of their routine was prayer. As Muslims they were expected to pray five times each day – one of the Five Pillars of Islam. No matter where they were stationed, their maulvi would identify a place to lay some carpets facing towards Mecca, and call the men to prayer. Only rarely did they have the chance to pray in a proper mosque, but used a tent or a building in or near the camp in which to pray. They also observed the festivals of Eid ul-Adha (when a sheep or goat is slaughtered) and Eid ul-Fitr (at the end of Ramadan). As the Muslim calendar is lunar, these festivals rotate through the solar British calendar, advancing by ten or eleven days each year. Eid ul-Adha was just after Christmas in 1941, and just before it in 1942. One might think that observing the Ramadan fast (involving total abstinence from food or drink during daylight hours)

Major Finlay with colleagues from the 47 SDS at a railway station near Abergavenny.

would be considered bad for military discipline and performance, and indeed one of the categories of those exempted from fasting is 'military personnel on active service'.[28] But these men had grown up with the practice of fasting and knew how to pace themselves and avoid becoming ill. The evidence is that the fast was observed widely. In 1942 a *hafiz* (one who has memorised all the Qur'an) from the contingent was permitted to officiate at the Woking Mosque for the duration of the month.[29] This was indeed an honour, for to memorise the Qur'an is a widely respected feat in itself, to be able to recite it at the country's premier mosque would have increased the honour to the individual and the contingent as a whole.

The officers' care for their men and their religious traditions and practices may have been motivated by humanitarian concerns, but was also driven by strategic military thinking. They were never short of good advice on such matters. Nawazish Ali, quartermaster dafadar for 42nd Company with a world of experience, offered advice to his younger colleagues. Among the basic wisdoms that could occur in any culture or religion, such as 'a wise man is respected everywhere' and 'forgiveness is better than revenge', we find religious ideas like 'good prayer should be offered all the time' and 'always consider death in front of you and refrain from sins'.[30] The men were also honoured by a visit from Sirdar Ikbal Ali Shah, the British-resident sufi, who had written to Hills in January 1940.

He came to Crickhowell to give a lecture about Mecca 'illustrated with lantern slides of photographs, taken by the Sirdar Sahib himself, of the holy city'.[31] Afterwards Finlay entertained him to lunch at the Angel Hotel in Abergavenny and put him on the train. It was clearly important to everyone that these men be allowed access to worship, and be encouraged to become better Muslims.

Beyond their spiritual needs, the men were being well looked after by an array of supporters and friends. Major Kelly of 42nd Company later said, 'welfare poured over the whole company. To such an extent that it had to be stopped in certain cases. Such as dances being arranged.'[32] There were always well-wishers at the local and national level who found ways to help them. In April 1941 they were presented with a mobile canteen – a tea van that could follow them round the country – and the photo of that event was a prized possession in Risaldar Major Ashraf's house long after the war.[33] Kenneth Hord of the *Daily Mirror* visited them at Llangattock and wrote enthusiastically about their 'glee party':

> Their *dols* and *seranis* – drums beaten with the hand and tin whistles – were lost in France. But others have been improvised and these provide the music for the Indian dances of which they are masters.
>
> The camp runs its own welfare organisation with canteens and a mobile cinema, where East truly meets West when George Formby appears on the screen.
>
> The Sepoys go into raptures over him, and the loss of every Hollywood beauty would cause no pain as long as George had a new film to show.[34]

A journalist called Morgan from an unidentified Welsh newspaper observed the tradesmen at work: 'Their camp life is extraordinary in the way they do everything themselves. They are experts in all forms of handicraft, and weavers, potters, leathermakers, carpenters and blacksmiths help to make the unit self-contained.'[35]

The camp at Llangattock was fairly buzzing with activity in the gentle Welsh sunshine. On top of that was the buzz of microphones and speakers, as the BBC continued to visit regularly, recording the voices of the men to transmit in India, and broadcasting to them every Sunday morning. The commanding officer of 7th Company wrote that 'the BBC invaded Llangattock camp today and many RIASC personnel were required to speak into microphone. Rained'.[36] Later Jemadar Ishtiaq Ahmed of Allahabad, the medical officer for 29th Company, recorded a special programme to be broadcast at Christmas 'on behalf of the parents of the Contingent to their children in India'.[37] Having been away from home for over two years at that time, the need was considerable.

A newer addition to their camp personnel was also remarked upon by Kenneth Hord: 'Their interest in education too, is great. They study under Indian teachers. Two English instructors are teaching them our language, and a British officer lectures to each unit in Hindustani every week on world affairs'.[38] The two English instructors were Warrant Officers Brown and Wallace of the Army Education Corps.[39] Many of the men were already accomplished linguists, having some command of four languages. Their mother tongue was Punjabi or Pushtu, they used Arabic at prayer, they could understand Urdu (the official language of the British Indian Army) and they had picked up some French. Men reported for English courses with Wallace and Brown 'in possession of one notebook – preferably SO Book 135, 2 black pencils, 1 red or blue pencil and one 12" ruler'.[40] With everything suitably in order, there was still room for jokes:

Amman: Hamid, did you wash your face before the English teacher arrived?
Hamid: Yes
Amman: And your hands also?
Hamid: Yes
Amman: And your ears?
Hamid: Yes, but only the one that had to be near the teacher.[41]

The exams, however, were no laughing matter. The paper for the second-class certificate that same month required the students to write 150 words on one of five topics, including 'Winter in England' or 'My experience of British people', and to answer comprehension questions on a passage about Subedar Richpal Ram, who had been awarded a Victoria Cross in the Middle East.[42] The hard work paid off, and that year Hills was delighted to report that 600 personnel had gained the army's third-class certificate in English, and were thus entitled to wear a special badge on their shoulder. A lack of English was not always a barrier, however: in

North Wales Edgar Parry Williams felt on an equal footing as 'they didn't have much English anyway and we didn't … either'.[43]

English, Welsh and Punjabi were not the only languages heard in that part of the borders in 1941. A correspondent from the *Abergavenny Chronicle* wrote a bucolic piece called 'On the Evening Bus' that winter. As the bus meanders through the rolling hills to Crickhowell in the failing light, he is surrounded by Indians, Belgians, French and British servicemen:

> as I sat there, the 'bus speeding along in the evening light, I felt a feeling of gratitude to these men who had come to fight alongside the British and to lay down their lives, if need be, in the defence of this country.
>
> One of the Indian soldiers, after searching in his pockets for some time, found that he hadn't enough money to pay his fare, but he needn't have worried. Almost immediately after he had said 'Sorry, have no more money' or something like that, a voice from behind said to the 'Nippy' [female bus conductor] 'Right-o miss, how much is it?'
>
> Although the Indians couldn't understand the Frenchmen, who in turn couldn't understand the Belgians, I noticed that when they saw something in the scenery unusual or very interesting they would point and smile with a familiarity which I have never seen between men of different countries before.
>
> It was as if they all belonged to the same fellowship.[44]

Which of course they did. In times like those, the job of the reporter on the local paper was to find such parochial stories, to make a connection to the bigger picture, and thus to keep up morale.

Another story in the same newspaper shows a very different angle on the Punjabis' stay by the Black Mountains. In September 1941, the *Chronicle* printed a letter from Raymond Lewis, the honorary secretary of the swimming club.[45] On the previous Sunday a 'certain lady' had complained about the presence of Indians in the Bailey Park open-air pool. The men had been ejected, as had several others throughout the week.[46] The reason is not given, but one can assume that the very presence of brown male bodies in the same water as white female bodies caused offence. Mr Lewis was writing to express the 'disgust' of the swimming club at the 'scandalous' ejections – he stood in solidarity with the Indians. The letter continues:

> These men, that lady may or may not realise, are our allies, who have come thousands of miles to fight by our side, to lay down their lives if need be, in the defence of Britain – and [of] that lady … I can only say, in conclusion, that her actions are without doubt entirely unsupported by anyone … for to let colour and creed prejudice one's minds in days like these, especially as these Indians are fighting for us, is almost too abominable to believe.

There is strong feeling here, a feeling of solidarity and equality, and another letter the following week supports Mr Lewis. One could dismiss the 'certain lady' as a one-off, as indeed this story is a one-off among the many press articles about K6. But it is part of a trend of racism around swimming pools – the US Army put a British swimming bath out of

Sada Khan and Charlie Edwards: two carpenters in Crickhowell.

bounds to black female soldiers, for example.[47] It is more likely that this is rather a thin end of the wedge, a hint of the unreported hinterland of private, unremarked racism. In public, people might have felt they had to be positive about the Allies from around the world, but when comfortable at home or in the pub, when the tie was loosened and the guard was down, we can be sure that racist opinions were felt and expressed. The spread of such quintessentially private utterances can never be known, but they definitely existed – the 'certain lady' of Abergavenny tells us that.

In Crickhowell itself there are plenty of stories that tell of good relations with the natives. A charming photograph shows two carpenters, Sada Khan from Punjab and Charlie Edwards from Powys, looking at the camera. The Punjabi had been helping the Welshman, working on timber lorries, for there were many forests in the area.[48] Meanwhile a local shop hosted an Indian tailor, who sat cross-legged in the window under the approving gaze of passers-by.[49] Nawazish Ali, who gave helpful advice to younger sepoys, turned his writing talents to poetry, under the pen-name Mushtaq. In one of the very few examples where a K6 soldier records his feelings about Britain, he later wrote:

> *After reaching England, we saw a new system there;*
> *The streets were clean and the behaviour of the shopkeepers good;*
> *Everything was placed in order, with the power of knowledge and skill;*
> *O Mushtaq! I saw lovers walking by holding arms and hugging.*[50]

This is the only part of his poetry that refers directly to the UK, and Nawazish is fascinated by what he sees on the streets – the cleanliness, the order, and well-behaved shopkeepers – perhaps this affected his conduct later as a shopkeeper himself. Most of all, though, he is fascinated by the spectacle of men and women in pairs, in close physical contact with each other, unimaginable in India at that time. After some initial doubts about how much his men could wander at will in the town, Hills was reassured by their good conduct. By September, all ranks were allowed to 'walk out' solo, provided they had a pass. British soldiers in camp were subject to the same regulations, so there was a levelling-out process here, and there was 'no objection to lady visitors' in the camp from 4 p.m. to 7 p.m.[51] With the three new companies in mind, Hills was careful to lay down some laws, however: British women should be treated with the same politeness afforded to Muslim Indian women, the men were not allowed to enter public houses or to spit in the street, and certainly the 'wearing [of] Sam Browne belts when not authorised to do so' was forbidden. They were required to wear their new badge: the 'Star of India, worked in yellow, white and blue on a pale blue ground'.[52]

Smartness and correct uniform were always held in high regard within the Indian Army and in K6 in particular, and the men's presence at marches and parades around the country continued. When men of 25th Company marched past the bricked-up façade of Exeter's medieval Guildhall in War Weapons Week, their photos appeared in *Fauji Akhbar* and the *Times of India*.[53] In November 1941 five VCOs and forty-eight soldiers were invited to march through the streets of London in the Lord Mayor's Parade, with the newly returned Tom Hexley at their head.[54] This was a tough period in the war, with the Luftwaffe bombing of British cities ongoing, no good news from the desert, and the Germans gaining the upper hand on the Eastern Front. Indeed, a photo of the parade looks like a shot of a ruined and depressed city in the rain. Nizam Din wrote up his experience of the march in an article that describes in detail the preparations, the journey to London and the Indian Contingent's third place in the parade, behind the navy and the RAF. He does his best to convince the reader of the joy of the occasion:

> Citizens of London were seen with happy faces. When we returned, His Majesty King and Exalted Queen were standing on a high terrace outside the Royal palace. We saluted them. It seemed that Their Majesties were expressing considerable interest in whatever is happening around them … On the way, a British regiment treated us with much love and served us tea. We thanked them a lot.[55]

Among the guests visiting Llangattock Park were two Indian officers who had distinguished themselves in the campaign in East Africa, where Indian divisions had formed a major part of the British effort: Captain K.L. Atal and Captain Shaukat Hayat Khan, both of Skinner's Horse.[56] Shaukat was a most distinguished Punjabi, being the son of Sir Sikandar Hayat Khan, the prime minister of Punjab, a prime example of an Empire loyalist. The secretary of state for India, Leo Amery, asked him to write 'a note' on conditions and morale of Indian troops in the UK and the Middle East. This note (unfortunately since lost) was to cause considerable consternation, as Shaukat himself described in forthright tones later:

> I was foolish enough to accept the assignment. For days I sweated over the report which ran to several pages. I pointed out the iniquitous treatment meted out to Indian soldiers as compared with others in the same theatre despite the fact that they fought and gave their lives just as valiantly as any other in the crusade [sic] against Fascism. As it was to be a secret document, I had to type it letter by letter on a borrowed typewriter. When it was completed I showed it in confidence to Col [sic] (later General) Akbar Khan of the Royal Indian Army Service Corps, who had been evacuated along with his men from Dunkirk. He literally went into a fit about the candid discourse. He warned me that I could be sure of a court Martial when the Indian Army authorities learnt of it. I was too naïve to take him seriously. I thought he was just a good-for-nothing old windbag, lacking in confidence, and decided not to heed his advice.[57]

It is a great shame that Shaukat's report does not seem to have survived, for it would shed a different light on the men's experience and their treatment. Although a loyalist at this stage, he went on to become a leading campaigner for Jinnah's Muslim League in Punjab after his father's death.[58] His move away from support for Empire may have been influenced by the institutional, embedded racism that he identified in this report.

* * * * *

The Indian General Hospital had moved in June 1941 to Dinas House in Brecon, fourteen miles up the river Usk to the west of Crickhowell.[59] There they continued their work looking after more than 150 patients, men injured in accidents or laid low by disease, of which tuberculosis (TB) was the biggest threat.[60] They established an isolation wing for TB cases at Allt y Ferrin near Llandeilo, and transferred some patients to Woolaston hospital in Newport and Lyonshall Red Cross convalescent home in Hereford, where 'personnel of the Contingent are immensely popular'.[61] There was also a special tent erected at Crickhowell for eleven soldiers of the new companies who had arrived from Bombay with venereal disease.[62] This was seen as a poor reflection on discipline; until that point there had been 'no case of venereal disease amongst the personnel either in France or in the United Kingdom'.[63] The personnel of the hospital continued to evolve, with two white nurses joining in February 1942 – Sisters Fraser and Crago.[64] Despite their best efforts there continued to be deaths among K6 personnel. There is one grave at Crickhowell itself, and eight in Brecon, including that of the poetry-writing bellows boy Aurangzeb.

Aside from deaths, the numbers of men in K6 fluctuated, with arrivals from India and departures, all of whom passed through the Reinforcement Unit, which was somewhat like a holding station. In July 1942 Hills and his officers compiled a list of members of the original K6, who had left India over thirty months before, who wished to be sent home. The list included nearly 1,000 men, the vast majority of the original members in the UK.[65] At the end of August 1942, Hills' total command amounted to 3,400 men and 3,400 animals, including two companies of white British men in the RASC companies.[66] Altogether, the total number of men who served in Force K6 at some stage during the war was 4,227.

Among the comings and goings were a number of officers. Many of the original K6 officers went back to India after they had been in the UK for a while, so by March 1942 there were only five such left (Hills, Hexley, Cole, Finlay and Fawcett).[67] The force included one woman – Driver I.M.L. Pitts-Tucker, wife of Captain Pitts-Tucker, secretary to Hills in 1942.[68] Meanwhile Major Akbar had left for India in August 1941 with two purposes in mind, as he explained in a letter to the imam at Woking: 'to do all I can to destroy Hitlerism and to help myself and my brothers, and to tell the public in India what excellent work you and everyone else is doing'.[69]

The tide of Indian officers was generally flowing in the other direction, though, reflecting the increasing Indianisation of the army during wartime. By February 1943 there were eleven Indian commissioned officers, including five Muslims, three Hindus and three Sikhs.[70] Hills was of the opinion that the Muslim officers had an easier time, which he couched in rather roundabout terms in his report:

the Hindus are much on the defensive and have a purely personal viewpoint, the reason for this is obvious. The Moslems, on the other hand, are keen, most of them of course have been appointed to commissions from the ranks of the Contingent and know their duties reasonably well, they do not suffer so much from a prestige complex.[71]

Clearly Hills thought the religious differences between a Sikh or Hindu officer and a Muslim soldier would be insurmountable. A man of his time, Hills was steeped in the old ways of the Indian Army and not quite ready for units that were integrated.

Among the Sikh officers was one Rattan Singh. He arrived as a lieutenant in April 1942 and was posted to 7th Company, then in St Austell. Margaret Woodhouse was a little girl living close to Duporth camp and remembers him well:

One evening, my father and an Indian doctor friend, who was staying with us at the lane, were out walking and got into conversation with an Indian Army officer who was out walking alone. The two Indians came from the same region of Northern India and the officer was delighted to have someone to talk to, as I understand that he was the only officer and, since he could not fraternize with his men, he was consequently very lonely.

The officer's name was Rut en Singh (the spelling is almost certainly incorrect, but that is how it sounded to me, a child, at that time!). He had been educated at a public school in England and was the son of wealthy parents, or so I understood. My recollection is that he was the only man to have a horse, and a splendid sight they were, he was a fine-looking man and the horse was magnificent.[72]

Later in Chepstow, another girl was also impressed by him:

The Commandant had been educated at Oxford. He was friendly with my parents and my mother's young sister. As a result, all the family, including my grandmother, were invited to a meal at the camp. We sat at a low table where chapatti-type bread was passed around, and curry was served on the bread. No cutlery! A great fuss was made of my brother, who was taken around the camp and put on a large horse. I, a mere girl, was largely ignored! The commandant translated part of letter from his mother in which she said 'remember my son, all the lads in your care, are some other mother's sons'.[73]

In July 1942 Rattan Singh was selected as one of eight to attend a course for servicemen from the USA, the Dominions and the Allies at the University of London on 'international good will, citizenship and postwar'.[74] Hills was keen to remind him that 'personnel who are attending the course are doing so not primarily for their own benefit but for India' and that he had to submit a 'thesis' on his return. In this way Hills, with his eye on public relations, hoped to advance the reputation of India and Force K6 among the professors and the other students on the course, and to gain valuable insights for the men. Rattan Singh continued to do well in the force, marching in the United Nations Day parade in London in 1943, and showing off his skills in jumping and trick riding.[75] Being an officer in a Muslim unit in the British countryside was a good opportunity for a young officer like Rattan Singh.

8

Hinges and fringes

We travel for various purposes; to explore the culture of soils; to view the curiosities of art; to survey the beauties of nature; to search for her productions; and to learn the manners of men; their different polities, and modes of life.[1]

Apart from their extended time at Crickhowell, units of the Indian Contingent were posted to other parts of Wales during this period, as well as Colchester in Essex. In May 1941, 32nd Company were spread around South Wales, with troops at the greyhound track at Pontypool (where Clement Attlee visited them), Caerleon and Ruperra Castle.[2] One troop were sent to work with the Staffordshire Regiment at Chepstow Racecourse. This little Welsh town is situated right on the border with England, where the winding river Wye meets the great river Severn, near the village of Beachley, the terminus for the Severn car ferry. The men are well remembered there:

> I can remember when the Indians were at the racecourse. They all had these turbans, and horses and mules. They used to go down through Chepstow with their carriage to pick up the mail from the station. I can remember going along to Prices, High Beech, when I was at Larkfield to collect milk for the cookery classes. One day they stopped me to ask 'Was I the milky lady?' We were carrying those carriers with about six bottles.[3]

Further up the Wye Valley, 25th Company spent some time at Monmouth in early 1943. Apart from training with the Hallamshire and Lincolnshire Battalions, they found time to play a lot of hockey and start a vegetable garden. They were handsomely entertained by the locals, going regularly to the cinema and 'afterwards entertained to tea, conjuror and games by the citizens of Monmouth'.[4] Their pipe band marched in the town in May as part of the Wings for Victory parade: Punjabi soldiers playing Scottish bagpipes in a Welsh border town. At the same time 42nd Company held a sports day in the park at Pontypool, featuring tent pegging, 'potatoes race', musical chairs, and a muleback tug of war.[5] Meanwhile 32nd Company were further west at Pembrey on the Carmarthenshire coast, where they watched the Abbott and Costello film *Hold that Ghost*, which 'was very much appreciated by all ranks'.[6] They held a public gymkhana, where children were allowed to ride the mules and the Indian sword dance (probably a Pashtun *khattak* dance) was enjoyed by the public. This was something of a farewell event for this friendly village, for the very same day the company started a sixty-five-mile march across the Brecon Beacons, travelling by night. They bivouacked on the hills during the day, at Llandybie, Ford and Cantref, and arrived at Llangattock at 0030 hrs on 21 April, when the 'personnel received a ration of hot tea and were in bright spirits'.

Even further up the river Wye is the English cathedral city of Hereford. The 29th and 42nd Companies were based at the racecourse in the summer of 1941. Postings at racecourses made sense, as such places had the facilities to accommodate horses and mules. In June they carried out exercises with the infantry near Hay-on-Wye.[7] These exercises were misremembered years later by Bruce Chatwin in his prize-winning book *On the Black Hill*.[8] The Advanced Remount Depot were also posted there, and the sepoys enjoyed swimming in the Wye at Lugg and Bredwardine, as well as a circus at Ledbury.[9] The ARD moved to Derby in October, where the men collected £16 selling Remembrance Day poppies.[10] At the end of the year it was decided that the responsibility of supplying new horses and mules would be taken by the British Remount Depot, so the remaining mules were distributed to Doncaster and Bawtry and the ARD men returned to India.[11]

While 29th Company were at Hereford they received a visit from an official war artist, Henry Lamb. In May 1941 Lamb had seen 'some fine-looking turbaned Indians about Salisbury' and was determined to paint them.[12] He followed them to Hereford and painted two canvases: one of Major Akbar and one of Driver Abdul Ghani. The portraits are clearly a pair: they show head and shoulders in front of a coloured background, designed to bring out the tones of skin and uniform. Akbar's portrait resides in the storeroom at the Imperial War Museum but is scheduled to join their new Second World War display from 2021.[13] In it, he looks to his left, perhaps to India. Abdul Ghani, currently on display at the Kelvingrove Museum in Glasgow, looks to his right. He is in full dress uniform, of course, with *pagri* tied carefully, lanyard on left shoulder, and bandoliers, which were used for rifle ammunition, across his chest (see cover image). Lamb recorded in a letter that 'he also has a frontier medal 1938 but to his chagrin this was eclipsed in the picture by his bandoliers'.[14]

Like Major Akbar in the partner portrait, Abdul Ghani is not making eye contact with the artist or the observer but looking somewhat dreamily to the viewer's left. Adding to the slight sense of disconnection is the plain, greenish background – a hue that matches the khaki of his *kurtah*. Lamb has not chosen a background that makes the sitter stand out, nor has he done what many portraitists do: put some tools of the trade in the background. It would not have been hard to paint a mule or a cart behind the driver, but Lamb instead puts the focus on the man rather than the job – the focus is his eyes, his face, his expression. On his head Abdul Ghani wears, not a steel helmet, which might signal imminent danger, nor yet a forage cap, which communicates a casual situation, but the formal turban, so beloved of those who photographed or painted the men of K6. Other than his service number (178415), we know little else of this soldier. We can assume he is in his 20s or early 30s, probably born in the 1910s, from the Pothwari plateau, and his name tells us he was a Muslim. He was included in Brown's seven-week English course in early 1942, suggesting that he had some aptitude for the English language, which may give a clue to the choice of him as subject for painting. Lamb would have needed to communicate with his sitters: having a translator in the studio would have been a waste of personnel. One wonders whether, like Major Akbar, the sitter received a signed copy to take home with him. Perhaps somewhere in Punjab the family still keeps this souvenir of their grandfather's time in Britain.

Lamb himself was equivocal about the pair of portraits, writing that he thought the two pictures 'all right & likely to diversify some future exhibition in a useful way'.[15] The paintings were exhibited at the National Gallery later in the year, hanging either side of a painting of a policeman by A.R. Thomson.[16] The review of the exhibition in *The Times* said that Lamb's two portraits were 'to be noted', but no other contemporary responses survive, although a later critic remarked that most of Lamb's Second World War portraits are 'extremely competent but unexceptional, those of the lower ranks tend to be livelier'.[17] During the war all the gallery's permanent collection of paintings was evacuated to Manod Quarry in Ffestiniog in Wales, and so the hollowed-out space was filled by the pianist Myra Hess and her lunchtime concerts, and temporary exhibitions like that featuring Abdul Ghani and Akbar.[18] The sepoys could stand in for the Old Masters for the duration: K6 had penetrated wartime British society to the core.

* * * * *

One of the most unusual postings for K6 men during this period was on Steep Holm. This uninhabited island lies in the Bristol Channel between Cardiff and Weston-super-Mare, with England in view a few miles away to the right, and Wales the same distance to the left. Previously used by Romans, Augustinian monks and smugglers, by 1941 it was a haven for golden samphire and wild peonies, seagulls and 'the largest earwigs I have ever seen', according to Private Harold Parr.[19] With a sou'westerly bringing gales and rain through the winter, this chilly rock must have felt a very long way from Punjab. In 1941 the narrow passage between Steep Holm and its Welsh neighbour Flat Holm provided a way to cover the sea lanes outside Cardiff and Bristol, and represented 'the defended gateway to Britain and a symbol of relief for those who had survived the treacherous South-Western approaches'.[20] So a joint force of Royal Engineers, Pioneers and Royal Artillery were sent there under Major Bertlin, to install searchlights and four six-inch naval guns which had been in storage since the First World War.[21] Bertlin recalled:

> our task was to fortify the islands to repel any possible enemy force coming up the Bristol Channel. Because of the steep path to the top of Steep Holm, mules were landed on the beach by tank landing craft and I planned a zig-zag railway to haul the guns up the steep cliff.[22]

The K6 war diaries show that ten men and twelve mules from 32nd Company disembarked at Steep Holm on 22 September 1941.[23] Their life there must have been very harsh indeed, dragging guns up the steep slope, living in difficult conditions with all supplies (including live sheep, of course) arriving by boat from Barry on the Welsh side.[24] When the tide was wrong or a gale blew, the supplies could not get through, and there was only one beach to land on. Water was rationed, as it had to be brought in by boat, and later there was an outbreak of typhoid. Gunner Cyril Stickland of the Royal Artillery found:

> of all his wartime experiences, including being wounded at Amiens, the short period he spent on Steep Holm was among the roughest of the war. Once, the island was completely cut off for thirteen days and by then they were living on hard baked ship's biscuit with a spoonful of jam.[25]

Rations were supplemented with rabbits, birds and gulls' eggs. Some of the men made a brisk trade collecting eggs, which they sold to their NCO for a penny. He in turn sold them for tuppence each to the boatman, who sold them on to the shops in Barry for threepence. The shopkeepers then sold them to customers for 4d.[26] During their six lonely months on the island, the sepoys and their mules performed prodigious feats, dragging guns and supplies up the slope to the 120-man barracks and batteries at the top of the hill: the island's name was well earned. They won praise from their British comrades. Regimental Sergeant Major Adams recalled that the Indians 'were a fine lot of men' who 'made a really good job of curried mutton'.[27] The men, under command of an English-speaking NCO, were visited regularly by British RIASC officers.[28] On 20 April Subedar Mohd Ibrahim made the crossing to give them their pay.[29] Given that there was nothing to buy on the island except gulls' eggs, this seems a surprising trip for the subedar to take, but there was a visit later that year from the Entertainments National Service Association (ENSA), the branch of the army that provided entertainment for the services.[30] The men left in May 1942, but there is a strange coda to this story. The island played host to other Indians nearly forty years later, when the Bollywood movie *Shaan* was shot on the island.[31] Perhaps the director Ramesh Sippy knew some of the K6 boys who had been stationed there.

During the summer of 1942, the three remaining original companies were posted to Snowdonia in North Wales, where the highest mountains reach down to the sea. They were stationed in and around the hamlets of Croesor and Nantmor, on the south side of Snowdon. These ancient counties of Merioneth and Caernarvon are haunted with old stories, such as the tale of the two dragons who battle beneath the hill of Dinas Emrys, until discovered by the young Merlin. Another local story would have been familiar to the Punjabis, for it is based on an old Indian tale. The story of the Brahmin's wife and the mongoose relates how a rural couple had one baby son and adopted a mongoose.[32] Returning one day from fetching water, the wife was met by the excited mongoose, blood smeared around its mouth. Imagining that it had killed the baby, she dropped her water jar on the pet, killing it instantly. She then found the baby alive and well, and a dead snake, which the faithful animal had killed to protect the infant. Her husband returned and they lamented the death, the result of hasty action. This story forms the basis for the story of the hound Gelert, supposedly buried in the village of Beddgelert, just up the hill from Nantmor. Gelert was the faithful hunting hound of the Great King of Gwynedd, Llywelyn Fawr. His story follows that of the wife and the mongoose, with the offending beast being a wolf. Llywelyn regretted his haste so strongly that he never smiled again, and built a special enclosure for the hound's grave, which still stands today.[33] The men of K6 would have heard and recognised the story, and seen the grave: perhaps they pondered on loyalty and the dangers of taking action too quickly.

The sepoys and the local people created new stories themselves, which many local residents took delight in recounting decades afterwards. In the small village of Croesor, with only fifteen houses and some scattered farms, the injection of 1,000 men all together had 'an amazing effect' on this community where everybody knew everybody.[34] During the four short months that the three companies were posted there they made a huge impact, on the fields, the local children and on the women, leaving at least three babies behind.

The three companies were in training with the three infantry battalions of 70th Brigade.[35] The infantrymen had been in Iceland, and their Icelandic experience was useful:

living in rather isolated camps among a few Welsh people speaking their own language, with place names long and unpronounceable, and large tracts of high land nearby, we might almost have been in Iceland. There was one difference – there was certainly a large amount of beer available, but the supply often ran out.[36]

Each mule company supported an infantry battalion, carrying their equipment round the mountains in exercises named 'Sheep', 'Lamb' and 'Drum'.[37] The men worked closely together: the Tommies loading the mules while the men of K6 held the animals' heads, and then led them up the hillside tracks.[38] Because of this close proximity, the men from the north-east of England were actively encouraged to 'fraternise with Indian personnel of affiliated Mule Coys'.[39] There were limits, however, as Brigadier Philip Kirkup reminded them:

> Attached Mule Coys are composed entirely of Mohammedans and in establishing liaison it should be realised by all ranks that there are, in some respects, limits to which fraternisation should be extended. British troops will not … persuade Indians to accompany them to public houses or wet canteens, both of which are out of bounds to Indian troops.[40]

There were other entertainments available. Apart from parades and marches, the men joined in sports with British troops, including playing kabaddi and 'putting the weight'.[41]

Despite such light-heartedness, the sepoys were distracted by events at home. The summer of 1942 was a difficult one in India. Following Japan's entry into the war in December 1941, the British Empire had suffered defeat after defeat in Asia, losing Hong Kong, Malaya and Singapore, and then Burma. In all these places, Indian sepoys had been among the defenders, and many thousands were now in Japanese POW camps, in conditions far worse than in any German *lager*. Refugees from Burma flooded into the north-east of India – around 300,000 of them by May 1942.[42] The British cabinet minister Stafford Cripps visited in March, on an unsuccessful mission to find a constitutional settlement that would suit Congress and the government, and that failure was followed in August by Gandhi's 'Quit India' speech, which triggered a wave of protests around the country. Indians were afraid, and rumours were everywhere, summarised as 'the Japanese are coming; the British are set to flee'.[43]

While sepoys yomped up and down the cwms of North Wales, their countrymen were suffering and fearful. The officers at least were well aware of what was happening at home. Yaqub Mirza came across Lieutenant Saifullah Khan weeping in his office and asked him if he'd received bad news.[44] The next day the officer explained in detail what had happened, and the failure of the Quit India movement. Against this background, Hills did his best to rally the troops and focus them on their work. In a letter to all the men, he wrote:

> time spent in fruitless political discussions during the hours when a soldier should be devoting his energies to the improvement of efficiency is not only neglect of duty but a waste of the money of the taxpayer. Discussion should … in off duty hours, be confined to the principle of how best can an Indian help his country … politics as such must be deferred to a more suitable time.[45]

He neglected to let them know when that time might be.

The men from Punjab were keen to supplement their rations with local Welsh delicacies. Edgar Parry Williams recalled their fondness for eggs, and his 13-year-old brother Eric heard that they would pay the black-market rate of ten shillings for a dozen. Eric and Edgar went to the camp and:

> Eric showed his eggs and instantly there was a crowd of Indians around us. One of them took an egg and broke it … and instantly swallowed it. One egg was gone … Eric said 'Ten shillings a dozen' and the Indian said 'Ten shillings! No ten shillings!' and … he pulled out a list and he knew from that list the price of eggs and he paid us whatever the price was for eggs – maybe half a crown. That was the end of that enterprise.[46]

Sultanas were in short supply in the villages, but the sepoys had ample. Dilys Rees' mother 'used to trade eggs for sultanas with the Indians, who also gave sultanas out to the children. Dilys remembers walking through the camp, quite unafraid, with a rice pudding her mother had made.'[47] Another local boy, Watkin Evans, was interested in their eating habits:

> They had a big canteen there. They were in tents. The only buildings were toilets. You know where Bryn Pandy is, there was a cookhouse there, Indian

cookhouse there. They used a pinkish lard. Every Sunday they were killing lambs. They did not buy them from the local farmers, the lambs came there by wagon. They killed the lambs by Min Afon a bit further up. They had their own butchers. I always remember going there to collect swill from the canteen and it went to Garreg Hylldrem and this Indian he was on the top of the table, square table, making the bread with his feet, standing there. They had this big oven, half round oven, and they used to make it [chapattis] flat like a pancake and drop it on of that and give it a turn and it was ready.[48]

As they had found in France, the men made friends with children easily. One young woman thought that they got on so well because neither group could speak much English and that seemed to make a rapport between them.[49] Carys Richards, 'the girl with the golden voice', made a radio programme for BBC Radio Wales years later, telling her listeners:

Us children were surprised that they were pleased to see someone strange coming along on the road past the camp. 'Look young ladies with red hair,' said one in English, ran a number of them out of their tents to stand politely, everybody smiling. My father had a conversation with one of the men, a tall one, and he looked taller again under his turban. He [my father] understood he was a member of RIASC and the name of the camp was Rawalpindi. 'Come on or we'll miss the bus,' said my father and we walked shyly through the rows of dark faces which were still smiling at us till we arrived back to Welsh territory.[50]

Jos Williams and his sisters made some 'mischievous, honest, clean fun' out of their Indian guests:

It was like this. The Indians used to come here for a cup of tea with mother, one at a time, many used to come. If there was one here, another one would not come … Lal Khan was the name of the batman – he used to come here every morning for fresh milk and eggs. They were not allowed to smoke in the camp so he would come through to this room to have a smoke, and every morning he would offer a cigarette to my sisters, Laura and Mair … What the wicked girls did! Laura told Mair, 'You take one tomorrow morning and he will put a light to it, I am sure he will do that, and you take a few puffs of smoking like that and pretend you go ill and fall off the seat.' Of course it worked well! She took the cigarette, he lit it, she collapsed off the seat and he shouted, 'Mums, mums, water, water, water.' He came back with water saying, 'Cleans, cleans, cleans.' Oh we had fun with them![51]

One soldier was particularly well remembered in the villages above Porthmadog: Malik Mohammed Khan, a veterinary jemadar. He rode a white horse and had a pockmarked face: qualities that would make him memorable. Edgar Parry Williams described him as a 'very quiet gentle kind of a man' who made them tea with lots of milk and sugar.[52] He was keen on singing and used to visit the school to hear Welsh folk songs. He also taught the children a Punjabi lullaby 'Sunate, sunate, Sunate krishana', that Edgar still remembered sixty years later. Nellie Woods, aged 21, whose father ran a garage, was also friendly with him. 'He seemed an old man … Spoke English well and was very well read. Malik asked for books to read [and] would come to the house with his valet … who did not speak English. Malik would sit in their front room for hours reading. Very intelligent. He had scars from smallpox.'[53]

Nellie had rather a poor reputation in the area. Giovanna Bloor (who conducted extensive K6 research in Snowdonia) called her the 'Polly Garter of Croesor', referring to the young woman in Dylan Thomas' *Under Milk Wood* who laments as she hangs up the laundry that 'nothing grows in our garden, only washing. And babies.'[54] Nellie liked to flirt with the Indian soldiers when they visited the cinema or the dances at the Memorial Hall. Another girl, Marian Roberts, recalled once coming out of the cinema when it was pouring with rain. She and her friend walked home under the capes of two Indians, holding onto their waists. She kept the autograph of Nowab Khan, written in English and Urdu, together with his service number 180697. He was just 19 years old.[55]

Interested as they were in the local women, the soldiers did not forget their duty to God. Edgar recalled that in the morning and evening, 'you would see them in rows, and they would be going backwards and forwards, putting their foreheads on the ground, making this humming sound, coming up on the breeze, and you were not supposed to interfere with them at that time.'[56] Watkin Evans recalled visits from Malik Mohammed Khan:

I remember there was a doctor there and he used to come up to the house, an Indian doctor, a tall chap, a big man, and he came up to Coed Ty nearly every day. And every time he comes in, straight upstairs and he wanted a towel and he was praying on the towel in the bedroom … I remember my brother and I was playing and I don't know how, I hit my brother with a stone and he was bleeding. And as soon as I did that, twenty minutes after, this doctor came up and took him up, and went down to the camp and came back and stitched it up for him … He used to pray for about ten minutes. We used to peep to see what was going on but he would close the door – one could not hear him. My parents didn't mind. He was a nice chap, a very nice chap. Very polite. With quite good English. Some of them couldn't speak English at all. And we all spoke Welsh. Communication was bit patchy! I don't know how it was he came up to the house – none of the other Indians did. I shall never forget him.[57]

For four months 1,000 men of the RIASC lived in those villages in North Wales, and the place was never quite the same again. A bridge below the Cnicht mountain is named Pont Traed y Mul (Bridge of the Mule's Leg) after a mule became stuck on the bridge and had to be killed, leaving the leg between the slates.[58] The children and the adults of the valley recalled the men for years afterwards, one of whom even came back after the war to thank Jos Williams' mother for her kindness. Thousands of miles from Punjab, the men clearly felt a connection with the hill people of North Wales. And after all, 'The Indians didn't come here of their own accord, they were away from their families. I made a lot of friends with them.'[59] The welcome was warm in this mountainous spot, and the memories are long.

* * * * *

During all this time the men were visiting Woking Mosque regularly in small groups on leave. Just as Henry Lamb had spotted some of them at Salisbury station, another artist was sitting and sketching at one of the busiest railway stations in the country: Waterloo. Helen McKie was known for her drawings of military figures during the Great War and had 'corresponded with soldiers on active service across the world'.[60] She continued that patriotic focus in the Second World War, doing large-scale works featuring women and barrage balloons, shipyards, and a study of Churchill in the Admiralty War Rooms. She was commissioned for what was probably her most famous work by Southern Railways in 1943: a view of Waterloo Station.[61] Positioned at a high angle, where shops are now found, McKie drew an action-packed scene of the hustle and bustle of people criss-crossing the station concourse at eighteen minutes to seven. Here, in one of the main hubs of wartime London, we see all human life: matelots pulling a loaded trailer, lovers kissing goodbye and a Highlander carrying bagpipes. All the 'types' of London wartime life are there – the provocation is for the viewer to recognise somebody just like them. And there, in the foreground, front and centre, just to the left of a pair of nuns, a couple of Indian sepoys with *pagri*s, rifles and kitbags. Standing between platforms eleven and twelve, not in conversation but watching the world go by, the two Indians are the only non-white faces in the crowd, as they would often have been during their time in the UK. Other allies are present: there is a Polish *schapka* right at the front, and two white Americans near the corner, but the central place of the two RIASC men suggests that McKie wanted to accentuate the importance of the Empire in the defence of the mother-land. Although the *pagri*s are perhaps not completely accurate, there can be no doubt that K6 men were her inspiration. They passed through Waterloo regularly on their way to their leave camp at Woking Mosque, and they went up to London every Tuesday and Thursday for sight-seeing and tea with the ICF.[62] McKie put them in the picture because she saw them at the station – they were a part of the everyday swirl of station life at Waterloo, one of the busiest stations in the land. So successful was this picture, issued as a poster by Southern Railways, that McKie returned in 1948 to make a companion piece, entitled 'Waterloo Station: Peace'. In this version, which matches the figures one by one, the two Indians are now in full dress red uniforms, without rifles, watching the world go by. Partition and Independence may have come and gone, but for Helen McKie time was frozen, and the Empire with it. McKie's picture has been made into a jigsaw puzzle, popular at the London Transport Museum, so the figures of the two unnamed sepoys are assembled by the hands of many people who know not who they were, nor understand their significance. Hiding in plain sight as they wait for a train to Woking, their units were soon travelling in the opposite direction, to Scotland.

9

Heroes and traitors behind bars

Prisoner of War ... a melancholy state ... Hours crawl like paralytic centipedes.
Nothing amuses you ... Life is one long boredom from dawn till slumber.[1]

In December 1941, Jemadar Rana Wali Mohamed Khan from Hoshiarpur
was a POW in Germany. He had been the medical officer attached to
22nd Animal Transport Company in France. According to a report from
a repatriated British army doctor, Rana had an interesting story to tell:

> Rana was sent for by the Germans and ... went in a private car with a
> German officer to an address in Stalag IIID, where he found ... [Indians]
> dressed flashily in civilian clothes. Rana discovered that some were from
> his old unit 22 AT Coy. They immediately jumped to attention.
>
> On the guise of talking about their health he questioned the men and
> was told that ... the man who had been their priest in 22 AT Coy and who
> had [led] them twice a day in prayer had been away for three months in
> Iran as a German agent there. These men were expecting to be dropped
> in Afghanistan to be helped over the frontier into India and they thought
> that they might be doing some 'secret broadcasting' in India itself. These
> Indians were given two Red Cross parcels per week and they offered Rana
> any amount of food.[2]

This report reveals a number of things about life for Indian soldiers in the
POW camps, and the choices that the sepoys of 22nd Company made.
Firstly the men jumped to attention, showing that they still held Rana
in high regard. They were dressed in civilian clothes, so they had not yet
taken the step of putting on German uniforms. They were still receiving
Red Cross parcels and had a surplus of food to share. Meanwhile their
maulvi had been parachuted into Iran as a spy, and they were hoping to be
dropped into Afghanistan. The Germans clearly had high hopes of these

men: they were being well looked after and attending an Urdu course with a view to broadcasting propaganda to India. As for Rana himself, he had stayed with 22nd Company after their surrender in France in June 1940, and his comrade-in-arms Tom Hexley wrote a report that is full of praise for his work after capture, including treating an outbreak of dysentery with Epsom salts, and performing an eye operation in Longvic camp. Professionally stretched and rising to the challenge, Dr Rana stuck to his loyalty to the British and his Hippocratic oath. Others had made very different choices.

Before we try to understand those choices, let us return to the summer of 1940, where we left 22nd Company at Gérardmer, having surrendered to the Germans.[3] The officers had been separated, and Hexley was now in charge of the 300 men. During the next three months their travels continued, on foot and by train, through four different POW camps. The speed and success of the German advances that summer had left them with the huge problem of thousands upon thousands of prisoners. As Hexley wrote: 'it was obvious that the enemy just did not know what to do with, or how to feed, the thousands of prisoners they were collecting in.'[4] This was to lead to all sorts of problems for the men of 22nd Company, which would take many months to be ironed out.

The fact that so many sepoys survived these difficult months intact is testament to the way they stuck together and supported each other in a disciplined and comradely way: it was business as usual for 22nd Company. Their maulvi led prayers daily, they cooked and ate together, they looked after the sick, including many cases of dysentery. The fact that Hexley chose to stay with them until the end of November – indeed on more than one occasion the Germans separated him from the men – demonstrates the loyalty that this remarkable man felt towards his colleagues. It seems that he was a man of real organisational talent, physical energy and charisma, with the ability to learn and use at least three languages, a man whom his comrades liked and respected, whom they would follow. His report is full of personal stories that reveal a strong bond and a warm relationship with the men that was unusual in the hierarchical and racially charged Indian Army of the time. As he put it, 'I lived with them under all conditions and they accepted me as one of them.'

For the first few days in captivity the men travelled on foot with their carts and animals, and the six remaining lorries with RASC drivers. One of the accompanying German officers cycled up and down the column, and Abuzar explained the reason to Hexley:

> hesitatingly in a round about way … It appeared he was a homeo-sexualist and was going systematically down the column trying to find a kindred spirit among the men by questions and signs. I doubted this at first but TD Abuzar called up some men and from their replies to my questions and imitations of the motions of the enemy officer was making to them, it was obviously what was happening.[5]

Later the men were subjected to what Hexley called a 'mild form of looting' by the Germans, who relieved them of knives, their wireless, swords and watches. When Hexley remembered the company 'treasure chest' which was concealed in one of the carts, he and a carpenter smashed it open, destroyed the papers and divided the remaining 30,000 francs (around £150) equally among the company. After their mules were taken at St Dié, the men marched off, each carrying a 'tremendous bundle of kit', using sticks or hockey sticks, and looking like 'a terrible crowd as everything was mud-spattered and wet but it could not dampen their spirits. They recalled to me a party of Scouts going for a week-end camp in the greatest of spirits.'[6] Quartermaster Dafadar (QMD) Barkat Ali made sure to take the gramophone under his arm but distributed the Hindustani records to men he trusted. At the rear of the column was Sweeper Basanta, 'carrying a large porcelain "hooka" which was still burning'.

Their next destination was Sélestat, on the hills descending towards the river Rhine. Here they were herded into a gigantic 'collecting centre' for 50,000 or more POWs, who 'appeared as thousands of ants wandering aimlessly about'. There seemed to be no organisation in the camp, and very little food. The Germans drove a lorry round outside the wire and threw four-pound loaves of bread 'over the wire like chicken feed'. There were no proper latrines and the ground was 'covered in human excreta'. The 22nd Company rapidly cleared and swept a space and set up their cooking equipment within clear boundaries. The rest of the POWs gathered round and 'we were being regarded as a type of Punch and

Judy show'. They also drew an audience when the maulvi led communal prayers, and next morning the men were 'quite cheerful and contented, wandering off around the camp making friends' as they had nothing to do for the first time in months.

A week later they marched again, to the town of Erstein, halfway to Strasbourg. This was a 'terrible' march: 'We were given no halts – our bundles of kits became as heavy as lead, the heat was terrific and our clothing soon soaked with perspiration. I do not think any man of the Coy who was there will ever forget it.'[7] Local women helped by giving water and dressing feet, and 'one enterprising young lady with a trailer arrangement fixed to her cycle, cycled up and followed us for some miles with buckets of water'. The following day they covered the final section to Strasbourg on the Rhine, with ciné and still photographers accompanying. This was probably the day that two photographs in the Bundesarchiv were taken, one showing the men marching, another at a halt, with Hexley and Barkat Ali in front.[8] Their destination was an old barracks, where they occupied four storerooms over a stable – their first proper camp since leaving Metz four weeks before. They were repeatedly visited by German staff officers with their wives, to gawp at the men and observe prayers. Hexley wrote: 'My own impression of the affair is that we were regarded as some new type of animals would be at the London Zoo.'[9]

They were also visited by one of their VCOs who had previously been separated, the veterinary assistant surgeon (VAS) Ishaq. He arrived in an 'enemy staff car with some enemy officers with whom he appeared to be on the best of terms'. Ishaq subsequently gave away chapattis to German NCOs, so Hexley rebuked him in the strongest terms. The next day Hexley was put in solitary confinement for 'instigating mutiny', but used the isolation to study French from a book, 'which proved invaluable in later days'. He was acutely aware of the possibility of the men developing strong feelings against the vanquished British, and the temptation to fraternise or even join the Germans, but he reckoned that for most of the men, 'the more severe the hardship became and arguments developed, so the more genuinely pro-British became the feelings of the Coy'.

A few days later Hexley was most perturbed to discover that, along with some other white French troops, he was to be taken to a new camp across the river in Germany, leaving his men behind. As he marched across the bridge, 'my spirits were low, being alone – but French prisoners were openly crying'. Soon afterwards he saw a mixed column of North African, Senegalese and Indo-Chinese French colonial soldiers marching the other way into France, looking cheerful. As he sat watching them, 'a sudden idea struck me and picking up my bundle I crossed over the gap, only some three or four paces, joined up with them and marched along'. Remarkably, his new column marched past 22nd Company, and keeping his face hidden, he 'struck off at an angle, walked over and joined them'. They were on their way to a new camp at Belfort, and for the next three months Hexley lived among the sepoys pretending to be Indian. From Belfort they proceeded to Frontstalag 155 on an old airfield at Longvic near Dijon.[10] After three months in captivity they were eventually photographed and documented, and Hexley gave his nationality as Indian and birthplace as Rawalpindi. This was a remarkable thing to do, as he could have been much more comfortable in a *Stalag*, but he wanted to stay with the men. They settled into a routine, keeping up their practice of cooking for themselves, but having to resort to eating whatever supplies were found for them. The exception was meat, which they never ate unless they could slaughter it themselves. October also saw the month of Ramadan, and Hexley reported that 'in spite of all the hardships and difficulties, Roza [fast] was carefully maintained by all'. At the end of the month came Eid, which:

> was celebrated in the best style possible. The Maulvi Sahib produced a new white smock and clothes from somewhere and led communal prayers. SWO Akbar Khan issued some of his closely guarded *ghi* and an attempt at a 'Barra Khana' made. Many of the Mohds in the camp paid the Maulvi Sahib their monetary tribute and he was able to clear off some old debts.[11]

As the winter approached, conditions showed no sign of getting better. Six French soldiers were discovered attempting to escape through a sewer trench and bayonetted by the German guards. Dr Rana stitched them up expertly, but two died. Barkat Ali had kept hold of the gramophone, but the needles were so blunt that the music was almost completely unrecognisable. Naik Roda Khan was made a camp policeman by the Germans and given a swastika armband to wear, which 'he religiously spat on … each time it was pointed out to him'. Although the French POWs regularly received letters and Red Cross parcels, none arrived for 22nd Company. Things were beginning to look desperate and morale was deteriorating. Hexley had had enough and was determined to escape.

* * * * *

After Hexley's escape from Longvic at the end of November, the story of the men left behind is much harder to tell, as documents are fragmentary. The men stayed at Longvic for a few more months, but by August 1941 most of them were in Lamsdorf (now Łambinowice in Poland), with Abuzar at their head as 'man of confidence', responsible for reporting direct to the Red Cross emissary.[12] The Red Cross report (written by a Swiss bureaucrat) includes a paragraph saying, 'their military bearing, their meticulous cleanliness and their smart appearance are the admiration of their captors'. The rest of the men were spread across eleven more camps.[13] At this stage, twelve months after capture, most of them were still together, Abuzar was in command, and most had stayed loyal to the British. While around thirty men chose to join the German Army, and ten managed to escape, more than 85 per cent of 22nd Company chose to wait stoically for the war to end. Their experience in captivity was the longest of any Indian POWs in the world wars, possibly the longest ever: nearly five years in some cases. The 320 men were among 15,000 Indian prisoners who in their turn were part of around 170,000 British and Commonwealth POWs in Europe: a vast army of men sitting and waiting.[14] Their story is seldom told and little known, partly because they are usually subsumed under the banner of 'British troops'.[15]

The common impression of the life of the POW in Germany is one based on films and TV series from the 1950s and 1960s: *The Wooden Horse, Colditz* and *The Great Escape*. This myth shows white officers in bunks, in huts in a forest or a castle, bored and frustrated, spending all their time plotting how to escape. This was not the experience of the majority of the men of 22nd Company. Although several of them managed to escape, their prison experience was characterised by hard work. Article 49 of the Geneva Convention allows the 'Detaining Power' to 'utilize the labour of prisoners of war', but officers (including VCOs) are exempt and NCOs 'shall only be required to do supervisory work'.[16]

As the majority of 22nd Company were not NCOs or officers, and the Germans needed vast amounts of labour to keep their war machine turning, the majority of the sepoys were working for most of the time. Hexley told an Indian newspaper that they were employed 'in working parties on road making, coal fatigues, unloading railway wagons and similar work near the camps'.[17] In 1943 a large group of over 300 Indian POWs, including around seventy from 22nd Company, were moved from Annaburg, south of Berlin, to Rennes, in north-western France.[18] In July they were moved again, back eastwards as far as Malschbach, just across the Rhine from Strasbourg. From here they were sent to various work camps, notably Steinselz and Schoenenbourg, both tucked in the north-east corner of France, where there were also Palestinian Arab POWs from the British Pioneer Corps, and black South Africans. In a twist of irony, the camp at Schoenenbourg was housed within a Maginot Line fort.

The prisoners in each camp elected a 'man of confidence' who would talk privately with the Red Cross representatives when they came for their regular visits. This camp had elected Barkat Ali, the QMD who had held on to the gramophone in 1940. Barkat Ali was later deposed from this role because he was 'too dictatorial with his fellow POWs and did not forward complaints against himself'.[19] The Red Cross reports on the camp at Schoenenbourg show how much conditions had improved since 1940. There was a room set aside for a mosque, and their maulvi requested copies of the Qur'an and carpets. The men had hot baths weekly, slept on bunks on palliasses filled with wood-shavings with two blankets 'of German origin', but were cold in winter:

> when the weather is bad and the days already sharply chilly, as is the case at this time of year, these prisoners wet and shivering with cold return to an icy compound which they have the greatest difficulty in rendering even temperately warm with the damp wood which they collect at the end of the day.[20]

As they were doing hard physical work, they were on the 'heavy worker' ration scale but were still not eating meat as 'German law forbids to kill cattle in the Indian fashion'. During the winter their work involved levelling the ground for roads and railways, for which they were paid seventy pfennigs a day. According to the Red Cross, they were well treated by their employers. The following summer they were digging out copper cables from the fort, working seven heavy hours per day, but coming back to camp 'in quite a happy spirit. They all look much better now than in winter, as they enjoy being out in the green woods during summer.'[21] Their transport was dangerous though; fifty of them were squashed into a truck designed to carry thirty. This led to two serious accidents, and on 3 November, Mir Alam, who had been Hexley's orderly, was killed when a truck overturned. He is buried in the graveyard at Schoenenbourg Church, alongside Ghulam Rasul of the Rajputana Rifles, who died the same day.[22] Their graves face towards Mecca, at an angle to the Christians buried nearby.

Although ordinary soldiers like these did not suffer the levels of boredom that officers did, they still needed to fill their leisure time. The ICF played a crucial role in their well-being, through their regular Red Cross parcels. Each week every prisoner received a food parcel containing *dhal*, *atta* and *ghi*.[23] At the packing centre at India House they reached a peak of 6,500 parcels per week in 1944. The ICF became the official next of kin for all Indian POWs in Europe and was therefore entitled to send monthly clothing parcels as well. The fund became adept at sourcing 'exotic' ingredients: in 1943 the Brazilian government donated fifty tons of banana flakes and 102 cases of tinned milk, while the Mexicans gave fifty-five tons of rice. All prisoners acknowledged how important the parcels were in keeping body and soul together: their arrival was 'a rare moment of pure joy'.[24]

Recreational pursuits in the camps included music and games, and at Annaburg at the end of 1941, 'two plays of a social nature' were put on by the Indian POWs.[25] An article in *Fauji Akhbar* in July 1943 appealed for books for prisoners, in order to 'keep their minds active and their interest unflagging', and listed suitable topics including religious books, poetry, historical novels and dramas.[26] A major source of anxiety was letters home. During 1943 only 15 per cent of the prisoners with Barkat Ali received mail from home, and when it did arrive it typically took eight months. Meanwhile in Britain, Hills and the India Office recognised the vital importance of letters in keeping up morale and preventing defection to the Germans, and so organised regular letter-writing sessions among the companies in Britain. Hills also enlisted retired Indian Army officers and dignitaries like Viscountess Chelmsford and Lady Ampthill to write to the camps.[27] Sometimes sepoys used code to convey hidden messages in their letters. Jemadar Siddiq Ahmed wrote to Hills from Spangenberg in July 1942:

> Letters from home are very few and very long apart (except of course from you) and the surroundings and monotonous life of captivity is proverbial. Now you might say it is the same with everybody in captivity, but to crown our misfortunes it has not been the same with quite a few of us, who have refused to play it. I wish you understand it without further explanation. Never mind all will be OK. We are glad that we have not fallen short in any way, and it is the only consolation that helps me keep cheerful.[28]

Hills picked up the coded reference and forwarded the letter to the India Office, giving his opinion that the men are being 'bothered by German propagandists'.

The sepoy prisoners were often concerned about their families at home. The Red Cross reported that the Malschbach contingent were pleased when they managed to arrange a process for transferring money from Germany to India in May 1944.[29] An example of the anxiety felt is in a letter from a 22nd Company farrier in a POW camp in Germany, dated July 1942. The letter is to the RIASC depot in Punjab and is concerned with domestic matters – his wife and son, and the money at home. The unnamed farrier asks the commanding officer to intercede for him and 'take special step against the above-noted fellows'.[30] But letters did not always get through. After the defeat of Germany and the liberation of its POW camps, Indian liaison officers found 22,000 undelivered letters from home to Indian prisoners.[31] Among around 15,000 Indian POWs, that averages three letters for every two soldiers, a considerable deposit of unread questions and expressions of love, and a store of undelivered anguish.

The routine for officers and VCOs was different, but not necessarily easier. At Oflag 79 near Brunswick, there were 246 Indians, including

Captain Anis. The secret camp history recorded: 'The Indians throughout the camp's existence hardly received any letters from home at all, and were not allowed by the Germans to write to India in their own languages, their cooking facilities were far from satisfactory and they suffered acutely from the cold.'[32] In 1943 a photo appeared in *Fauji Akhbar* from Spangenberg showing five VCOs or NCOs from 22nd Company, together with an unidentified British soldier, which may have been Hitchcock.[33] The men look thin, and frown awkwardly at the camera. To distract themselves from hunger and boredom, some camps excelled at arts and literature. Eichstätt camp, near Munich, delighted in a library of 15,000 books, with a further 60,000 belonging to individual POWs; Laslett was a prisoner there.[34] The same camp hosted a music festival in February 1944 that ran for thirty-three days. There was also an elegant camp magazine called *Touchstone* that ran from the autumn of 1943 until February 1945.[35] The contributions were generally not about camp life but focused more on culture and life after the war, including articles on the Beveridge Report (which laid down the blueprint for the post-war welfare state) and Home Rule for Scotland. With orderlies to look after their physical needs, and long hours for reading and studying, the life of an officer POW was very different from that of the ordinary mule driver.

The better facilities at the Oflag are illustrated by the troubles of one 22nd Company soldier, Supply Warrant Officer Akbar Khan. Along with eleven other Indian warrant officers he was treated as an NCO.[36] In their letter of complaint, they listed the advantages of a 'proper Oflag' as follows:

In an Oflag there is usually a good library, containing many books of a scholarly and interesting nature. The study of these books may take up several hours in a day, and constitutes a pleasant means of passing the time, which is of the utmost value for a prisoner of war.

In an Oflag, there are also provided the means of finding relief in sport, such as hockey, volleyball and tennis, and indoor activities such as table tennis, playing the piano, etc …

Meat products provided in our rations, such as beef and bacon, are forbidden for both Hindus and Muslims. But they could be swapped for cigarettes with British officers, who tend to receive large quantities of such items in their private packages.[37]

It is not clear what happened to that complaint. Warrant Officer Akbar's name did, however, appear on a list from British military intelligence of those 'known, reported or suspected to have gone over to the enemy'.[38] He was clearly keen to improve his situation.

* * * * *

In order to understand the processes that led some of the men to join the German Army, we must go back to before the war and meet again Subhas Chandra Bose. This balding bespectacled Bengali was a key figure in the Congress Party, a man of 'strong martial inclinations' but also a 'heart-throb'.[39] He is a figure with a contested reputation, with clear fascist sympathies.[40] At the outbreak of war in 1939, Bose's stance was simple and logical: he favoured an armed struggle against the British state. He was therefore put under house arrest by the British, but escaped via Kabul and Moscow, and arrived in Berlin in April 1941, where he found a small group of Indian emigrés, ready to work against Britain.[41] In November 1941, the Zentrale Freies Indien (ZFI – the Free India Centre) was inaugurated. At this stage it had a staff of four, and its main job was daily radio broadcasts to India in seven South Asian languages. One of its members was Girija Mookerjee, later a professor of history. In his memoir, *Europe at War*, he expressed doubt about their alignment:

> I was not quite sure if we were doing the right thing. We did not approve of National Socialism and none of us felt any attraction for it … Subhas' theory of England's enemy being our friend was all right so long as such an enemy stood for some broad political principles with which we could agree. But our whole political attitude was against all that Nazi Germany represented … none of us seriously believed in German victory or even wished for it.[42]

From the German point of view, an active unit of Indian soldiers on their side was something of great potential value, for both military and propaganda purposes. By the summer of 1941, after the invasion of the Soviet Union, the situation in the Middle East looked very favourable for Germany. Despite Hitler's much-quoted position that he would 'rather see India under British domination than under that of any other nation', the German High Command envisaged a three-pronged thrust towards Afghanistan and India: through Egypt, through Turkey and over the Caucasus.[43] This was known as Operation Tiger, and was the foundational purpose of what was to become known as the Legion Freies Indien – the Indian Legion or 950 Regiment.[44]

In March 1941 the men of 22nd Company were in Lamsdorf. Here there were visits from 'various Indians', after which, a small group of eight Pushtu speakers, led by the company maulvi, Said Ahmad Shah, 'all comparatively uneducated men from NWFP', volunteered to help the Germans.[45] According to a post-war interrogation report, the maulvi 'overruled the objections of the Muslims to breaking their oath of allegiance to the British by telling them that the Quran exempted a Muslim from an oath if he starved for three days'.[46] These nine were sent to the Regenwurm (Earthworm) training camp, where they 'were trained by German officers, commanded in English, and given special training for clandestine commando operations, such as wireless technology, sabotage, parachute jumping, mountain warfare and ciphering'.[47]

The men were to be dropped into the North West Frontier, their native land, where they would set up resistance cells and carry out operations against the British 'occupation', like British Special Operations Executive (SOE) spies in Europe. Dr Rana's report at the start of this chapter claims that the maulvi had already spent three months in Iran prior to December 1941.[48] If this is true, it represents a remarkable coup for German intelligence, at a time when Iran was under occupation by the Indian Army, following the German invasion of the Soviet Union.[49] These nine men of 22nd Company became the first Indians in the German Army, before the trickle of Indian POWs became a flood after the surrender in Crete.

What was it that persuaded men like the maulvi to join the Germans, while others like Rana resisted? There were four interacting factors at play: idealism, material gain, pragmatism and peer pressure. Bose's speeches to prisoners of war were focused on the principle of freedom from the British, he wanted to inspire sepoys with nationalistic ideals towards an independent India. Rudolf Hartog, a German interpreter in the legion, was clear that the main selling point for joining the legion was

Bose himself: 'it was Subhas Chandra's personality and conviction that won most of the men'.[50] There might have been a legion without him, but it would not have become so big. Auchinleck, the commander-in-chief of the Indian Army, himself wrote, 'It is no use shutting one's eyes to the fact that any Indian officer worth his salt is a Nationalist.'[51] Some historians believe that material conditions were the main motivation, specifically food, money and access to women.[52] Testimonies from ZFI workers support the pre-eminence of such factors, this time acting in the opposite direction, against the recruitment of NCOs. The interrogation report states that 'little success was achieved with the NCOs or with soldiers of long service, as they were unwilling to forfeit their pensions and family allowances in India'.[53]

Another strong reason for the decisions taken by individual sepoys was peer group pressure. One account describes how two of the ZFI men were 'particularly successful in bringing a large flock of rank and file to the legion like shepherds', a sense of men following a strong lead.[54] The historian Yasmin Khan, writing about Bose's later enterprise in Burma, the Indian National Army (INA), adds in a level of complexity and nuance: 'Soldiers may have been broadly sympathetic to Indian freedom but they were irritated by the timing of a movement that could derail their efforts against the Axis at a delicate moment in the war.'[55] The 'best of a bad lot' is the argument here, the lesser of several evils. Individual soldiers weighed up these factors over time and made decisions which they may have regretted later.

* * * * *

The word 'legion' carries considerable linguistic power, recalling both the Romans and the French Légion Etrangère. The Indian Legion, recruited mostly from Indian POWs taken in North Africa and Italy, was one of many such 'legions' established within the German Army from non-German citizens. There was also a much-forgotten British Free Corps, whose members included Leo Amery's eldest son John, one of the last Britons to be executed for treason.[56] In line with his ideological purpose to end British rule in India, Bose set clear conditions for the legion: that it should be kept separate from other units, that the terms of service should be the same as for Germans, and that it should only be sent for combat in India.[57] Another innovative idea was that Muslims, Sikhs, Gurkhas and Hindus would be mixed up in companies together, going against the British idea of separation. This policy was initially strange to the men but proved surprisingly successful.[58] A programme of intensive 'propaganda' was carried out in POW camps, and then the recruits were concentrated in specific camps for training, notably Annaburg and Königsbrück. There they had their own magazine, *Bhaiband* (Brotherhood), and were issued with standard German uniforms and weapons, which may have also been part of the motivation for RIASC men, used to handling just animals and fodder. Indeed, the list of those who joined includes a blacksmith, a cook, a saddler and a sweeper, so the chance for promotion was also a factor. The numbers were slow to rise, however, with just 1,169 having signed up by the end of 1942.[59]

Their number was not to include the blue-blooded Captain Anis. Unusually for a K6 man, there is a wealth of material about Anis and his wartime experience, as I was lucky enough to meet his daughter Zeenut in Islamabad and interview her with her African grey parrot Golmatol (Roly Poly) on her arm. As the highest-ranking Indian officer in German hands in 1940, Captain Anis was clearly something of a catch, with considerable propaganda potential. He quickly found he was being very well treated, with good food and lodgings.[60] He was also subjected to less welcome visits. Swaleh from the ZFI came to visit him on a monthly basis, accompanied by a German officer. On his first visit Anis told him who his father was, so Swaleh:

> jumped up, came and hugged him, kissed him on both cheeks and said, 'Your father is one of the people I most admire in the world because I was at Aligarh.' Then he turns round to the German officer and says, 'This man is not going to be used, we're not going to put him into the situation, I cannot allow this.' So [Sahibzada Aftab] saved his son's life.[61]

The Indian old boys' network could stretch all round the world, even into a POW camp. After the war, Swaleh became a friend of the family in Karachi: the new political reality of Pakistan could embrace such ambiguity.

The ZFI had not finished their efforts to recruit this officer, however. A few months later Anis received a visit from Subhas Chandra Bose himself. Bose was building the legion at this stage and said to Anis, 'You are the most senior Indian officer, I would like you to take command.'[62] As a nationalist at heart, Anis was tempted, and when he told his daughter the story many years later, she could not understand his response. He refused to join. Anis explained his decision to Zeenut by saying that he had taken an oath to serve King George. By receiving his pay he had 'tasted his salt' and a Muslim could not betray his word, nor could he resign his commission. Layers of identity and loyalty were at play – loyalty to God, to King and employer, to his military heritage – too complex to explain to his young daughter. 'At some point in life you'll understand,' he told her. Nevertheless, Anis' refusal to fight for the Germans did not mean he ruled out being friendly with them. Determined not to waste his time inside prison walls, he learnt German. Although some fellow officers wanted him to try to escape, he was not prepared to take the risk of being shot, with a wife and four young children waiting for him in Delhi. Other officers were suspicious of him. The senior British officer at Oflag 79 wrote an adverse report about Anis, though it has not survived.[63] Anis came from a very different background and took a very different position from his British comrades, saying, 'I've got nothing against Germans … this is not my battle … [but] a battle between the European powers.'[64] In fact, the British were also equivocal in their attitude towards him. In September 1943 he was promoted to the rank of major, even though he was still inside the camp.[65] The mechanics of promotion by seniority continued, despite incarceration.

Dafadar Abuzar meanwhile had reached a different conclusion. As we have seen from Hexley's report, Abuzar's reputation in 22nd Company before and immediately after capture was that of a reliable soldier prepared to take on extra responsibility. On 19 June 1940, shortly before their surrender, Abuzar took over command of 'A' Troop due to Jehan Dad's illness, and Hexley writes that he carried out these new duties 'most efficiently and cheerfully'.[66] Later Abuzar made a draughts board with his colleague Roda Khan, and they played games on a cart as the column meandered through the French countryside. In July, when the company were held in an old barracks in Strasbourg, Hexley wrote of the 'usual rivalry between troops for best kept barrack room', and that Abuzar's troop took the first prize. He was the 'man of confidence' at Lamsdorf the following summer, still loyal to the King and his salt. When Abuzar met Bose in December 1941 at Annaburg camp, his interrogation report says that he saluted him and shook his hand, but that he still preferred to 'remain neutral' at that stage and told the men of 22nd Company to do the same.[67] That he saw his position as 'neutral' is interesting, as one could classify it as loyal, at least at that stage. A few weeks later, after a row about the withholding of Red Cross parcels, Abuzar and seven other NCOs were sent to the famous Colditz Castle, home for the 'bad boys'. There Abuzar acted as interpreter, so his language skills must have advanced considerably. Not long after that, he went to Frankenberg POW camp, where: 'He was very well treated … Gurbachan Singh and Dr Madan talked to him at length, suggesting that he should volunteer, and that if he failed to, he would be subjected to contemptuous treatment. [Abuzar] yielded and put on German uniform.'[68]

After two years in German hands, with the German advance going well in North Africa and the Soviet Union, Abuzar had weighed up his options and taken what he believed was the sensible path. His decision to join the legion involved a demotion to the rank of private: all legionaries had to start at the bottom. If he were solely influenced by his promotion prospects, he might have taken this as a factor against joining the Germans. In fact he rose rapidly, being promoted to *Gefreiter* in July 1942 and *Unteroffizier* in October (lance corporal and corporal respectively).[69] Having been restricted to the inside of camps for two years, he now had much greater freedom, going in September to the Brenner Pass to receive a delivery of 1,400 Indian POWs transferring from Italian camps.[70]

It is difficult to be precise about how many of the 320 men of 22nd Company joined the legion, but it could be as high as thirty. There was and is an understandable reluctance to admit to joining the Germans. In one case I was able to interview a relative of one of the members of 22nd Company who was suspected of having gone over. This soldier is mentioned as a possible legionary and 'propagandist' in two separate documents.[71] Over seventy years later, his son and nephew were keen to rebut any suggestion that he may have joined the Germans, and his son pointed out that he was a keen scholar of Allama Iqbal (poet and spiritual father of Pakistan), a pursuit he took up in prison. Up until the 1970s he still received letters from Germany, offering him a job (he was at the time in the Islamabad police). Even though the INA and the 950 Regiment are generally not considered traitors in South Asia, individual family members do not want their relative to be under suspicion, especially by a British historian.

Another turncoat was the VAS Sayed Mohd Ishaq, who had given chapattis to German NCOs, later going on to become a *Leutnant* in 950 Regiment.[72] Abuzar's interrogation report talks of his 'intimate' relationship with a French woman who taught English, Josette Destang, to whom he became engaged.[73] During their training in Germany, local girls and married women 'threw themselves at these Indians', partly due to the shortage of German men around, but also as the men of the regiment continued to receive parcels via the Red Cross, containing chocolate, coffee and other hard-to-find treats.[74] It also attracted some of Germany's upper crust, including the aristocratic diplomat Adam von Trott zu Solz, who found the legion useful as 'a handy means of removing his friends, and family, from the Eastern front and despatching them to France where they were relatively safe'.[75] Meanwhile Bose had left Germany to set up the much-better-known INA in Asia, travelling by German U-boat into the Indian Ocean, where he transferred to a Japanese submarine.[76]

By the spring of 1943 the men of 950 Regiment were trained and ready for action, and received orders to proceed to Beverloo in Belgium.[77] Forty men, however, refused to go to Belgium due to the worsening military situation and the absence of Bose, their *Netaji* (esteemed leader). These men were court-martialled and sentenced to at least two years in military prison.[78] This rapid response by the German authorities had the required effect, and the men departed for Belgium. Soon after that they were posted to the Atlantic Wall at Texel and Zandvoort in the Netherlands, where they were repeatedly photographed and where they left behind at least nine babies.[79] In September they were transferred again to France, to the area west of Bordeaux known as Les Landes. This was an easy posting to begin with, as their interpreter Hartog wrote: 'their billets in the French villages and charming seaside resorts were comfortable; there was no shortage of good wine and the shops offered a relatively wide choice of food and other items. The Indians, as also the Germans, soon felt at home in this hospitable country and pleasant climate.'[80]

Hartog evidently enjoyed his time with the Indians, having previously been on the Eastern Front. As a linguist, he was one among many attached to the legion, and he reckoned that such service 'helped three of Germany's leading orientalists to survive the war'.[81] While in France, Dafadar Abuzar's career really hit the heights. He was promoted to *Leutnant* with Ishaq and nine others in October 1943 and put in command of a company near Lacanau.[82] In November he was part of the grand launch of the Berlin branch of Bose's Indian provincial government and appeared in the official German photograph of the occasion.[83] He even achieved sporting success, captaining the legion's hockey team in games against German teams in Bordeaux and Paris.[84] Ishaq, meanwhile, was rumoured to be calling himself *Graf* (Count) and living with a French wife on the outskirts of Bordeaux. It seemed as if everything was going swimmingly for these young ambitious soldiers in the prime of their life.

10

The great escapes

May this reminder of times past,
(So near to us yet floating away!)
Speak, without fear of being effaced
So that our heart may quiver a while.[1]

At least ten members of the 320-strong 22nd Company escaped and made it back home: a success rate of around 3 per cent. And yet their stories are almost completely unknown. The myth of the Second World War escaper is that of the aristocratic English gentleman with moustache and uniform neatly pressed, outwitting the dim German guards. This stereotype is neatly expressed in a scene from the 1955 film *The Colditz Story*, where two Guards officers, played by Richard Wattis and Ian Carmichael, perform an elaborate slow march in the courtyard of Colditz Castle in order to distract the Germans from an escape attempt involving French orderlies loading mattresses on a truck.[2] This was not the experience of the men of 22nd Company, although Abuzar at least did spend time in Colditz.

The fact is that those moustachioed gentlemen wrote their stories after the war, and the sepoys did not. A typical example is *I Walked Alone* by the Earl of Cardigan, which details his journey through France and Spain in 1940, one that closely mirrors Hexley's journey a few months later.[3] Cardigan's yarn was published while Hexley's is unknown, and those of the nine Indians are even further back in the mists of forgetting. Even with only the bare facts of the archival documents, these stories are a remarkable record. Helped by French women or travelling solo, scaling walls and getting through barbed wire, jumping off trains and avoiding German soldiers, these Indians travelled hundreds of miles to reach neutral territory, scared, hungry and always vigilant, not speaking the language, but determined to be free.

Of the quarter of a million Allied soldiers and airmen in prison or behind enemy lines, a maximum of 5,000 managed a 'home run'.[4] A large proportion of those followed one of the established routes to neutral countries: Sweden across the Baltic Sea to the north, Switzerland in the middle of Europe, and Spain in the south, through the Pyrenees. To get to Spain there were two well-known lines. These were the 'Pat O'Leary line' from Paris to Marseilles or Toulouse, across the mountains to Barcelona, and then on to British territory at Gibraltar in the far south; and the 'Comet route', which ran from Brussels down the Atlantic coast, thence to Bilbao in northern Spain and on to Gibraltar. Both routes were run by networks of French and Belgian volunteers, supported by a new branch of British military intelligence: MI9. After the fall of France, all of the north as well as the west coast was under German occupation. The south and centre, however, were still under French government – albeit a puppet one – known as the Vichy regime. This meant that the Mediterranean port of Marseilles – where the sepoys had first landed in Europe – was a prime attraction for any soldier on the run. The border between Vichy-controlled territory and the German north was strictly controlled in some places, more permeable elsewhere. Once through that border, the Indian escaper would need resilience, a good pair of boots, and money. One British diplomat was paying £40 for each British officer and £20 for other ranks brought into Spain.[5] The experience of being escorted hundreds of miles through hostile territory must have been strange for somebody of European heritage; for an Indian it would have been doubly odd, and doubly difficult. For a Punjabi from a rural background to walk like a Frenchman or talk like a Frenchman, and thus avoid the police, was a tall order. And yet they managed. Despite their darker skin, their different religion, their lack of knowledge of European customs or geography, they got back home. This is testament to the women and men who helped them, but also to their own spirit, determination and damn good luck.[6]

The first K6 man to make it home was Jemadar Jehan Dad, recorded by MI9 as one of the very first escapers to make it out of a permanent POW camp, after Private Coe of the Dental Corps.[7] Jehan Dad was from Chauntra, fifty miles west of Rawalpindi, had joined the army at the start of the Great War as a sepoy and worked his way up.[8] In 1939 he was in his mid-40s, a jemadar in command of 22nd Company's 'A' Troop when they landed at Marseilles. At the time of their surrender, Jehan Dad was suffering from acute sciatica and had to be carried on a stretcher everywhere, so Abuzar was put in command of his troop.[9] The day after their surrender, Jehan Dad was in a lorry that was separated from his comrades. He was taken to hospital at Sélestat, and thence to a camp in Germany. Here he pulled off a trick that was to enable him to get to England. He managed to acquire a French uniform from a fellow prisoner and passed himself off as a North African French soldier. This was a stroke of genius, as the Muslim Algerian and Moroccan troops were being held in large numbers and were soon to be repatriated. This was precisely what happened and on 21 September Jehan Dad crossed the border back into France. In November he proceeded into the Vichy zone to Marseilles, where he stayed in a safe house.[10] From here his journey became easier, via Spain, Gibraltar and then by ship to Scotland, arriving on 17 February 1941. A few weeks later he joined 25th Company in Devon, and Hills reported, 'Risaldar Jehan Dad … reported his arrival on 20 Mar, he is fit, unshaken and cheerful.'[11] He had been promoted to risaldar as a small reward for his exploits. Later he was further rewarded, with an MBE presented by the King in March 1942.[12] He eventually returned to India in January 1943, his sciatica no obstacle to continuing his career in the army.[13]

Donald Caskie, who looked after Jehan Dad as he passed through Marseilles, was an extraordinary character who was instrumental in helping hundreds of Allied servicemen escape.[14] Born on a croft on the Hebridean island of Islay, from the age of 6 he knew that he wanted to be a Christian minister. His first parish was in the southernmost part of Scotland, at Gretna, famous as the place to which English couples ran away to get married without their parents' consent. In 1935 he moved to Paris, where he became the pastor of the Scots Kirk on Rue Bayard. When the Germans occupied in June 1940, he joined the streams of refugees going south, making his way to Marseilles, which was full of British and Allied soldiers on the run. A French detective pointed Caskie towards the British Seamen's Mission at 36 Rue de Forbin, near the Vieux Port. The rest is escapers' history. Using this building and a growing network of contacts, the quiet vicar 'laid the foundations for the first properly organised escape line out of France'.[15] Britishers on the run were housed in the mission and given clothing and false papers – officially the French police allowed Caskie to help British civilians only. When a new escapee arrived, Caskie sent a telegram to the Church of Scotland head office in Edinburgh. The Church then sent a standard letter to their relatives, saying that Caskie had cabled their name and address and that 'the needs of all the men are being met'.[16] This was a dangerous business, and Caskie did not want to receive letters for the escaping men in his charge that could incriminate him. To increase secrecy, his notes were written in Gaelic, not a language that was widely spoken in Marseilles or among the Gestapo. Arrested several times, sentenced to death by the Germans, Caskie survived the war, was awarded the OBE and even had a Strathspey dance named after him.

In November 1940, one of the Church of Scotland's standard letters went to Irene Hexley at 55 New Street in Birmingham. This was Tom Hexley's sister, on tenterhooks since the German blitzkrieg. She wrote back confirming Hexley's rank and regiment, and saying: 'The last six months have been anxious ones indeed, but now we can face Christmas with glad and grateful hearts. Would that all mothers, wives and sisters may be as fortunate as we are.'[17] For Irene Hexley as for hundreds of others, Caskie's actions gave joy and relief from uncertainty. Hexley had left Longvic camp at Dijon at the end of September 1940, in the early stages of the Vichy regime, when there were thousands of people on the roads, and a continuing sense of uncertainty in the country. A few weeks before, in order to stop French ships falling into German hands, the British had attacked the French Navy at Mers El Kébir in Algeria, killing hundreds of French sailors and hardening attitudes against the British. This was 'not quite the act of a friend' and the relationship between Britain and France had fundamentally shifted, so Hexley's journey was not always straightforward.[18] A report in the *Birmingham Post* made it sound easy: 'Lt Hexley is a typical "Gary Cooper" he-man. Posing as an Indian, he was sent to a German prison-camp, but Nazi barbed-wire and bayonets could not hold him.'[19]

All the accounts agree that he escaped Longvic in disguise and on a bicycle. His son Colin simply says he 'made out he was mad and just walked off'.[20] Whatever the exact truth may be, he cycled and walked sixty miles south through occupied France, until he reached Montceau-les-Mines. Here he was helped by Polish coalminers to cross over into the

Tom Hexley (right) in Miranda de Ebro camp with Baron Rothschild's secretary and unidentified prisoner.

Vichy zone, and continued his journey to Marseilles. He was then arrested by French gendarmes who thought he was Polish, and sent to a collecting centre for Poles.[21] This is where Caskie stepped in, for at some point in November, Tom Hexley's name and address appeared in the Scotsman's list. On 27 October Hexley left Marseilles with Captain Wilkins, an MI9 agent, to cross the Pyrenees into Spain.

Even in neutral Spain he was not safe, for he was arrested by the Spanish authorities (the third nationality that had imprisoned him) and thrown into the notorious concentration camp at Miranda de Ebro, south of Bilbao. This camp had been established by the Fascists during the Civil War, and at this stage was mostly used for Republican political prisoners. As the war went on it was increasingly used to house Allied escapers and evaders. Lord Cardigan passed through there before Hexley, and reported very tough conditions, with inmates having their heads shaved and forced to salute the Fascist flag every evening. As Cardigan put it, a prisoner:

has no eyes for fine ceremony of for romantic scenery: he only knows that his muscles are stiff and painful through toil, that his stomach is heavy with a supper of still-undigested beans and that there are a couple of fleas at work somewhere under his coat-sleeve. For him, the horizon is bounded always by the petty miseries of his captivity.[22]

While Cardigan complained about the monotonous diet of beans, Hexley's son remembers that his father always refused cabbage soup.[23] A photograph of Hexley in the family album shows him with two other men, smoking and smiling at the camera, cups in hands and caps on heads with a letter 'P' for '*prisionero*'. The caption in the family album reads: 'In a Spanish prison. Secretary of Baron de Rothschild as a companion. He assisted others to remove all of Tom's bad teeth with pliers and a pen knife.'[24] The stay was not indefinite, for the Spanish government had agreed to 'deport all stray Britons to Gibraltar and to set them free at the boundary of that small strip of British territory'.[25] Hexley arrived at Gibraltar and sent a telegram to his sister on 12 May 1941 saying: 'Arrived here safely Milly's birthday. Well and happy hope to see you soon.'[26]

The family must have breathed a huge sigh of relief, but his adventures were not yet over. On 22 May he embarked on board HMS *London*. The *Birmingham Post* takes up the tale:

> It seemed as if his adventures were over, for he was bound for England, home and beauty.
>
> But Fate again took a hand, and when the warship was in sight of England orders reached the captain to put about and join in the ocean-wide search for the Bismarck.[27]

Hexley witnessed the sinking of that great German battleship off the Irish coast, but the *London* had to turn back and Hexley ended up in Bathurst (now Banjul) in Gambia, from where he telegraphed his family again and sent his first letter to his wife in India 'imploring her to look after Noel and June's feet'.[28] He made his way from there to Freetown in Sierra Leone, picked up another ship and finally arrived in Glasgow in the middle of July.[29] Within weeks he had been made a lieutenant, he was back with his friends in K6 and marched at the head of a detachment through Birmingham City

Hexley and Ashraf 'swinging along Broad St' in Birmingham, summer 1941.

centre.[30] The photo of that parade is captioned by his sister: 'Our Proudest day'. Soon afterwards, he had lunch with Leo Amery, who described him as 'a fair blue eyed young man, with a simple straightforward manner, but unlimited in resource ... [with a] demure little golden haired sister'.[31]

Hexley's trek had taken him from Rawalpindi to France, briefly into Germany, to Spain and West Africa, to Glasgow and home to Birmingham: over 15,000 miles in nineteen months. The local paper summed it up:

'Join the Army and see the world' says a familiar recruiting poster. That is what a Birmingham man, Lieut TW Hexley did.

And did he see the world? I'll say he did![32]

His epic voyage was to stay with him and his family long after the war, and when he chose to settle in Scotland, he was pleased to have found a home in Caskie's native land.

Driver Buland Khan's voyage was equally long and equally tortuous, and would be completely unknown were it not for a report held in the Indian National Archives in Delhi.[33] Buland Khan came from Mianwali on the North West Frontier and was a Pashtun-speaker from the Niazi tribe. He was a member of the Reinforcement Unit in May 1940 and was put on a train to join 22nd Company near Metz – the train that was bombed by the Luftwaffe, leading to four deaths. Buland Khan was injured in 'the left fore-arm, face, right knee and thigh. He states that his life was saved by his steel helmet. He was taken to a French hospital at Bar-le-Duc and was shown every kindness there.' After a week he was transferred to a hospital in Paris and his left arm was amputated below the elbow. He was then taken to Bordeaux, during which time the Germans took over that part of France. He was discharged in the autumn, and made his way to Marscilles, where he may have been helped by Caskie, although his name does not appear on any of the lists. He stayed in the barracks at St Jean along with other British troops, from where the American consul arranged for his evacuation with sixteen Britishers through Spain to Gibraltar. There he had a choice of going to Britain, where he could have joined his comrades and perhaps found work suitable for a one-armed man, or home to India. Unsurprisingly, he chose the latter. His route around Africa was leisurely, involving stops at Freetown and Lagos, and eventually on to South Africa, where a friendly civilian gave him £6. From there he proceeded slowly up the east coast of Africa by passenger ship to Aden and then across the Indian Ocean, arriving at Bombay on 28 August. He duly reported to the RIASC training depot at Jullundur, where he found Wainwright, recently the commanding officer of 25th Company, who wrote this report in October 1941. Wainwright concludes:

> Buland Khan does not smoke and so he has a nice credit balance in his account. He has not been sent to his home as yet as his Medical board proceedings have not been received back. He has made requests for a new artificial arm (his arm is off well below the elbow) and to have four teeth replaced. He is very good at heart and speaks some English and French.

After an epic voyage all round Africa, Buland Khan remembered the kindness shown to him. He had lost half of his arm, but was happy to be back home in Punjab, nearly two years after he left.

By an extraordinary coincidence, the next escaper was also called Buland Khan. He was a young man from Chakwal, south of Rawalpindi, a cook in peacetime. In December 1939 he joined 22nd Company as their mess servant, responsible for cooking the meals for the British officers.[34] Although the job of an army cook might not seem very adventurous, this Buland Khan was to prove his ingenuity over the next few years. After capture, he found useful employment cooking for Dr Rana in Longvic.[35] He then went with the rest of the company to Lamsdorf, Annaburg and finally Rennes in the north-west of France. There, in February 1943, Dr Rana intervened and asked him to take up a new trade, as a nursing orderly in a hospital for colonial POWs: Indians, Moroccans and Senegalese. The hospital was housed in a primary school, 'surrounded by barbed wire, with a German sentry on the front door'. One day:

> when I was standing in the window of the hospital, a French girl, passing on the road outside the barbed wire, spoke to me. The Germans had nailed the windows down, but we had managed to remove the nails, and were able to open the window when the sentries were not looking.
>
> The girl asked me if I knew a Senegalese called Kulubali in our camp. I said I did, and called Kulubali. When he told the girl that I was a British Indian soldier, she spoke to me in English …
>
> One day when I was talking to a French Moroccan, he hinted to me that this girl might be able to get me a forged identity card, and facilitate my escape, and that she had helped other prisoners before.[36]

Buland Khan was clearly a man with ideas. He spoke some French and some English, he was a skilled cook who could turn his hand to working in a hospital, he had made friends with fellow Muslims from other countries. And he was saving money for his escape. The unnamed girl said that she could help him, and he said he would like to bring his friend Sergeant Shah Zaman:

> We arranged that on the morning of 23 Nov she would be in the door of an orphanage opposite our hospital at 1900 hrs.
>
> I had collected 8000 francs, and on the evening in question, Sgt Shah Zaman and I managed to get through three lots of barbed wire, which

being loose, we were able to separate. We managed to climb a wall and jumped over it. The girl, who was waiting in the door as arranged, with another girl and a man, then came forward and took charge of us.

At this point, Buland's MI9 report finishes with the customary sentence: 'From this point we were helped on our journey.' We can only conclude that the two girls were from one of the escape lines, possibly the Comet line, and that they took the two Indians 400 miles south to Spain. Buland reached Britain on 20 March 1944, by which time the rest of K6 were back in India. We can assume that he returned to India by troopship in due course.

The frustrating lack of detail in the official reports is even more pronounced for the next four escapers. The only source for their escapes are brief reports in the National Archives in England, among the recommendations for awards. Bashir Ud-Din Ahmed was a nursing sepoy, part of the Indian General Hospital when it arrived in France. He was commended for his 'excellent' work in January 1940 at the newly opened hospital in Dieppe.[37] He was attached to 22nd Company on 2 June, to support Dr Rana, and from then on he was part of their medical staff, looking after Jehan Dad and others. Like Buland Khan, he was working in the hospital in Rennes from December 1942.[38] At some point in 1943 or early 1944 he escaped 'with the aid of a French woman', quite possibly the same one who had helped his colleague. He was recaptured not far away at Taupont and was then 'extremely badly treated, being kept bound and without food and water for several days'. He escaped again and hid in the hills until August 1944, when he was very happy to see General Patton's Third Army advancing through Brittany after D-Day. For this exploit, he was Mentioned in Dispatches.

As a lance naik with five years' experience on the North West Frontier, Mansab Dar was in charge of a section of six drivers and their carts. He went through POW camps at Lamsdorf, Annaburg, Neuburg and Nancy.[39] He was targeted by the Germans for recruitment, and in August 1942 he was taken to Berlin, where he met Bose face-to-face. Mansab Dar spurned his advances, saying that he and his comrades would 'adhere to their one duty, allegiance to the British Government'. As a result, he was badly treated, put on hard fatigues for ten hours a day, and consequently became ill and was taken to hospital in Nancy. After D-Day, he broke out of camp, was concealed by another helpful French woman and then waited for the Allies to arrive, which they did in the shape of General Patton a few weeks later. The ending of his citation is interesting in its understatement: 'There was nothing very spectacular about Mansab Dar's escape but his general behaviour, his unflinching courage and loyalty, and the example he set to the others during his long and hard period of captivity, should not go unrecognized.'[40] The fact that there was 'nothing very spectacular' in escaping from a POW camp shows just how commonplace such extraordinary exploits were in wartime.

Both Mohd Ashraf Khan and Mohd Sarwar escaped in Italy, where some members of 22nd Company had been sent to work. Sarwar was a lance naik in 'C' Troop, and in September 1943 he was at Bagnoli, a suburb of Naples, loading stores and ammunition and digging trenches. When the Italian Army surrendered, many POWs escaped, some with success. Sarwar was recaptured twice and escaped thrice, hiding out in the hills until the Allies reached him.[41] Mohd Ashraf Khan was the troop dafadar in 'B' Troop, along with Mansab Dar. Prior to being sent to Italy he was subjected to 'a great deal of [German] propaganda, but to no avail. Maltreatment for his refusal was consequently severe.'[42] After the Italians surrendered, his work gang was marched northwards towards Capua. He feigned illness in order to evade the guards, collected forty-one other escaping Indians and, 'never staying long in one place, he brought his party to American lines a month later'. He was awarded the Military Medal.

The final two K6 escapes were from trains. Driver Mahmud Khan was a Pushtu-speaker in Abuzar's 'A' Troop, and probably joined 950 Regiment. Abuzar's interrogation report talks of a Mahmud Khan (and there was only one in 22nd Company) as the orderly for Harbich, who ran the Regenwurm training camp, a forerunner of 950 Regiment. Abuzar said that Mahmud then seduced Harbich's daughter and committed 'an unnatural offence with one of [Harbich's] good looking German orderlies' – a reference to gay sex.[43] He was 'sent away', but Abuzar said that subsequently he was believed to have escaped from Rennes and married a French woman. In fact, a telegram from the British consul in Berne, Switzerland, dated 22 November 1943, reported that Mahmud had 'escaped from the train at Le Mans when travelling from Rennes to [Strasbourg] on August 24th 1943 and arrived in Switzerland October 26th but was only reported by Swiss today'.[44] Telegrams to the India Office at that time often included phrases like 'Presume you have no adverse records' and 'May we convey C in C's congratulations'. Such wording indicates that the British officials in neutral countries were aware of the fact that Indian soldiers had joined the Germans, and that escapers might have a murkier record than first appeared.

Those questions also cropped up in a telegram from the War Office to India about Siddiq Ahmed. Like Dr Rana, Siddiq was part of 22nd Company's medical detachment and had written a coded letter to Hills in July 1942 about German overtures to Indian POWs. Siddiq Ahmed was from a village called Santhawari, sixty miles south of Delhi.[45] As a jemadar in the Indian Medical Service he was classified a sub-assistant surgeon and had to work entirely independently as a doctor.[46] As a POW, he was still expected to look after the sick, which he did in several camps, including Oflag IXA and Stalag IXC.[47] In February 1943 he was being transferred with two VCOs of the 2nd Royal Lancers. They were on their way to Frontstalag 222, a camp situated just forty miles from the Spanish border, near Bayonne. Clearly the temptation was too much for them, for they sneaked over the frontier and were in Gibraltar by May, then in Cairo and back in India not long after. The War Office telegram was doubtful of their story and questioned the genuineness of the escapes, saying, 'some assistance by the Germans in these escapes cannot be regarded as out of the question.'[48] Given Siddiq's close relationship with Hills, this is highly unlikely.

* * * * *

These stories are of individuals and small groups. But in May 1944 there was a mass breakout of Indian POWs that was among the largest of the whole war, a tale which is completely unknown outside a few elderly citizens in the Vosges mountains. During the American air raid on Epinal, several bombs had fallen on the Indian POW camp up the hill from the railway station. Many were killed, including Muhabbat Shah from Syed Kasran village. Those not killed or injured were ordered by the guards to go into the nearby forest.[49] As Captain Dewan of the Mahratta Light Infantry reported, after the initial panic, the camp commandant told the prisoners to: 'carry as much food, clothing and necessities as we could, and go out into the country outside the camp not more than five or six miles away, as he understood more air raids were likely'.[50]

Many men spent that first night in a ravine outside the camp with a small detachment of German guards. In the morning, they were ordered to disperse, which 'was too good to be true for we saw the chance of escape … Without map or compass and with only a rough idea of the direction of the frontier, we made off'. The next few weeks saw hundreds of Indian POWs walking south then south-west through the forests of the Vosges mountains, like a Bollywood version of *The Sound of Music* with the von Trapp family replaced by groups of Hindus, Muslims, Sikhs and Gurkhas. They were helped everywhere by the French and hunted everywhere by the Germans.[51] From Epinal to the Swiss frontier at Delle (where there is an outcropping of Switzerland into France) is seventy-five miles by road, but longer through the forests. The RAF dropped strips of khaki paper, which the French citizens then arranged in the woods to point towards Switzerland. Some escapees acquired a compass and others used landmarks to find the way:

> one old French lady stopped us, and without any explanation from us, said we were escaped prisoners and she was very pleased; she gave us some excellent bread and cheese and advised us not to follow the main road as it was patrolled by the Germans but to take the power line as a guide.[52]

The word had got round the population, and networks of assistance were mobilised. After a week or so the escapees started to arrive in Switzerland. The Swiss authorities and the newspapers were astounded at the volume of men arriving. By midday on 20 May, nine days after the air raid, 186 had arrived, with 100 more over the next three days.[53] One Muslim soldier had been shot by the Germans, but his companions refused to abandon his body and carried it across the frontier in order to bury it in a Swiss cemetery.[54] The final number who made it to Switzerland was at least 300: the British embassy telegraphed London on 6 June to say that 853 were missing from the camp.[55] Indian escapees continued to come across for weeks afterwards, but some decided to resume a more active role in the war, and around thirty were reported to be helping the French Resistance in the hills.[56]

One place where the men found an especially warm welcome was the village of Etobon and its neighbour Chenebier, in the hills west of Belfort. Etobon was a small village in rolling farmland, with a population of around 260, a Protestant village that had converted in the seventeenth century under Swiss influence. Indian POWs started to arrive on 14 May, having walked about fifty miles from the camp.[57] Jean-Louis Pernon was 11 years old at the time and recalled:

I was a country lad, I liked climbing, running in the woods and on the hill we called 'Chateau' with its 'round stone', a crumbling summit rock.

On that day, I heard somebody whistle several times. I was ready to scarper in case of danger when I saw, walking out under the leaves and the branches, a bearded man who came forward slowly in order to reassure me.

He was dressed strangely. He had a large smile which fascinated me, because on each tooth a shining pearl was incrusted.

I wasn't frightened, he sat down with legs crossed, and then with gestures and French words he explained to me that he was a soldier, a prisoner, that aeroplanes had destroyed the prison and that he was in flight in the forest.

He asked me if there were any German soldiers in the village. I said no. He seemed reassured. I showed him my house, and he said that the next day he would be there in order to eat. We parted with a finger on the lips. 'Chut, silence!'

The next day he was in front of the house, but not alone: with two soldiers like him. I gave them some bread and some fat bacon which he refused without saying why. My mother came out and offered him a live rabbit, or a chicken. The rabbit chosen, he explained he wanted to cook it outdoors. So I watched, in the broad sunshine, as he drained the blood from the animal, skinned the rabbit and buried the entrails. Then with a casserole to cook in, I helped them cook it in their fashion with vegetables and garden herbs. They ate it all outside, scrubbed the casserole, and said their thankyous with hands joined together.

They left for the other forests, the finger 'chut' on the lips – a final wave of the hand.

And the carefree nature of my eleven years returned to daily life.

But I have always kept the image of this kind bearded man, his teeth encrusted with … diamonds.[58]

Pernon's three soldiers were Muslim, evident from their dislike of bacon and their method of killing the rabbit. At no point did the 85-year-old man who gave me this story, written in pencil in the present tense as if he were still 11 years old, state that the soldiers were Indian; to him they were simply the gentle bearded people who emerged from and melted back into the forest.

Local man Jules Perret kept a detailed diary at the time. On 14 May he recorded:

What a drama! As I was coming in, driving the cows, at the bend by the Côte, I found myself face-to-face with six men, almost black, one with bare feet, completely dressed in rags. I said 'whoa!' to the cows and we tried to speak with each other. I finally understood that they were five Hindus and one American redskin, escaped from a camp in Epinal after it was bombed.[59]

Later he recorded:

Us with these men from Asia! They are trusting. They believe they've been saved. Not yet! Their big beards, their uniforms, their hair in a bun under their turbans, could all compromise them. And no more clothes to give them … That night we decided to take them to the parsonage, two by two, three groups in three minutes. Suzette brought the last group, with a youngster with a broken big toe. There they were in the living room where M. and Mme. Marlier [the pastor and his wife] were waiting for them. We built a fire, gave them camp cots. Mme. Marlier washed their feet and bandaged their wounds. Then we let them sleep.[60]

The tiny village was to extend a welcome out of all proportion over the coming months, with up to 200 POWs receiving food and shelter. As Perret points out, not all were Indian. The 'redskin' was a Canadian paratrooper called Melvin Nichols, who left a bracelet with one of the girls.[61] By 17 May the village had a system for the onward transport to the frontier, involving a small truck from the local syndicate. The POWs rested for a few days, ate and drank, had their photo taken in front of the parsonage and made friends. Jules Perret liked their company: 'It's funny to hear them talk. It's very sweet, like birds singing. They come from Nepal, Delhi, Bombay, very black. Few eat bacon.'[62]

A few weeks later, farmer Emile Bonhotal received a letter from liberated Marseilles, written in French but signed by Mahal Singh. It was addressed to 'Chers Papa et Maman' and signed 'Vos amis Malassé et cie'.[63] Emile and his family had looked after a group of Indians for a few days, and Mahal Singh would always remember their kindness. The letter has a special place in the family archives. The Indian soldiers, recruited by the British, captured by Germans and Italians, imprisoned in France, bombed by Americans, helped by French, finally found safety in Switzerland.

The story does not finish when the Indians moved on. After D-Day, the activities of the local Resistance were stepped up. Following the assassination of a German general in an ambush, German troops arrived in Etobon and Chenebier on 27 September. Thirty-nine local men and boys were rounded up and taken to the church at Chenebier; their families thought they were being taken for forced labour. The pastor Pierre Marlier begged the Germans 'on bended knee' to take him instead, but they refused.[64] In batches of ten, the men were arranged against the church wall and shot without trial. The pastor was later deported to Dachau, returning after the war a broken man. He is buried next to the thirty-nine. Although Epinal was liberated soon after, the fierce fighting in the Vosges continued into the winter, and Etobon itself was not freed until 18 November. Devoid of so many of its menfolk, the village was in mourning. It was awarded the Légion d'Honneur soon after the war, and Jules Perret was given the MBE by the British government in 1949 – his grandson showed it to me when I visited in the summer of 2017. The cemetery on the hill outside the village has a special section for the thirty-nine murdered by the Germans, and in September 1947 a plaque from the Indian government was inaugurated there.[65] The text (in French and Roman Hindi) reads:

Memorial plaque from the Indian government at Etobon Cemetery.

This plaque is a testimony of gratitude from India to the citizens of Etobon and Chenebier for the help which they brought to Indian Prisoners of War who escaped from the enemy in 1944–45 during the German occupation of France.

India mourns for the noble sons of these two villages who gave their lives for the common cause.

The kindness of the people of Etobon and the surrounding villages towards the escaping Indians has not been forgotten. The ageing citizens of the village carry their memories and guard their artefacts with care, for they know that the heroism of their parents will stand the test of time. India, Pakistan and France were united then in a common cause, and the decency of the French civilians saved many hundreds of lives.

11

Should auld acquaintance be forgot?

Strangers are always welcome when they visit Scotland. We are interested in foreign countries, and the viewpoints and customs of foreign peoples, and try to make our guests feel perfectly at home.[1]

The bulk of the men of Force K6 spent the last eighteen months of their European stay in the Highlands of Scotland. They became used to the shape of the countryside and the taste of the water, and the accents and warm hospitality of the Scottish people. The tradition of playing bagpipes spread more widely among the Punjabis, and the dour Highland idea of not playing sport on the sabbath was supported and embraced. One of the many imperial connections between Scots and Punjabis is the Martial Race Theory. Just as Sikhs and Punjabi Muslims were seen as being 'naturally warlike', so were the Highlanders, and their regiments had formed the backbone of many a British force around the Empire, including the relief of Lucknow in 1857.[2] So there may have been a kindred spirit between the Punjabis and the Highlanders which helped explain the warmth of their welcome. Of course, the Scottish climate is colder than that in Wales and England, and more snowy, and the mountains grander. That was one of the reasons for the force's deployment there – it was more like Norway, which was still their intended destination. The harsh winters were testing for the men, but Hills thought they could survive or even thrive, reporting in February 1943 that he had no doubt that 'the Highland climate is suitable for Indian troops … visited a unit near Balmoral coming back from 15-mile march in sleet with snow on ground … personnel were fit and cheerful, the majority had rosy cheeks.'[3] They were to be sorely tested during this final period, and some did not stand the test.

Most of the units arrived, complete with their mules and horses, at Dalwhinnie station in July 1942. The rail journey from Wales and England took all day, with the last few hours from Perth following the road through the

Highlands as it climbed up until it reached the watershed at Dalnaspidal and descended the river Spey. Here the men found themselves in wild country, the home of grouse and salmon, as well as whisky distilleries (all closed for the duration due to restrictions on the use of barley). At this stage the companies were reorganised into two 'pack groups', each of four transport companies, including two from the RASC composed entirely of white British soldiers. They were spread out in the villages and towns around the Spey in camps 'snugly nestling among the heather hills'.[4] The men were soon hard at work training for mountain warfare with the men of 52nd Lowland Division. Mountain warfare in Norway would require all transport to and from the front line to be by mule, so part of their job was working closely with the field ambulance unit of 156th Brigade.[5] Casualties were loaded on stretchers attached to mules, and transported away from the front line.[6] The men of 3rd Company were reported as being 'very fit', and when they entered the brigade sports competitions in July: 'This unit won all competitions entered for ... mounted wrestling, tent pegging and team equitation. 156 Field Ambulance with which this unit's B troop is working, won the packing and loading competition.'[7] One can sense Major Cole's pride in his unit. The round of work and rest continued, interspersed with visits from photographers and VIPs. Among the latter was the King's sister, Princess Mary, and the Jam Sahib.[8] The Jam Sahib was Digvijaysinhji Ranjitsinhji, the Prince of Jamnagar, on the west coast of India, and the only Indian in the British cabinet. The local paper remarked that he wore an Urquhart tartan that day and was recorded by the BBC saying of the countryside, 'they remind me of the hills of the North West Frontier provinces of India'.[9]

As 1942 went on, the companies spread out over a widening area that extended northwards to the Moray Firth and beyond, and eastwards to Aberdeen. Part of 32nd Company were posted to the Mountain and Snow Warfare Training Centre at Glenfeshie near Kingussie, where they were used as part of the training process for infantry officers.[10] In October, during Ramadan, 32nd Company embarked on an epic march to their winter quarters in Golspie. Their officer reported that 'all personnel were in happy spirits. The going was good and message writing was practised en route', and later when they went through the centre of Inverness, they were 'given a warm welcome. Traffic was excellent and units left their proper intervals.'[11] It seemed as if the men were ready for anything.

They were even ready for a change of diet, for their tastes had evolved since coming to Europe. In September 1942, when many of the men had been in Europe for close to three years, Colonel Hills wrote a detailed letter to the War Office suggesting a new scale of rations. Pickles, black pepper, jam and margarine were to be introduced, reflecting foodstuffs that the men had enjoyed around the country. Garlic was to be left out as its 'keeping quality [was] poor' and it was not grown in the UK. The menu of spices was extended to include a mix of coriander, cumin, cinnamon and cardamom.[12] There was an 'overwhelming demand for cigarettes of British manufacture – particularly Woodbines or Player's Weights' to replace the Indian *bidis* they smoked at home. There was also a proposal that chapattis should be supplemented with English white bread, which the *Daily Mirror* had reported was very popular and named 'double roti'.[13] Even in their consumption of meat it was possible to see a change of habit. Supplies of live sheep were not always easy to maintain, especially in winter months, so there were a number of experiments in preserving meat. Hills wrote in September 1942 of a plan for canned 'Halalled mutton' which would be 'killed by butchers detailed from 47 SDS in the correct Muslim fashion … The mutton itself will be very palatable, and not as dry as BT Corned beef'.[14] This proved to be a success, with Heinz canning thirty-seven and a half tons – ninety days' supply for the whole contingent – and Hills reporting 'they like it'.

Among their scattered postings in Scotland, one of the most remote was at Loch Ewe in Ross and Cromarty on the west coast. The tiny villages around the sea loch were swamped with servicemen of many nations from February 1942, when the Admiralty decided to use it as a terminus for the Arctic convoys transporting tanks, raw materials and food to the Soviet ports of Murmansk and Archangel. The loch filled up with merchant ships and navy escorts, so many that a person could walk a mile across the loch from vessel to vessel without getting their feet wet.[15] Among the sailors preparing for that freezing, hazardous voyage were many Indian lascars, including Aftar Miah, who would be buried in the graveyard at nearby Gairloch. He was from Calcutta, 35 years old when he died in 1942, a fire-man on the SS *City of Keelung*.[16] In June the Punjabis of the Reinforcement Unit arrived on the shores, staying for just seven weeks.[17] Their role is not clear, but they may have been transporting supplies on difficult sections of the land route around the shores of the busy sea loch. Surprisingly, the reputation of the men in the villages is not as positive as elsewhere. There is one rumour of sheep rustling, which may be explained by an entry in the war diary which reads '17 sheep wandered from camp … search parties out all day'. Local girl Dolly Cameron remembered how the men used to:

> bring their mules down the hill behind the house. These were taken down to the shore at the spit and they would be exercised with full packs in the sea. The men would call at the house for eggs, live chickens, corn and hay. Only the officers spoke English and they would carry crop sticks. The Indian soldiers used to bring Dolly's mother sheeps' heads and also chapatties but these were felt to be too greasy and oily so they were fed to the hens … One soldier gave Dolly a photo and asked her to be his 'little cabbage'. Once after school when she was working in her father's shop counting coupons and weighing the rations an Indian soldier came in. He grabbed her by her blouse collar and said 'kissie kissie'. When she pulled away he took out his knife and hit the counter.[18]

They were lonely. A story from a city-born British soldier who was posted to this remote place demonstrates the problem: 'When you've been here six months you start talking to yourself; after twelve months you start talking to the sheep and after eighteen months, the sheep start talking to you.'[19]

The Reinforcement Unit moved to Speyside at the end of July, but they did not take everything with them. Seventy years later, local man Donald Matheson was using his metal detector around his family's croft in Inverasdale on the west side of the loch and discovered 'a series of curved pieces of metal'.[20] He took the fragments to a local blacksmith who confirmed they were parts of mule shoes, a physical trace of K6's presence in that windswept cove.

The village of Golspie is situated on the east coast halfway between Inverness and John O'Groats, close to Dunrobin Castle, the home of the Earl of Sutherland. The 32nd Company settled there in October 1942 and stayed three months, with two months more in 1943.[21] With a peacetime population of around 1,200, the village was swelled by around a quarter when the Punjabis arrived. There is an RIASC sword in the local museum and Urdu graffiti on the walls of the Old Drill Hall, where the men slept. John Melville, then aged 8, used to throw stones at them 'to annoy them', which led to their officers having a stern talk with his headmaster.[22] The village children used to trade with the Indians, exchanging cigarettes for rice and sultanas, joking that the Camel cigarettes were made from camel dung. But their parents were somewhat wary, warning their children not to touch the chapattis or the strong mutton curries. Local crofters found a ready market for sheep, and they even noticed the famous Movick wild goats were disappearing. When Eileen, Duchess of Sutherland, died in August 1943, men of 32nd Company formed the Guard of Honour at her funeral and led the procession, after which Pipe-Major Campbell played 'Flowers of the Forest'.[23]

Just along the coast is a larger town called Dornoch, home to a small cathedral and a colony of harbour seals. The Reinforcement Unit were stationed south of the town from June 1943 (most of that time with Hexley as their commanding officer) and the Indian General Hospital was at the Dornoch Hotel. As in so many other Highland settlements, they made friends here. Alasdair Will has a picture of his uncle Leonard

Unidentified sergeant at Dornoch.

as a very young boy smiling while holding hands with an Indian sepoy and an older Scottish boy.[24] There is a lovely photo of an unnamed dafadar in the online history archives of Dornoch Museum.[25] The picture was taken indoors, probably in the sitting room of a house. With his trim, greying beard and his round-rimmed spectacles, his warm smile directed at the camera and his seated pose, he looks rather avuncular, like an old schoolfriend visiting for the weekend. He sits next to the family radio, with the switches in easy reach. Clearly this is a figure who is so well integrated in the house that he is given the seat of honour; one can imagine him sitting here every evening, drinking tea, eating shortbread and listening to the Home Service. He has crossed 7,000 miles, but he has found a home in this coastal Highland town.

As Dornoch was the last location for their hospital, there are two graves in the local cemetery. They are of Driver Ghulam Nabi and Naik Abdul Rakhman, who both died of TB.[26] Surprisingly, there is another Indian grave between them, that of Ram Bhopal, who died in 1960. Locals remember him as a pedlar, selling clothes and fancy goods door-to-door around the Highlands and Islands before and after the war. He was not the only Indian in that trade: in fact there were hundreds similarly engaged.[27] The three graves lie together outside Dornoch, reminders of a shared imperial past that came home to even the remotest British communities.

Inland from Dornoch and Golspie lies K6's northernmost posting: the village of Lairg. With its own railway station, stables for the animals and a hotel and school gym for the men to sleep in, Lairg was well equipped. It was also a good place to find meat, with its own cattle fair, and the largest lamb sale in Europe every August; selling 40,000 lambs in a single day at its peak.[28] There was a suitable place to use for prayers: a corrugated tin building, previously used as the United Free Church. Joan Leed remembers hearing the call to prayer and seeing the shoes lined up neatly outside.[29] This was also an area known for its bagpipers. Donny MacDonald recalled that his father, who was from an old piping family, gave lessons to a sepoy who 'spoke reasonable English'. In due course, the BBC came and recorded the two men playing traditional Scottish airs together.

At the end of 1942 the WVS put on a special party for the sepoys. According to the local paper, 'a splendid and bountiful supply of eatables was available'. Songs, stories and dances were performed by Indians and Scots and the medical officer 'spoke eloquently in reply. Dr Fazal emphasised the strong bond that would always exist between Scotland and India as a result of the kindness and hospitality shown to Indian troops by the people of the Highlands.'[30]

The evening concluded with a rendition of 'Auld Lang Syne' by an Indian bagpiper, which 'showed more than anything else the strength of the tie that links Scotland with India'. A week later, the honorary secretary of the Lairg WVS, Isobel Fraser – a young pretty schoolteacher – wrote to Colonel Hills. In her eloquent and beautifully worded letter, she writes how sad the people of the village are that 25th Company has come and gone twice, and hopes they will return again 'for we had hoped these fine officers and men would be our guardians for the duration of the war'.[31] She gives an account of the party, including home-made cakes and three cigarettes for each man, 'setting them on the table in "V" formation', and continues:

> We felt like your men were very much like our people of the Highlands in many ways, and on their return to Lairg in October last, we felt that they were just coming home again. I cannot tell you just how pleasant they have been, how kind to the children, and how helpful to us all. For my own part, on my daily treks to school, I had often to pass horses and mules on the way to and from the watering-troughs. Being very nervous of these animals, though delighted to watch them at a distance, I was ever chary of passing them. Your men had not been two days in Lairg when they discovered my weakness, and never once did I appear but an officer or N.C.O. came to my rescue, halted the animals, and escorted me past them on my way …
>
> Lairg is bleak and deserted now that they are gone, and the empty stables are a mute reminder of the happy faces and busy figures that were ever seen there. The children have lost their 'good companions' from whom they were never separated during the months of the Indians' sojourn in Lairg, and the great majority of firesides have an empty chair tonight. No 'Khuda hafiz' is softly spoken as the door closes on the beloved Indian friend. Lairg is a village of memories.

This letter speaks of such deep levels of mutual warmth and care between the people of this small village and the sepoys so far from home. Indeed, one might almost read it as a love letter for one going away, a promise not to forget the 'auld acquaintance'.

Further south near Aberdeen, the men and their animals made an impression on the local children. Veronica Lancaster was just 5 years old and remembers a column a quarter of a mile long marching up from the railway station. She went zooming down the hill in her pedal car as they came up, and they 'all had to wait for me'.[32] A young man was staying with Turnbull the butcher of Broomhill Road and recalled: 'When Indian Troops were training at Milltimber House he had a contract to supply them with mutton. I accompanied him on several deliveries and was given my first taste of curried mutton on pilau rice almost 60 years ago and I've enjoyed Indian food ever since.'[33]

Sheila and Brenda (with glasses) Bideau with Sergeant Khan in Ballater. The Bideau sisters were refugees from the German occupation of the Channel Islands.

Local fisherman William Milne was angling in the broad river Dee one summer evening and got cut off from the bank, in danger of being 'marooned for the night'. A water bailiff called to a sepoy nearby, and:

> Believing that someone was drowning no fewer than twenty-four of the Indians rushed to his aid … 'The Indians were delighted to have rendered me assistance, but seemed almost disappointed that I was not in more serious need of their help,' said Mr Milne, who apart from being rather wet, was none the worse for the experience.[34]

Alongside their military preparations, the sepoys could provide a valuable service for local children and adults.

Not everything was easy for the sepoys – there were occupational hazards in their work. The winter training conditions were hard indeed. Yaqub Mirza wrote: 'We had had our training in Mountain Warfare in the North West Frontier Province and a bit of jungle warfare at home, but it was nothing like this. This was freezing alive. Those who had one, had to shave off their beards to cope with the ice.'[35] On 15 October 1942, the men of 3rd Company were on a training exercise called Exercise Sphinx in the mountains south of Aviemore. While coming round above Loch Eanaich Ruadh, on the slopes of the mountain Carn Ban Mor, a mule driver called Khan Muhammad became separated from his mates. This mountain is one of the Cairngorms, now part of Britain's foremost ski resort, and can be 'like the arctic in wintertime'.[36] The next day a search party found his body on the hillside. According to the official report he had 'died from shock following exposure. The body was not clothed in the full scale of mountain warfare clothing, contrary to unit orders issued.'[37] He was duly buried at Kingussie Cemetery, at the bottom of the mountain. As the Indian General Hospital was based at Aviemore for many months, this same cemetery saw several burials, and in fact holds the largest number of K6 graves anywhere: nine in total.[38] For many decades those graves were cared for by local woman Isobel Harling, who said later: 'I have loved doing it. My brother died in Belgium and kind people there tend his grave for us, so here I can only do the same for those who are so far away.'[39] At the end of 2019 Harling was awarded the British Empire Medal for her dedication.[40]

* * * * *

With postings in the north of Scotland, Woking was now too far away for a leave club. Accordingly a new club was opened in November 1942, at 13 Westercoates Terrace in Edinburgh, a typically expansive stone house above the Water of Leith. The building was run by the YMCA under the management of Mrs Taylor-Grant of Turiff who, according to Hills' report, 'has meals with personnel, who are treated as if they had always been used to the standard of living … tablecloths, sheets and pillows'.[41] The house was in constant use, with a party of seventeen men there every week, given tours of the city and meeting local dignitaries. As the *Scotsman* reported, they used part of the building for prayers: 'The conservatory of the house has been converted for use as a mosque, with special arrangements made to enable the soldiers to wash their feet, in accordance with the Moslem ritual, before entering the Mosque.'[42] In such a manner Edinburgh's first mosque came into being.

As well as the death of Khan Muhammad in the Cairngorms, there were other tragedies during this period. One such was the murder of Naik Muhammad Sadiq by Driver Mehr Ali on 28 June 1942.[43] Two days later Muhammad Sadiq was buried at Kingussie, and at the end of September Mehr Ali was brought before a civil court in Inverness. Hills and Ashraf attended, the public gallery was full, and Lieutenant Khanna was present to interpret for Mehr Ali, who was being tried in English.[44] The court heard that Mehr Ali held a grudge against the corporal, had first shot him in the leg and then later found him in the canteen, where Sadiq told him to go away. Mehr Ali's statement to Police Sergeant Alexander Stewart read, 'I tried to shoot at his leg … but accidentally shot him in the heart. I had no intention of killing him.'[45] Mehr Ali was found guilty of 'culpable homicide and assault by shooting', a lesser offence under Scots law. As the judge delivered the sentence, Mehr Ali 'bowed unemotionally'. We can assume that he served his sentence at home, and that Sadiq's family accepted his martyrdom. Thus the only member of Force K6 killed by a rifle during their time in Europe was shot by a colleague after a petty dispute. That they were never subject to sustained attack is indicative of their good luck in their posting. Plenty of other RIASC mule drivers were killed or wounded doing their job in Italy and Burma.[46]

Another drama occurred ten months later at the camp in Ballater, close to the Royal Palace at Balmoral. On 24 April 1943, Lieutenant Shaw of the RAVC, attached to 3rd Company, was inspecting the animals.[47] He saw some horses standing uncovered and ordered two sepoys to put rugs on them. The men refused, Shaw swore at them and was assaulted by two or four soldiers (accounts vary) with helmets and stones. The commanding officer, Captain Kedge, promptly arrested two of them. The next day, twenty-eight sepoys refused to parade without their two comrades, and conducted a 'sit-down strike'. Kedge panicked and called in British troops, forty men of the Royal Scots Fusiliers, who disarmed the Indians and took them to the army jail in Knock. Hills subsequently relieved Kedge of his duty, placing the blame on him for not controlling the incident internally. He wrote a report sharply critical of some officers, including Shaw, who, he wrote, 'had made himself hated', adding that Indian troops are 'sensitive to atmosphere and appreciate sympathy' but in this case had been 'goaded'. This unusual event, the worst example of indiscipline during their time in the UK, shows that the men were sensitive to the way the officers treated them and were tired of being so long away from home. It also indicates the degree of training and orientation that these officers needed. Shaw was a young British veterinary officer without Indian experience, who knew how to look after animals, but not men. Hills, by contrast, not far off retirement, may have been old-fashioned and paternalistic, but he was also caring and sensitive towards the men under his command, and willing to take their side against the officers.

There were other outlets for the men to express their feelings. One was the regular *durbar* or gathering, also known as 'Any Questions'. The *durbar* was an old Indian Army tradition, a monthly meeting of officers and men, to air grievances and ask questions. The only K6 officer to record *durbar* questions in detail was Captain Gurdial Singh, during his time with 42nd Company in 1943. Perhaps as a fellow Indian, he saw the questions as being more important than his white British colleagues did.[48] Among questions about milk and sugar and razors, we find Driver Ghulam Ali asking, 'Why do English gentlemen take off their hats when they meet a lady?', indicating the men were aware of what happened around them in the Scottish towns and cities.[49]

An example of a more political question came from Driver Fateh Muhammad in January 1943. His question was simple: 'Will India be free after the war?' The answer given by his commanding officer was a typically evasive official one: 'India is free. No nation that is not free could possibly make the war effort that India has. There seems to be little doubt that after the war India will obtain some form of self-government.'[50] The year 1942 had seen the fall of Singapore, the Quit India movement and the 'shiver' that ran through the subcontinent.[51] All of which would have been known, to some extent, by the men of K6, 7,000 miles away. Perhaps Fateh Muhammad was emboldened by these events, perhaps his friends encouraged him to ask the question. The end of that year had seen Allied victory at El Alamein, and by 14 January Paulus' Sixth Army was surrounded in the *kessel* at Stalingrad. The course of the war had started to turn, at least in the west. Perhaps Fateh saw this as an opportunity to ask the question on everyone's lips. His motives are lost, the precise wording is lost, and nothing further is known about Fateh Muhammad himself. But the question remains, as an assertion that even for a humble sepoy in far-off Blighty, freedom was something to be hoped for. Fateh Muhammad's words are filtered through official channels, but the spirit of the query comes through: a free India was something to be desired, and that Fateh Muhammad was not too scared to ask the question, even if he could probably predict the evasive nature of the answer.

One of their final postings before returning to India was the remote west coast village of Kinlochleven, just north of the mountains fringing Glencoe. This rainy alpine place at the head of a sea loch has a 'dour aspect' and was one of the first locations in the UK to have a permanent supply of electricity.[52] The British Aluminium Company opened a factory there in 1908 and dammed the River Leven in the hills to form the Blackwater Reservoir. Following the famous Dambuster raids of May 1943, there was concern about possible reprisals, so a decision was taken to construct a smokescreen around the Blackwater Dam to protect it. Arthur Hames of the Royal Engineers was part of the team:

> Our task was to erect an electrically fired chemical smoke screen circuit around the Blackwater dam. Getting to the dam was not easy. First we had to climb a narrow winding metalled road … (we later had a couple of jeeps

for this part but that was pretty hair-raising especially as it was winter time and we had ice and snow to contend with) ... the route lay along a rocky, winding, and severely undulating path which roughly followed the line of the aqueduct. We had to carry the more portable items in back packs, but the heavier items had to be conveyed by horseback. These horses were driven by men of the British Army Service Corps, but due to the roughness of the track several of the horses became frightened and bolted, shedding their loads everywhere ... eventually they managed to bring in some mules, which were more sure-footed but of surly temper! I think these probably came from a unit of Indian troops stationed not very far away ... we did manage to chat a little with one or two who could speak English. I do have a photo of a laden mule near the Blackwater dam, taken by one of my mates who had a clandestine camera.[53]

RIASC sepoys were posted there in October 1943, under Captain Singh.[54] Although the village barely features in the official war diaries, the men are well remembered by the small population. One popular story is of a 'mascot', a boy called Sunshine with 'pearly white teeth and a big smile' who spoke no English.[55] When he became ill, the villagers organised a *cèilidh* (a traditional barn dance) to raise money to send him back to India. Apparently the boy died onboard the ship. Sheena McDougall's sister Georgia went out with one of the soldiers, whom she called 'Tani' (possibly short for Tanweer). They went to the local cinema together and he used to come every morning for a cup of tea, and to bring them toilet rolls. These stories point towards very strong friendships in this cut-off loch.

The force's high profile at this time is illustrated by a cartoon by Philip Zec in the *Daily Mirror*, a newspaper with a circulation of over 2 million.[56] Zec was, in the words of his colleague Hugh Cudlipp, future editor of the *Mirror*, 'the people's cartoonist'.[57] As such, he had a keen eye for what would please and what would offend the Labour-voting readers. On VE Day, 8 May 1945, the *Mirror* turned to Zec to sum up the national mood. He drew a wounded soldier among the rubble of Europe, presenting the reader with a wreath called 'Victory and Peace in Europe'. The caption read, 'Here you are! Don't lose it again!'[58] In September 1943, Zec had chosen to respond to a contemporary scandal using K6 as a model and exemplar. The scandal revolved around Learie Constantine, the noted West Indian cricketer, who was refused entry to a hotel in London as a 'nigger'.[59] The home secretary protested in the House of Commons, and the case went to court. Zec's cartoon, published on 4 September, showed a black airman from the Caribbean together with an Indian soldier, recognisably based on K6 by the style of *pagri*. Carrying kitbags, they are seen in the palm court of an hotel, where a notice declares 'No coloured people admitted: by order'. One turns to the other and says, 'We didn't see that notice in the trenches.' Zec's message is clear: these men have been in the UK helping, answering the call, and a colour bar is not the way to repay them. There is a sense of solidarity bleeding out of the drawing: the depiction of both African and Indian is humane and sympathetic, unlike some other cartoons of the time which pander more to racist stereotypes. Overall, Zec is giving a clear call to the British people: the struggle for freedom and democracy is universal, and the British public should live up to the talk of national and imperial unity that was being preached so widely.

By the end of 1943 the international situation had changed radically. Britain was no longer the target of aerial bombing, the Allies were creeping slowly up through Italy, and the defeat of Germany could be contemplated. Meanwhile in Asia the Japanese Army was still attacking India itself. Operation Jupiter was not on the table any longer, and the British troops who had been training with the Punjabis were now being trained for France, not Norway. There was no longer a role for Indian mule companies in the UK. The need in Italy and in Burma was paramount. The men were restless too. A complaint came to Hills in a letter:

> We left India three years ago and some of us have not seen our families for more than six years as no leave was granted on the eve of our proceeding overseas.
>
> Those VCOs whom we considered as our best leaders are now being repatriated leaving us behind … and we poor and doomed soldiers who don't possess any voice have been overlooked and thus our sentiments and feelings have been very badly hurt. This policy has led to a good deal of deterioration in our morale.[60]

This politely worded request represented a serious grievance, and was one stage of a long-running saga about repatriation. Since the end of 1940 there had been a stream of men returning to India, to be replaced by reinforcements coming in the opposite direction. The last draft of replacements was a large one: nearly 1,200 men including seven officers.[61] They arrived just three months before the whole force left the UK, indicating the continuing lack of clarity about their role. By this point, Hills had been replaced due to ill-health, and the force was commanded by Lt Col. J.H. Sykes. As ever, Hills was concerned for his men, writing in his final report:

> personnel have missed promotion. Many men … would undoubtably be Daffadars or even VCOs in the expanded Indian Army of today had they been returned to India … [they] now feel they have been seriously handicapped in their careers by being kept overseas, with the knowledge that they were the first Indian troops to proceed on active service.[62]

The unit war service diaries tail off after Hills' departure, after which time all the units were exclusively in Scotland. Surprisingly there is not even a mention of the visit to Buckingham Palace by Sykes, Major Gurdial Singh, Captain Syed Amir-ud-Din Jaffery and Risaldar Ghulam Mohd.[63] There is a sense of fatigue, of a desire to return home, of readiness for a new venture. Their last appearance in the British press was a story in the local paper about K6's presence at a service in Dornoch Cathedral in September 1943 – they had long dropped off the national papers.[64] They were ready to depart.

12

Doing what comes naturally

Praise be to God who made love the foundation of the world.[1]

Among all the stories of welcome and friendship, there are other tales of deeper relationships, especially with British women. With so many young husbands and boyfriends away in North Africa, Asia or elsewhere, and the depression caused by bombing and bad news, it is hardly surprising that British women sought solace and warmth in the arms of the handsome moustachioed Punjabis who were staying nearby. Perhaps, like the artist Philip de Laszlo who had painted Indian soldiers during the Great War, they were attracted by the 'deep colours and deep eyes' of these warm, friendly, charming men.[2] For their part, the sepoys found they were interesting and attractive to the local girls, and 'women offered them ice-creams and more illicit pleasures' because, as one veteran said, 'they loved our uniforms, the colour, the turbans'.[3] The evidence from the German 950 Regiment, which contained a handful of men from 22nd Company, is similar, with several stories of long-standing relationships between K6 men and local women.[4] However much the India Office may have wished to keep the 'race' pure, the people on the ground did as they did around the world, and formed personal relations 'out of sheer loneliness and the need to be loved'.[5]

One story concerns Yaqub Mirza, the clerk who had noticed the girls' bare legs when he arrived at Crickhowell. In 1943 he was stationed at Knock with 3rd Company, with their base in the Knockdhu whisky distillery, closed down for the duration.[6] The local girls came to the railway station bridge 'for a chat, for a laugh or for an argument till evening. Snow or rain would not deter them.' One evening Yaqub and a friend went to a dance in Gordonstown. Yaqub was interested to see girls and boys dancing together: 'How would they keep discipline, I wondered? They drink as well and go mad, I had heard. "I am not going to drink and

I cannot dance either. What shall I do there?" I asked my pal. He replied, "You can watch them, warm your heart at least."'

They arrived at the village hall, full of young people and music which was 'noise to me'. Yaqub was transported:

> looking at the faces and the flowery shapes of skirts swinging in rhythm to the music. Never before had I seen a pair of legs of the opposite sex, let alone a jungle of them in one hall. They were talking and laughing while dancing about like butterflies … I was amazed.

The band leader asked the girls 'to talk to that Asian boy who doesn't dance, drink and doesn't talk either. For your courtesy's sake he deserves to share your happiness.' So Yaqub and his friend became a focus of attention, and girls 'tried to talk and touched my hair and put their arms

Chaudry Wali Mohammad (seated left),
Yaqub Mirza (standing right) and two
unidentified colleagues.

around my waist'. Yaqub had been welcomed to the dance. But his eyes were for one girl only, a girl in a blue satin blouse: 'Her beautiful legs carried her around the floor while I watched with my eyes and mouth wide open. Her brown silken hair dangling over her cheeks attracted my eyes like a magnet. Her fresh delicate lips, beaming brown eyes and inviting overall femininity stunned my senses.' Yaqub was captivated – 'she had succeeded in wounding a soldier and she was utterly unaware of the casualty.' At the end of the evening he followed her home 'like the little lamb of Mary' and so discovered where she lived, although no words had passed between them. Back at the barracks, his friends brought him food that they'd saved, but Yaqub could not eat and could not sleep.

The next day was a Sunday. Yaqub combed his hair, cleaned his teeth and put on his smartest uniform to return to her house. The door was opened by an old lady. Unsure of how to introduce himself, Yaqub fell back on a well-established conversation opener and asked to buy some eggs. The lady invited him in and gave him tea, sandwiches and boiled eggs. They chatted, and Yaqub asked if he could wait for her daughter, who had gone to Elgin. He waited as long as he could but had to return to barracks before she came. On his return he found that everyone knew about his situation, and an older soldier, whom they called 'Chacha' (uncle), advised him to be careful, for he was playing with fire. Yaqub knew, but 'whispered to my heart – what a lovely way of burning yourself!'

A few days later, Yaqub was playing table tennis in the recreation room. Bending to pick up the ball, he saw the girl with the blue satin blouse, and promptly lost the game. She suggested a walk along the railway line, and he finally learnt her name: Isobel. As they walked, she took his cold hand in hers. Back at her house, there was a coal fire glowing and her mother made tea while they talked about the weather. Yaqub was tongue-tied and shy, but he managed to whisper in her ear:

'I like you'. Isobel did not mind, instead she went to the kitchen to tell her mother about it. Both of them brought tea with hospitable broad smiles. I was surprised by their attitude of friendship but I was still as shy as ever, shy to pick up a piece of cake from the table. Isobel said, 'Yaqub does not like the cake because I have made it.'

Yaqub's Punjabi manners had not accustomed him to the flirtatious styles of Banffshire, and so he 'devoured' the cake. Later her younger brother arrived and rushed out again, and her mother went to collect sticks for the fire, so they were left alone. Yaqub touched her shoulder and pulled her closer, and she responded:

> with a kiss which I felt was a miracle of man's ancient invention yet the most modern. The kiss is not poetry and nor it is a music. It must have been cultured in heaven, and when paradise was ruined and man was cast out of heaven, he must have stolen it and brought it with him. The kiss is something of a blind vision not yet measured, neither written nor spoken, and such was my experience of the first kiss of the girl I was in love with.

Yaqub was torn. He felt that what they did was 'immoral' – his mother had warned him about the magic that women have that can 'transform your personality' – and Chacha had reinforced the warning. But he could not help himself: he was 21, far from home, with a beautiful girl who liked him as much as he liked her. What could be more natural? He returned to his comrades: 'utterly transformed. I made jokes and picked up on the funny sides of almost everything. "You are in a good mood today, aren't you?" my friends observed.' Yaqub and Isobel saw each other regularly, but one evening she resisted his advances and called him an 'awful boy', and they argued. Yaqub stormed off on his bike and did not visit her for two days. She came to the bridge the following day with her friends Alice and Agnes, and they explained what she had meant by calling him 'awful'. Eventually they kissed and made up 'amidst the giggling of the on-lookers' who again called him 'an awful boy' to tease him. They went together to her house, where her mother stayed in the kitchen while Isobel sat on his lap and they kissed and cuddled. 'It was the greatest evening ever of my young life,' he wrote.

When he returned to Knock that evening he had been reported absent, and his commanding officer, Major Lindoorn, wanted to see him. Yaqub was worried that he would be put on report or even locked up, but Lindoorn, who answered the door in his pyjamas, told him to leave a note next time, and to report next morning. The following morning Yaqub was informed that he had been promoted and posted to the Reinforcement Unit at Dornoch, 100 miles up the coast across the Moray Firth. Yaqub did not know what to do, he was ambitious to move up in his career, but he was in love with Isobel. He made his decision and agreed to go. Isobel was understandably upset. He told her that he was a soldier and must do his duty, and that he would have to leave her at some point. Isobel's mother put the kettle on and 'silence prevailed all over the house until the kettle whistled'. Isobel agreed to come to the station the next morning to see him off.

The next morning Yaqub was at the station early, kitbag in hand, waiting for the train that would take him north to the coast before joining the main line to Inverness. With fifteen minutes to go, Isobel had not arrived, and Yaqub was getting anxious. He found her and they had a last embrace: 'My heart bled and broke. I entered the train, found a seat and hid my face in between my hands.' At Dornoch, Yaqub started his new job and tried to forget about his heartache. On the third day his new commanding officer, Tom Hexley, sent for him and gave him a telegram which read, 'Congratulations on your promotion – love and kisses – Isobel.' Yaqub's heart was content, and for the rest of his time in Scotland he focused on his work. He would carry her image and their encounter in his heart for the rest of his life.

* * * * *

Yaqub and Isobel were not the only ones to fall in love. That such unions should lead to babies – at least eight are reported in the UK – is to be expected. In the context of over 90,000 marriages between British women and Poles, Canadians and Americans, it was part of a general trend.[7] But there was also a countervailing feeling of 'sexual patriotism' – that you should not have sex with foreigners, that 'British women belonged to British men'.[8] The Mass-Observation directive on 'coloured people' in 1943 shows a general opposition to mixed marriages and mixed-heritage children, although office-worker R. Gundry was an exception, writing, 'If my son or daughter wanted to marry a coloured person, I would welcome this.'[9] He was not the only one with enlightened views.

One story is particularly illuminative and inspiring: the story of Gladys, Jamal and Jeff.[10] Gladys Trump was born in Budleigh Salterton in Devon

Gladys Shapland in 1930, soon after her marriage.

in 1907, the daughter of a master carpenter. Her background was strict and Victorian – her Methodist mother had a stick on the dining table to rap the children's knuckles with. Gladys was a talented woman with untapped skills; she played the piano well and offered tuition later in life. In 1930 she married an electrician named Albert Shapland, who had been born in Shahjahanpur in India, and they moved to 104 East Hill in St Austell, Cornwall. This was a 'primitive' terraced house, made of cob, with two bedrooms, an outside toilet and no running water inside. Gladys would live there until she was 80. She was not happy in the house, and probably not happy in the marriage: Albert was a heavy smoker and a serious drinker. They had two children together, Edna and Nigel. When the children were still very young, Gladys' sister Julia came to stay. She gave birth to a baby girl Janet 'out of wedlock', and they lived with the family for a while – a taste of things to come. When the war came, Albert found work in Plymouth docks, and would stay away from home for long periods.

On 9 October 1940 in St Austell:

an extraordinary event took place. That morning several hundred Indian troops from the Punjab in full battle dress, wearing the headgear known as a pugree, marched from the railway station; a few hundred yards from where Gladys lived; with mules and horses to Duporth holiday camp just a mile or so away. Local people were astounded.

These were the men of 25th Company and the Reinforcement Unit, hotfoot from Ashbourne in Derbyshire. Over the next few weeks they would become a regular sight in the town, as would the photographers and journalists who followed them. A local girl recalled a column that went past her house every day, until:

> one day one of them just came into the house and sat down when he saw [my mother] putting a record on the gramophone. After that he came nearly every day … He often brought his friends. They used the outside tap to water the mules. [My] mother made him pasties and gave him cigarettes as she said he was somebody's son, and fighting the war just like her boys. They used to sit on [the] doorstep and sing.[11]

Gladys Shapland, however, took the friendship to the next level. At some point in the next few months she met and fell in love with one of the Indian soldiers. Her son wonders what happened, writing that 'she was almost certainly a very unhappy woman and looking for adventure' and 'perhaps he was well-educated, charming and fun, and swept her off her feet'. What is certain is that in the spring of 1941, a baby was conceived, and Gladys gave birth to her third child, Jeffrey Malcolm (Jeff, now called Paritosh) on 21 January 1942. But that was not the end of the affair – in May 1943 another 'dark skinned baby with black hair and brown eyes' was born, to be named Ronald Clive. From that moment onwards, as Jeff wrote, 'she lived with the lie', and indeed she never told her youngest two sons who their father was; she took the secret with her when she died. Albert accepted the two children as his own, but he died soon after the end of the war, in 1948. After that, Gladys lived 'as someone who in her eyes, and I suppose in the eyes of many people around, had done something unforgivable'. Her crime was to love somebody, to help somebody in a dark time, and to have two children. Gladys lived a long

Ron (left) and Jeff (right) Shapland in their
back garden at 104 East Hill, early 1950s.

life, eventually dying in 1994 at the age of 87. Jeff writes, 'she had never
set foot outside of Devon or Cornwall but brought India and England
together in two of her children.'

Jeff Shapland grew up in the house at East Hill with his elder sister
and brother and his younger brother Ron, but with no father. He was a
bright child, went to the local grammar school and became the first one
in his family to go to university, studying chemical engineering at Leeds.
After graduating he worked at Avonmouth and lived in Bristol, where he
married. In 1967 he became a science teacher, first in Grimsby and then
in Leicestershire. Later he became a deputy head and in 1984, principal of
Winstanley Community College in Leicester, at the young age of 42. And
for all this time, he thought his father was the white electrician Albert
Shapland. How could that be?

The process of finding out about his father was a gradual one. When he
was at school, people would remark that he was 'darker than most people',

and he always got a good suntan in summer. This was explained away by people talking about how Cornish folk have mixed ancestry, and perhaps there was 'some Portuguese blood in the family'. At Leeds University in the early 1960s he started to encounter people of colour, from South Asia and the Caribbean, and he was amused when South Asian men would approach him talking Hindi or Urdu, and he answered in English with his broad Cornish accent. A little later in Bristol, his landlady insisted she bring him meals in his room. When he complained to a fellow resident, he was told 'it's only you, we eat in the dining room … she doesn't think you should eat with us because of your colour'. Again, Jeff thought she'd made a 'huge mistake' and felt 'dumbstruck … they were mistaking me for an Asian person'. The 1972 influx of Ugandan Asians into Leicester caused 'uproar', and the atmosphere in his school became threatening. He was kicked and punched by students and called an 'effing paki'. So, although he did not see himself as in any way Asian, his students did. However much he is able to look back now and put all these clues together, at the time each one was a separate incident in everyday life, and did not have such a great significance. Later still, after he had become principal, one of the governors told him: 'really glad you got the job, but you nearly didn't … not all the panel wanted you, a couple of county councillors thought you were too short and too dark to command respect'. And as principal, young Asian girls would come to him in the corridor and say, 'Mr Shapland, my mum wants to know, are you Asian?'

It was around this time that he expressed his feelings of confusion to his big sister Edna. In the course of a long conversation, she told him:

> in the war there were hundreds of [Asian people] at the Duporth camp, and one of them was very friendly with Mum and he used to sometimes stay the night and sleep downstairs in the small front room. His name was Jemal Khan, and he wore a turban she said. Well, we looked at each other and we didn't say anything. But I think we both thought mother would never, I mean you can't imagine your parents having sex let alone having an affair, can you? So that was the seed that was sown.

Jeff was astounded. But even though his mother was still alive, he found it impossible to talk to her. 'My sister had remembered it for forty-odd years, how come she had not said anything?' he wondered. The idea began to grow in his head that his father was not his father. A doctor told him that he had the pigmentation that people of colour have, and when his son was born, his wife noticed a dark patch in the middle of his back, as many South Asian babies have. Eventually he persuaded his siblings to take DNA tests together, which proved that Edna and Nigel had a different father from Jeff and Ron. They found it hard to process the news:

> the struggle for me and my sister was to believe it. I knew it … the scientist in me needed it. [It] took me years to come to terms with this is what happened and my mother never told us. That felt very hard that she took that secret to the grave. She did tell my sister and my brother when she was very, very old that she had a terrible cross to bear.

A little while later there was confirmation from another source. His cousin Janet, who had been born 'out of wedlock' before the war, told them: 'we've always known that the boys had an Indian father because my mum … went down to help with their births. The knowledge was in the family, in the neighbours … [there was a] huge thing about secrets and lies.' She later wrote to Jeff: 'How sad though that you were not able to hear it from your mother, but in those days it was almost impossible to talk about such matters … Life is such an unknown path – when we are born in all innocence, we just don't know where it will take us.'[12]

Along the way, in parallel to this extraordinary narrative of discovery, Jeff underwent another transformation. He became a follower of the Osho branch of Hinduism and took the name Paritosh. He also did a lot of deep thinking about his family and is now very comfortable with his story. He wrote: 'I now have an easy confidence about explaining to people why I look the way I do … I feel comfortable in my skin and at peace with myself.' When I asked him if he sees Jamal Khan as his father, he answered: 'Yes, definitely … whatever that means … In some ways he's a sort of fictional character … I feel a sense of pride in him, coming all that way, fighting in France, coping.' Recently he has been speculating about his mother's choice of name for him. She called him Jeffrey Malcolm, the first syllables possibly drawing on the name of his father, Jamal.

So who was Jamal Khan? As Paritosh was conceived in April 1941, and the first draft of reinforcements arrived in May 1941, he must have been part of the original K6. There is only one Jamal Khan in the archives, a driver with service number 180617, who joined 25th Company from the Reinforcement Unit on 23 July 1941.[13] Whether or not he was Paritosh's father (and this speculation is shown in order to give the reader an idea of the detective processes involved), sister Edna remembered some other facts about him that she later told Paritosh, who recalled: 'Jamal Khan had something he couldn't read one day and came to the door to ask for help. She remembers him being in the house when I was a baby on the sofa; that would be in 1942 presumably. She said he had come to see the dark baby.'

She also remembered 'packets and parcels coming from India after the war –mostly, she thought, containing spices'. Most poignantly, Paritosh wrote:

> When I was a few months old my father returned to St Austell to see me and a photograph was taken of him holding me. Edna tells me how she found it one day when she was rummaging about, as she calls it, and recalls that mother was furious with her for having seen it. The photo has long since disappeared.

The only link to his father is gone, presumably destroyed by the woman who loved him, out of shame. The fact that Jamal and Gladys had two children together indicates that this was not merely a hurried liaison under the covers. He came back to the house often enough that big sister Edna remembered him. He had his photo taken with the infant Jeff and he sent parcels from Punjab after the war. We can speculate about how much his colleagues in 25th Company knew or guessed – after all, he must have been absent from his work on numerous occasions. We can wonder about how far he would have liked to be involved in the life of his Cornish sons: did he have a hand in their naming, perhaps, did he give Gladys money? But what is clear is that the relationship between Jamal and Gladys was something significant for both of them, and that the two boys were loved by both their parents.

Paritosh Jeff Shapland's story is an extraordinary one that speaks volumes about his family and about how Britain has changed in his lifetime. The shift from a time of gossip, of 'secrets and lies' to a time when 'the cupboards can be opened and the skeletons are let out' is a shift that he values.[14] It is a movement away from two forms of prejudice – against illegitimacy and against people of colour – a slow movement, and one that is not irreversible. Paritosh's story is inspirational, sad, human, ultimately uplifting in his attitude. In the twenty-first century we can get over the prejudices of previous times and be proud of who we are. As he says, 'I know I didn't find my father, Jamal Khan, through all this research but in a very real sense I found myself and it doesn't get much better than that'.

Paritosh himself is comfortable in his skin, as are his immediate family, although others may still find his parentage hard to accept. After his realisation, Paritosh went through a 'coming-out' process that involved local media coverage in Leicestershire and Cornwall. In its turn, that led to many letters and phone calls from people who remembered K6 in Cornwall and elsewhere, people who remembered 25th Company in St Austell, and even people with similar stories to tell. The vast majority of those communications were positive and supportive. As Paritosh said, 'We've come a huge way, haven't we?'

* * * * *

Paritosh and his brother Ron are not the only 'K6 kids' that research has found. There are similar stories of two other mothers in St Austell, one who was married, one unmarried.[15] Giovanna Bloor knew of three babies born after the short months the sepoys were posted beneath Snowdon. Illegitimate babies were always accepted as part of life there, and Merioneth was the only county in Wales without a home for unmarried mothers because 'the girl got denounced in chapel and the grandmother brought the baby up', according to Giovanna's mother.[16] No K6 offspring have yet come to light in Scotland, but given the numbers in England and Wales, it is likely that there were some. These babies were part of a wider group of mixed-heritage children born during and immediately after the war, their fathers mostly African-American soldiers. The official history of the war reported 554 children born to black American fathers and white British mothers, although other estimates are around 1,000.[17] Growing up in the 1940s and 1950s may have been difficult for these children and their mothers, with the attitudes illustrated above, but not in every case, and sometimes reunion with the father was possible. Among the smaller group of K6 children, Jeff and his brother Ron had a happy childhood, albeit in straitened circumstances, and we can hope that the others did too. The eight 'K6 kids' are the tip of an iceberg of affection and warmth extended to these men. Although there are also some more doubtful stories relating to sexual desire, the massive weight of evidence points towards handsome young men and lonely women coming together in cottages and barns and village halls, flirting and then sometimes making love. Paritosh Shapland and his seven contemporaries are part of the living legacy of K6, rejected or accepted by post-war society, but growing in confidence and pride as the years continue.

13

The end of the Indian Contingent

The times have changed; the world has changed its mind.
The European's mystery is erased.
The secret of his conjuring tricks is known:
The Frankish wizard stands and looks amazed.[1]

The remaining 1,950 men of Force K6 set sail from Liverpool onboard RMS *Maloja* on 14 January 1944, five months before D-Day, a few days before the assault on Monte Cassino.[2] The country was flooded with over 1 million American soldiers and there was a mood of optimism around, but there was to be a lot more blood spilt before the end. Before their departure, K6 had set their house in order. Although forbidden from letting anyone know where they were going or when, they had presented their flag to the ICF 'with the wish of all ranks, that eventually it should pass into the personal keeping of our chairman, Mrs Amery. This wish has been fulfilled.'[3] They had each received a final Christmas present from the ICF, in the shape of a tin of hair oil, and the men in the hospital were sent 'a Christmas Stocking filled with comforts'.[4] Mrs Taylor-Grant, who ran the leave centre in Edinburgh, was presented with a cheque, and the remaining kitty was divided between the ICF and the Bengal Famine Fund – some for home and some for away.[5] Their horses and mules were all left in the UK, put into the charge of the two RASC companies and the Remount Depot, and would subsequently be used in Italy, but the men took their rifles and ammunition with them, for all troops on the Burma front could find themselves called on to fight at any moment. It was a very different group of men who left from those who had arrived four years previously, and they were going home to a very different India.

They arrived in Bombay on 13 February – just three weeks before the Japanese attacks at Imphal and Kohima, a pivotal point in the Asian war – to a heroes' welcome: 'The band of a British regiment played military music as the vessel that conveyed them berthed at an Indian port, and in fine fettle and style the men marched off.'⁶ As in Marseilles at Christmas 1939, a film crew and a group of journalists were there to record the event. The pressmen waxed lyrical about the force's military contribution and their universal welcome in France and Britain, and interviewed individual soldiers. Remarkably, three filmed interviews survive in the archives of the Imperial War Museum.⁷ In an indoor studio, Subedar Major Ghulam Ahmed and Lieutenant Nizam Din (he of the gap teeth) speak in Urdu, and Subedar Nasir Rahman, clearly the most relaxed of the three, speaks in excellent English. Their words are scripted, and they all cover much the same ground: their time in France, meeting the King, working with British units and being invited to spend their leave with British families.

Among the wider returnees, praise for British hospitality was widespread and fulsome. 'Almost every member of the party had autographed pictures of men and women whose friendship they had won,' wrote the *Times of India*.⁸ Lance Naik Fateh Mohd of Gujerat had enjoyed his time as a tourist, visiting London Zoo and Madame Tussaud's, and spending hours 'joy-riding up and down the escalators' on the underground.⁹ Jemadar Abid Ali Khan, who had picked up a Scottish accent, said that he found Lairg very much like his home in the North West Frontier, and Subedar Mazumdar of East Bengal was delighted that 'at the dances we could dance with girls simply by asking them'. The men were inspected by a general, and then entertained at the canteen with gifts of sweets, fruit and cigarettes. Breathing the air of India and tasting the fresh fruit must have felt wonderful after weeks on a ship preceded by months or years in cold rainy Britain. In fact, most of the original K6 men had already returned: this ship brought only Hexley, Nizam Din and a few others from the class of '39. A few days later in Delhi they were inspected by the 'Auk' himself – General Auchinleck, commander-in-chief of the Indian Army, who had these words to say:

All of you have worthily upheld the traditions and enhanced the reputation not only of your respective Corps but of the Indian Army, and your stay in England, Wales and Scotland will, I hope, long be remembered by the many friends you have made there. The war will not be ended until Japan is utterly defeated. After the leave, which you have well earned, you will be called upon to play your part in her defeat, side by side with those of your comrades already in the battle area.[10]

Their job in Europe was finished, their role in the East was just beginning, but their stay in Britain would prove to be long forgotten rather than long remembered. They returned to their base in Jullundur and went on leave, and on 25 April Force K6 was formally disbanded.[11]

* * * * *

Over the next few months the men adjusted to life back home. They visited family and caught up with news, they changed their pounds to rupees, they enjoyed chapattis made from home-milled *atta* and the taste of real spices. The many micro culture shocks that they had experienced on going to Europe were reversed. Reports from the officers show the impact of their time in Europe. Captain Rattan Singh writes of 7th Company: 'There is a mixed feeling of happiness and disappointment. Happy to be back home to meet relations, friends and families, disappointment because the hygiene and social life in India is not the same as these men have been accustomed to for at least two to three years.'[12]

Although thousands of miles from home, these men had witnessed and experienced a lifestyle outside the war zone that appealed: a softer, easier life. Captain Saifullah, who had also been in the UK, was interested in how they might bring their experience home:

> The men have been to UK – a very advanced and all-round very nicely run country in the world. I am sure they do feel the difference between this country and UK. They all seem to appreciate the way of living in UK. It is yet to be seen what practical changes if any they can introduce in their villages and if they try to raise the standard of living.[13]

But there were troubles at home. Men were 'overstaying their leave' or deserting, to deal with the harvest or to sort out 'domestic affairs' such as the seizure of their land by relatives, or in reaction to rumours that they would be posted overseas again.[14] Captain Jaffery of 32nd Company reports on new attitudes and friendships that had developed, such that 'in

UK the Indian Soldier had made many friends in the British army as well as the civil. Some still correspond with them.'[15] Jaffery also reported that the experience of Europe was a positive one in terms of the relationships between the sweepers and the other men, writing, 'interesting to note that the men have no objection to a sweeper eating with them on the same table'. The men back from Britain brought new ideas and experiences to add to a rapidly changing India.

* * * * *

As 1943 turned into 1944, the sepoys in German uniforms in 950 Regiment, the Indian Legion, were still in the south-west of France. Abuzar and some of his fellows were acutely aware of the direction the war was taking, wondering whether they had backed the wrong horse. In February Abuzar made friends with a local member of the French Resistance, Max Joiris, and stole twelve German rifles for the French to use when the time came.[16] Abuzar was keeping his options open, aware that his decision was reversible. As a mercenary soldier, he knew when the time was right to move on. The Allies invaded France in June that year, and on 25 July Abuzar made up his mind. He deserted with two comrades and took shelter with Max Joiris in Bordeaux.[17] In December the 'notorious' Abuzar tried to cross the Pyrenees into Spain but was intercepted and flown under escort to England for interrogation.[18]

After the Allied invasions of Normandy in June and Provence in mid-August, German troops in the south of France were in danger of being cut off. Having been transferred to the Waffen-SS in August, the legion set off on a hazardous journey across the diagonal axis of France, in an attempt to reach Germany.[19] At Poitiers they were alleged to have committed some atrocities against French citizens.[20] As the Resistance troops took control of the city, many members of the legion fell into their hands, 22nd Company men among them.[21] The German officers were handed over to the Allies in due course, but the Indians were shot in the market square and subsequently buried in the Fond de Misère.[22] The rest of the legion continued their retreat across France, dodging Patton's army advancing from the west, the British along the coast and the Americans and Free French from the Mediterranean. On 16 September they crossed back into Alsace – now German territory – at the Col de Bonhomme near Gérardmer, where the 22nd Company had surrendered four years previously. They spent the winter and spring in southern Germany, waiting with increasing irritation in an 'end-of-the-world mood'.[23] They saw no more action; the majority of the legion were captured by the French Army as they tried to escape into Switzerland in May, and were then handed over to the British, who took them to the UK via Marseilles.[24]

* * * * *

The rest of 22nd Company, except those who had managed to escape, were still scattered in fifteen different POW camps across France, Germany, Italy and Poland, with the bulk of them in Epinal or Offenburg.[25] Conditions in camps deteriorated towards the end of the war: the winter of 1944/45 was a harsh one, the Allied bombing of Germany caused concern about reprisals, and food was short, with starvation 'a genuine

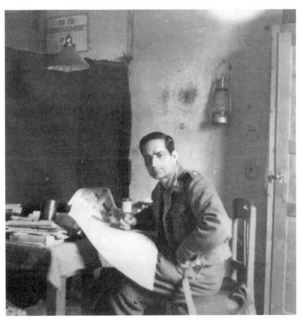

Anis Ahmad Khan in a POW camp: Stalag IIIA Luckenwalde, September 1943.

and terrible possibility'.[26] Anis' daughter Zeenut recalled one especially striking story that her father told of the food they ate towards the end of the war: the men were sitting round a cauldron, waiting for the soup to be ready, watching a 'horse's head bobbing up and down' – their only source of protein to add to the potatoes and black bread.[27]

Allied POWs took precautions, with those in Lamsdorf being 'secretly organised into fighting units' in case the German guards turned on them at the end.[28] Many POWs had to make forced marches away from their camps: Major Hitchcock spent a week on the road marching from Spangenberg until liberated by American troops on 4 April.[29] Meanwhile Captain Anis had been moved around from camp to camp, ending up at Oflag 79 at Braunschweig. In March 1943 he had written to his cousin Shahid Hamid from Annaburg to say, 'I am quite well by the Grace of God'.[30] Clearly the tough conditions had not yet started to bite. A year later, things had changed considerably, as the RAF and the USAAF were now carrying out regular bombing raids in Germany – the Americans by day and the British by night. A fellow Indian prisoner wrote, in August 1944:

> the camp was picked up as target and was raided at 11.20 a.m. The scene was horrible; nearby barracks, German guardrooms and kitchen were reduced to ashes. Seven bomb craters were created and a good number of anti-personnel ammunition was dropped on the camp … The dangers of really heavy air raids are only known to those who survive these terrors of war, half-starved for years enclosed by barbed wire fences.[31]

For a white British officer like Major Hitchcock, surrounded by hundreds of men like him, such privations would have been easier to bear. Anis was different: he was a fish out of water, and an odd fish at that. He was one of very few Indians and fewer Muslims, with a sneaking feeling that he was only still in the camp because he had not given that one word 'yes' to Bose, a word that he could so easily have given but for his sense of *izzat* or honour. His life must have been lonely: one can feel his need for company in his cards to his cousin Shahid. Even his batman, Driver Dost Mohamed, had been taken from him, having died in the camp at Berlin in November 1941; his name is inscribed on the Dunkirk memorial as one of the Indian soldiers whose grave is unknown.[32] Soon before the liberation of Oflag 79 Anis was moved around with other prisoners by train, and as an intensely private man, was revolted by the sordid reality that there was no toilet in the cattle truck, so 'if you had to pee, there was one can that was passed around.'[33] The camp was liberated by the US Army on 12 April 1945, and Anis was horrified when he saw the newly freed prisoners looting cameras, binoculars and radios: 'like children let loose … breaking into homes and shops and carting away lots of stuff'.

As the prisoners were liberated and sent home camp by camp, many found it hard to readjust to life outside bars. Prisoners had been affected by the intensity in different ways: 'Never again would men feel so bored, so hungry, so watched, so uncertain of their future.'[34] At Moosburg, where Jack Laslett had been imprisoned, the Indians were described as being the smartest and best disciplined of any nation in the camp, and were the first to fly out, on 2 May.[35] The Indians were not being sent home, however – at least not yet. The India Office wanted them all to come to England first.

* * * * *

In 1945 the men of 22nd Company were reunited in East Anglia, those who had joined the Germans and those who had chosen to sit it out. The India Office and British military intelligence had known of the existence of the Indian Legion for some time, and their plans were ready. A new intelligence unit had been set up: the Combined Services Detailed Interrogation Centre (CSDIC). From July 1943 they were talking about the men as 'Hitler Inspired Fifth Column (HIFs)' and had devised a colour code for grading POWs and legionaries according to their loyalty – black, white and grey: the darker the colour, the deeper the treachery.[36] In January 1944, Molesworth of the India Office saw a report in the *London Evening Standard* with a photo of a Sikh in German uniform. Molesworth's response was to have lunch with the editors of nine prominent British newspapers and ask them not to publish anything on HIFs.[37] They concurred. When the Allies invaded Europe in June, a Major de Gale from MI5 accompanied them with the specific purpose of 'security screening of Indians'.[38] The

British were taking no chances: all POWs would be questioned and sorted before being allowed back to India.

Several camps were established in East Anglia in the summer of 1944, with their HQ at Thetford. As the POWs started to arrive in the autumn of that year, many were found to be in poor health and:

> had lost all sense of proportion and had forgotten what discipline was. They had to be [handled] with firmness combined with tact. They took about two weeks to settle down and showed a great improvement on receiving new clothing and equipment. Many were sanctioned special diet after medical inspection.[39]

A separate hospital with 600 beds was made available, and all POWs were treated well, with special provisions for their welfare. As they were liberated, they each received a Red Cross gift bag from the ICF, with more waiting for them in the camps.[40] They were given money to send home and spend at the Navy Army and Air Force Institute (NAAFI) shop, and could earn more by volunteering to help with the potato and beet harvest.[41] There were trips to London and to Woking Mosque and a Sikh *gurdwara* (temple), and as it was a cold winter, there were snowball fights and a snowman competition.[42] The King visited in June 1945 and inspected 4,000 released POWs – the India Office was being very careful not to impugn the reputation of those who had remained loyal to the Crown.[43] The old K6 newsletter *Wilayati Akhbar Haftawar* was restarted in November 1944 with the usual mixture of news from India, war news and photos of the men themselves. In keeping with the new end-of-war mood, there was also a spread of photos of the newly liberated Belsen concentration camp.[44] The very last photo was a symbol of post-war British hope: St Paul's Cathedral lit up for the first time since 1939. The sepoys, itching to get back home to India, probably did not share this sense of national optimism.

One of the camps – at Cranwich, north of Thetford – was designated as a 'black camp' and housed the CSDIC men.[45] The team of Indian and British interrogators worked their way steadily through the captured legionaries and civilians. 'Grey' was split into dark and light shades, and the precise definition of black and grey evolved. By August 1945 grey could include those who had served in 950 Regiment, provided they had been 'misled by their leaders or persuaded to join the enemy by torture or the hope of better conditions'.[46] CSDIC even requested that Anis be sent for questioning, but that he should not be sent under escort.[47] They wanted to talk to him, to hear his story, but they did not wish it to appear that he was under suspicion. In fact, he was back in the army in a few short months; clearly he was not deemed to have crossed the line to black 'traitor' status. Abuzar was a different matter. His interrogation report is one of the most detailed, and its conclusion is unequivocal and damning. Abuzar was branded a 'traitor who, on his own showing, has been one of the leading recruiters and a prominent member of 950 Regiment ever since June 42'. It added that there was little doubt he had used violence in recruiting men to the legion, and that the Germans considered him 'thoroughly reliable'. Although he had later acted in support of the Allies again, through his work with Max Joiris, the author of the report considered this was due 'not to a change of heart, but to a desire to feather his nest'. Finally, it concluded, 'It is considered that he constitutes a permanent danger to security and it is recommended that he be categorised Black.'[48]

By October 1945 the camps had done their work and were shut, with a grand total of 9,711 recovered prisoners (black, grey and white) having been processed and returned to India.[49] In some cases the black and the white were sent home together on the same ship, like the SS *Aronda* in July 1945.[50] Either CSDIC were unconcerned about the troops' loyalty now the war in Europe was over, or they did not have enough shipping to worry the point. A report by the adjutant-general in India clarifies that all returning POWs would get an advance of seventy rupees and that they were 'likely to be in a rather pleased and excited frame of mind'.[51] It goes on to distinguish between those recovered in Europe and those from Asia:

The bulk of the HIFs appear to be completely imbued with Bose's propaganda and to be thoroughly anti-British. It is probably the fact that HIFs fully realise the enormity of their crime in becoming HIFs which makes them display bravado such as shouting *Inqilab Zindabad* [Long Live the Revolution] and scrawling this and similar slogans on railway carriages.[52]

The status of the 'loyalists' and the 'revolutionaries' of the Indian Legion was changing, and would shift further in tune with India's wider movements.

One young sepoy from 22nd Company didn't make it home. Having spent more than four years in POW camps, including Epinal, Driver Qaim Din from Rawalpindi died onboard *SS Amapoora*, the ship that was to take him home.[53] Like so many of his comrades, he had contracted TB. His body was brought ashore and buried at Thetford Cemetery. He was the last of the K6 men to be buried in Britain.

* * * * *

The 'blacks' of 950 Regiment, with twenty or so from 22nd Company among them, returned to India in the summer of 1945. They found that public opinion was in a state of flux. The men from Europe, Abuzar among them, were imprisoned at Bahadurgarh, just outside Delhi.[54] From there they witnessed the extraordinary procedures of the Red Fort trials. In November three of the INA's senior officers were put on trial for treason – one Hindu, one Muslim and one Sikh: Prem Sahgal, Shah Nawaz Khan and Gurubaksh Singh Dhillon. Public opinion swiftly moved against the British, with Nehru part of the defence team, and Gandhi expressing his support for the men in jail.[55] The men were found guilty and sentenced to death, but the public furore was considerable, with the INA men 'widely admired', and Auchinleck ordered the sentences be commuted.[56] This was a decisive victory for the nationalists, and the chant in the streets was:

> *Lal Qila se aayi awaaz*
> *Dhillon, Sahgal, Shahnawaz*[57]
> (From the Red Fort comes the cry
> Dhillon, Sahgal, Shah Nawaz)

Soon after that, all the remaining men of 950 Regiment (and the INA) were discharged. By May 1946 half of the RIASC 'greys' had been reclassified 'white' and sent on leave.[58] The 'traitors' were in the process of being recast as 'heroes'. British rule in India had passed the point of no return.

* * * * *

By the end of 1945, all the men of the Indian Contingent were back home, except those left behind in graves in Europe. Between them they had seen the highways and byways of Wales, England and Scotland, camps in France, Germany, Spain and Poland, army bases in Belgium and the Netherlands, and safe havens in Switzerland and Gibraltar. Driver Buland Khan, with one hand missing, had sailed slowly round Africa, and Maulvi Sayed Ahmed Shah had apparently been parachuted into Iran. Now they were all home in Punjab. Older, wiser, and perhaps a little plumper. A senior officer visiting 32nd Company in May 1945 was frankly disparaging of the men and the influence that the soft European life had had on them:

> Some of the [sepoys] of this unit have served with the Force K6 and have stayed in England a long time, where they were made much of, and consequently they have returned to India as spoilt children. They want concessions here which are not possible.
>
> I have had a talk with the VCOs and NCOs of this unit, and they have given me the impression of a disgruntled lot, specially those who have returned from England, and in my opinion these men are having a bad influence on the rest.[59]

For this officer at least, these men were different from the average Indian soldier, even a year after their return: England had softened and weakened them, and they were making bolshie demands that were impossible. They were like spoilt children whose *mabap* had over-indulged them. As in the old Punjabi tale of the jackal who falls into a jug of blue dye and pretends to be a peacock, these men were brought back down to reality, and sent off to wash in the stream.[60]

Colonel Noon, the author of the report, was an outsider, not part of K6. Officers who knew the men better and had been to Europe had different views. Some reported on grievances. Captain Saifullah said that the men of 3rd Company felt they had missed out on promotion by being posted to Europe and were aggrieved not to be awarded the 1939–43 Star.[61] Men of 25th Company were struck by the hostile attitude of civilians towards them:

In the UK they had grown accustomed to being regarded with respect. They have been mortified by the contempt, or at best indifference, with which they are received by civilians in this country. Two specific instances are (1) A soldier who tried to air his views on world affairs in a railway carriage was told to 'Shut up, you are an ignorant soldier, what do <u>you</u> know about it[']; (2) A civilian at Jullundur station to whom admission to a crowded railway carriage was refused by a leave party, began to abuse them, saying '*Qurbani ke bakre*' [sacrificial goat].[62]

Politics impinged on their lives in a way they had been able to avoid in Europe. After the Red Fort trials there was some concern that ex-members of the INA (including the legion) were being employed in government jobs, thus taking jobs from soldiers who had stayed loyal to the British.[63] But the attitude towards the INA was a nuanced one, according to a report from 32nd Company at the end of 1945:

INA Trials are arousing a great deal of interest. The general feeling is that under duress of hunger and mal-treatment the action of the majority in joining the INA is understandable. The recent Govt announcement that clemency will be shown to these people was greeted with enthusiasm. Whilst all agree that leaders who mal-treated their own countrymen should be punished, there have been no sign of real hate against these people.[64]

The reconciliation with the INA and its legacy was an indication of the increasingly questionable status of the army in post-war India. The men were back at home, amid a world at turmoil. Their unique experience in having travelled 7,000 miles to help was overlooked by their neighbours and would soon be overtaken by the rush of events. Only the men themselves carried the memory in their hearts. In far-off Britain, scores of people who knew them did the same, nurturing a small cache of stories of these smiling turbaned strangers who had come into their lives, changed them forever, and then disappeared.

Epilogue

Forgetting and remembering

Speechless and dumb I am,
Like a blown-out taper on a dismal night,
Enveloping in dark obscurity
the tombs, unlit, unepitaphed,
Of the unknown poor, lying underneath.[1]

In a Granada TV studio in Manchester in March 1998, the actors Richard Wilson and Caroline Aherne met to record an episode of *The Mrs Merton Show*.[2] Mrs Merton was a character played by Aherne, a faux Mancunian old lady in wig and glasses who sometimes asked cutting questions of her guests. The other guest was Bernard Manning, a northern comedian in decline, known for his casual old-fashioned racism. During the show an audience member called Miles (possibly a plant) asked Manning a question, recalling a time thirty years previously when he'd been 'thumbing a lift' home from Manchester to Rochdale, and Manning had stopped and taken him home. Miles then posed a killer question: 'What I want to ask Bernard is a) does he still drive a Jaguar and b) would he have picked me up if I'd been black [laughter].' After some badinage and some prompting from Aherne, Manning said: 'I don't drive a Jaguar now; I drive a Rolls Silver Spirit [audience 'woo'] and if you'd have been black, you'd still be stood there [laughter].' Wilson and Aherne both questioned Manning on this, which prompted Manning to switch the topic by way of justification, reaching into the ragbag of racist tropes: 'It's a free country. That's why all our troops – *our* troops – died at Dunkirk, and Anzio, and Arnhem, and Monte Cassino.' When Wilson protested that Commonwealth troops were also involved in the war, Manning intensified his attack:

Not for us. They fought for theirselves. You don't think Hitler would have let them off the hook if they'd won the war. There's no Pakis at Dunkirk, right up …

It is possible that Manning had never heard of the substantial Indian Army presence in the Italian campaign, at the battles of Anzio and Monte Cassino. Or he may have heard about them but chose to ignore them as inconsistent with his prejudices. It is almost certain that neither he nor Wilson nor Aherne knew that there were in fact 615 Muslim Indian soldiers – 'pakis' in his reckoning – on the beaches at Dunkirk.[3] They didn't know that those men went on to march in the very first UN Day parade in London in June 1942, appeared in the *Illustrated London News* and *Picture Post*, and left children behind when they departed. Manning was undoubtedly a racist, but in common with the vast majority of the British public, he did not know anything at all about the story of the men of Force K6, their time in France and their longer time in Britain. Outside a few people who had met them and a few military historians, they had been comprehensively forgotten.

To understand how and why this forgetting took place, we need to look at the concept of collective memory: what is generally understood within a culture about a particular event or person or period in the past.[4] What is remembered is what fits within the social framework or self-image of a society; if it doesn't fit, it slips away. Feature films and other visual forms can be particularly influential in shaping what is recalled, and it is quite possible that without personal experience of a particular time, a film or TV series can become the entirety of your knowledge, your version of that time.[5] Within the UK in general the Second World War continues to hold a dominant position in collective memory: the 'two world wars and one world cup' school of historical thinking.[6] This tends to include significant elements like D-Day, the Holocaust and the Home Front, but those elements shift into and out of prominence as time and fashions change. In South Asia, by contrast, there is very little of the war that is generally recalled.

The process of forgetting has been different in South Asia and in Britain. In both cases there was a need to create a new society after the war, to focus on the internal rather than the external. In South Asia these men were never widely known. They are part of a wider tide, the general forgetting of the 2.5 million men of the Indian Army. The simple explanation of this is Partition: by the summer of 1947, two years after the war ended, there were two countries where there had been one, and there was a need for new state narratives. In order to create new countries and new memories in India, in west and east Pakistan, some inconvenient truths had to be set aside. Bookshops in Britain have large sections devoted to the Second World War; not so in India or Pakistan. In the interviews I conducted in Punjabi villages in 2018, most people knew very little about the course or even the dates of the war.

In Britain the story is different, for there the men of Force K6 were widely known. The coverage in the press and on newsreels, as well as their appearance in parades across the country meant that they were in the public gaze from the start of 1940 through to 1943. In the summer of 1945, everything changed. This was a beginning as well as an ending, the start of a new post-war world. British society had become 'classless for the duration' of the Second World War, and some sections of the public had been able to move beyond the colour-bar racism of the time.[7] But when peace came in 1945 attitudes and priorities shifted quickly, and the desire to remember 'our boys' was paramount in a rapidly changing world where British prestige and the Empire were in slow, constant retreat. The new Labour government under Attlee was focused on domestic issues, keen to change society. Those British people who had only seen the sepoys in a newsreel or in the paper had a multitude of other visual images to process by August 1945: North Africa, D-Day, Burma, the liberation of Belsen, atom bombs. The war was gone, the need was gone, the relationship with India was in rapid flux. There was a new frame in place. Men like Nizam Din and Dr Rana were no longer needed, they had lost their currency. They had served their military and propaganda purposes.

Within the UK there is an element of racism in the general forgetting of the Indian Army, although the Gurkhas have managed to dodge that by continuing to be part of the post-war army and thus fit into the frame of collective consciousness. Just as the contribution of French colonial soldiers was rubbed out even while the war was going on, in a process known as *blanchiment* or whitening, British Empire soldiers, sailors and airmen from the Caribbean, Africa and Asia continue to be ignored.[8]

The particular circumstances of the K6 story only serve to bring out the injustice of their forgetting. They were here, at Dunkirk and in the UK, they left traces in the memories as well as material traces like horseshoes, graffiti and graves. They were unique, so for British people to forget them feels more poignant. Added to that, on another level, they were involved in the business of supply, not front-line fighting, and such support troops are rarely remembered. In addition, people may not have realised that those marching before them in parade in Exeter or Edinburgh were the same men as had been in France, the same men who appeared in *Picture Post* and the same men used for a cartoon in the *Daily Mirror*.

Of those men, 615 had also marched through Dunkirk, the story which brought me to write this book. Christopher Nolan's blockbuster film *Dunkirk* omitted any mention or glimpse of an Indian, and that particular forgetting was the subject of considerable media controversy in the summer of 2017.[9] Nolan is a filmmaker not a historian, and he chose to focus on air, sea and land, to intercut stories and to blend three different timescales, thereby leaving out K6. There is an interesting contrast between Nolan's film and two other recent visual portrayals of Operation Dynamo. In Joe Wright's 2007 film *Atonement*, James McAvoy arrives into the chaos of the beach with two comrades, one played by Nonso Anozie, a British actor of Nigerian descent.[10] The film's historical advisor later revealed that she had been uneasy about this casting decision as 'it was almost impossible for there to have been a black soldier in the British Expeditionary Force'.[11] Miranda Kaufmann, who specialises in black history, argued that it could sometimes be acceptable to 'bend the truth' in order to 'make the wider point that there were many soldiers of African descent fighting in World War Two'.[12] Kaufmann believes that the job of educating the public – through popular culture – of the role of minority populations in British history is so important that we can 'bend' what is shown in the record. Meanwhile in the BBC's 2019 series *World on Fire* writer Peter Bowker made an explicit choice to show an Indian with a British accent at Dunkirk, indulging in banter with a black British musician travelling from Paris to London via Dunkirk.[13] This inaccurate portrayal shows that there is still a gap, an opportunity for an enterprising filmmaker to come forward and make a movie or a documentary drawing on the wealth of visual material and the true stories of the men of K6 and their encounters.

* * * * *

The post-war true stories of the men of K6 vary widely, with the Britishers easier to trace than the Indians. Tom Hexley finished the war as a lieutenant colonel, left the army in 1947 and bought the Sutherland Arms in Golspie. He married again, to a woman from Inverness, and died at the young age of 58, after a heart attack while out riding.[14] In India meanwhile, Punjab split violently in two in 1947 and the country was in 'freefall', with many demobbed soldiers joining in the Partition riots.[15] Many K6 veterans were still in the army, which was divided between India and Pakistan. The mule companies of the RIASC were also split, and 7th Company still exists as an animal transport unit in the Pakistan Army, carrying supplies in the mountainous and frozen parts of the country, where they face their erstwhile comrades of the Indian Army.[16] For most of the individuals who served in K6, we simply don't know what happened to them. In some cases where a record of their home villages still exists (often thanks to the Commonwealth War Graves Commission) I was able to visit the village, in hopes of finding a head full of stories and a cache of letters and photos in a drawer or suitcase. Sadly, with a few exceptions, this was not the case.

There is one soldier for whom a wealth of material does exist: Major Akbar. He left behind a large quantity of documents and photographs, and his family members in Karachi and elsewhere were very generous with their time. After leaving Britain in late 1941, Akbar was posted to Burma, and in 1944 he was sent on tour round India, making speeches in support of the army. His promotions continued and his confidential report in the new post-war world of June 1946 reflected his continuing place in the Empire's good books: 'He showed considerable tact and administrative ability at a difficult period … An officer of the old school, and one in whom I had the greatest confidence. Is not afraid to express his views, and has a balanced outlook. Respected by all ranks.'[17] At the time of Partition he was the senior Indian officer in the new Pakistan Army (still commanded in 1947 by a white British man) with the number PA1. In common with most of the army, Akbar had reservations about Partition and wrote to Leo Amery in September 1947, when his new country was just three weeks old: 'We in Pakistan have got a very hard task in front of us. We have to start an entirely new show and under very difficult conditions. However we are confident that we will achieve our object.'[18]

Here is the officer of the old school, admired by the British establishment, with a solid thirty-year career behind him, among the chaos of the division of Punjab, putting on a brave face. In many ways this period was the pinnacle of his career. He was made aide-de-camp to Jinnah, the Quaid-e-Azam or great leader, who referred to him as 'my *aclota* – my one and only general'.[19] His retirement just a few years later seems strange, but may have been a combination of disappointment with not being made commander-in-chief, and a dislike for politics. More than once he wrote, 'being a soldier by birth, by choice and by profession also, I cannot indulge in politics', and his granddaughter expressed the family consensus in saying, 'he was too honest to be a politician.'[20] He was ready to move on to a new phase in his life: a thirty-year period of writing and family. Over the next decades he saw twenty-five grandchildren arrive, all were indulged with sweets and stories. He remained a devout Muslim, going on *Umrah* (pilgrimage) to Mecca in 1965 with his eldest daughter Razia.[21] He wrote over forty books under the name Rangroot, which signifies 'enlisted man' or 'private soldier', showing his pride in the fact that he had risen from the lowest rank to the very highest. In 1959 he went to China, taking his wife Kudsia and their youngest daughter Amna with him, and met Chairman Mao and Zhou Enlai. It is fitting then that his home 'Lal Kothi' now has a Chinese-language school on the ground floor, and his great-granddaughter studied in the People's Republic. Within six generations and 150 years his family, while remaining all the time in the same place, moved from independent Punjab, through British rule to independent Pakistan and is now looking east towards the new world power, China. His great-grandson Jawad summarised his legacy as being located before 1947, followed by a 'self-conscious move stepping away from society, cutting off his public exposure, distancing himself from army'.[22] Akbar was a career soldier and Empire hero in classic mould, a relic of the Raj, a much-loved grandfather and a prolific writer, and a key member of Force K6 for two of his eighty-seven years on the planet.

The only other Indian officer in the original Force K6 was Anis, and his post-war story was very different from Akbar's. He came home in 1946 after five years in prison: the longest imprisonment of any Indian officer in the war. His health was affected – he lost many teeth, for example – but he bounced back. He attended staff college in Quetta for five months at the end of 1946; this was an essential requirement for progress from a regimental officer to higher rank.[23] His final report praises his intelligence and common sense and describes him as 'a loyal officer who mixes well, and is tolerant and tactful'. Any lingering sense of his having been any kind of 'traitor' during his stay in the camp had gone. His fifth child Zeenut was born in January 1947 in Lucknow, by which time he was an acting colonel. Soon after that, Anis made a decision that seems remarkable in hindsight, but which made perfect sense at the time: he chose to join the Indian Army, not that of Pakistan.

At the partition of the army he was fourth in the seniority table of Muslim officers (Akbar was first), so could have expected to advance quickly once the armies were under their own national control.[24] The vast majority of the men of Force K6 became citizens of Pakistan, even if their homes had been in East Punjab, now part of India. Anis made a different choice. Aligarh, where he had grown up, was in Indian territory, and his siblings were divided in their decisions: three went to Pakistan, three to India. For Anis, according to his daughter, the clincher came from a conversation with Jinnah, who told him: 'there are going to be vast numbers of Muslims in India … your family is so well known and admired here … if you decide to stay you will be providing that kind of encouragement to the Muslims.'[25]

Indeed, he was a supporter of Jinnah's All India Muslim League, making a donation of 500 rupees to the party just two weeks before Partition.[26] Anis took that fateful decision and stayed in India, trusting that the new country would carry out the promises made by the Congress leadership to be secular and inclusive. At first it looked as if he had chosen well: by 1949 he was a major general and director of supplies and transport, running all the service corps operations.[27] Thus, in a way that is hard to believe in the increasingly polarised world of India in the twenty-first century, he became the first Indian Muslim to become a major general in the Indian Army.[28] This was not to be the end of Anis' remarkable twists and convolutions. In 1953 he decided to go to Pakistan after all. Frustrated at his lack of promotion, observing younger men rising to the rank of lieutenant general around him, Anis left the army and moved to Karachi. There was an outcry in the press and the Indian parliament: both were convinced that he would betray all of India's military secrets to the enemy and questioned the loyalty of all Muslims in Indian uniform. In fact, according to Zeenut, he remained loyal to the Indian Army and died a few years later at the age of 64 in 1966, 'of a broken heart'.[29]

At the end of the war, Risaldar Major Ashraf had been in the British Indian Army for thirty-two years, and was an honorary captain. In 1946, he applied to the Viceroy's office for the position of aide-de-camp, a position of great honour, and one fitting for a soldier with such a track record.[30] However, the job went to another risaldar, and a letter from Simla explains that 'there are many aspects to be considered' and realises that Ashraf 'will be disappointed'. With thirty-three years' service, with the Indian Order of Merit and having met the King at least twice, he was indeed disappointed at this outcome. He retired soon after and settled down as a respectable country gentleman in his home village of Dubran on the North West Frontier. He married twice and had six children; he went on the Hajj in 1952, and he became a member of the local *jirga* or tribal council.[31] He was also a moderately rich man – he employed several servants and had enough surplus funds to lend 2,000 rupees (worth around £150 in 1946) to a mine owner in Rangoon.[32] He was even a friend of Ayub Khan, general and later president of Pakistan, who hailed from a village nearby.[33] He was a loyalist of the old school, who had met the King-Emperor and looked forward to a long and prosperous retirement, surrounded by family in his home village.

Listening to Ashraf's son Abdul Jalil in the house of the poet Omer Tarin in Abbottabad, I got a strong sense of disappointment, nostalgia for a vanished lifestyle, even betrayal. Abdul Jalil spoke with some bitterness about 'nouveau riche' classes of people who rely on money, often from illegal sources, while older families 'fade away'. This betrayal seems to have reached its pinnacle in 1997, as Abdul Jalil revealed at the end of the interview. In that year Queen Elizabeth came to visit Pakistan. Abdul Jalil took his mother, Ashraf's widow, and set off to Islamabad, aiming to meet her. As he says, 'we didn't want anything – just recognition. We still have the old loyalties – a sense of Queen as symbolic figure.' He hoped that his mother could meet her woman to woman, and he took along a photograph of Ashraf shaking hands with King George – two fathers together. The junior officials around the royal party would not listen, Abdul Jalil and his mother were unable even to get near the Queen and went away disappointed. Fifty years earlier, a retired risaldar major's widow would have been held in high esteem and admitted to the royal presence, but sensitivities have changed. In the eyes of the world, the *izzat*-heavy identity of a retired risaldar major in the British Indian Army no longer carries weight, and all that remains is a set of photographs and a few family memories.

Some veterans found themselves treated with more respect. Hockey-playing Chaudry Wali Mohammad, who remembered Woking Mosque so vividly, lived a long and contented life in Pakistan, dying in 2011. He regaled his nine children with stories of his time in the army, and his son Zubair wished he had listened better, saying, 'he had a great memory, great stories to tell, but when you're younger you want to go and play'.[34] Zubair migrated to Britain in 1979 with a ten-pound note in his pocket. He bought two cartons of duty-free cigarettes, arriving at Heathrow with just four pounds. He now employs 150 people at a taxi firm in Woking. When his father Chaudry came to visit in 1995, Zubair took him on a grand tour to revisit his youth and the places he remembered: Abergavenny, Crickhowell, Bulford (where they talked to some current soldiers), Stoney Castle. Later they were hosted at the House of Commons by Humfrey Malins, the MP for Woking. Malins had allocated them twenty minutes, but when he met Chaudry and started hearing his stories, he cancelled his appointments and spent half a day with them. Recognising how much Chaudry respected Churchill, he showed them Churchill's chair and desk, and then the Churchill statue in the Members' Lobby, with its left foot polished by years of MPs rubbing it as they pass. Chaudry carried with him an affection for Britain and its people, picked up during his stay. He said, 'We were fighting for the British with heart. In those days Britain was the biggest power in the world and we were proud to fight for the country.'[35]

Chaudry's great friend Yaqub Mirza stayed in the army until 1959, rising up the ranks and retiring as a subedar.[36] He married his cousin Resham Bee and by the time of Partition they had a baby daughter. After leaving the army he was still a young man, so he migrated to Britain at the same

Yaqub Mirza in 1990, aged 69.

time as many other Mirpuris, settling in Nottingham. He found a job in the Raleigh bicycle factory and lived a long and happy life, turning to writing and translating Urdu poetry in his later years. Although happily married with four children, he never forgot his first love: Isobel from Knock. One night in the late 1960s he saw her mother in a dream, and she asked him why he had never been to see Isobel. Feeling 'fifty years younger', he wrote a letter to Isobel's old address. It came back marked 'Gone away', so he wrote to the village post office, giving his address and phone number. For weeks there was no answer, and then one evening the phone rang:

'Are you Indian?' 'No, I am not, I am a Pakistani.' 'Are you Mr M. Yaqub?' 'Yes, I am speaking.' I interrupted her to know if she was a police-woman. The voice of the caller turned emotional. 'I am Isobel.' No, oh no, I can't believe it. 'Yes dear, it is me, only me.' I eagerly asked her to tell me, 'Are you married? What is your weight? Do you smoke? Do you wear glasses? Are your teeth your own? How many children have you got?' In return she asked me similar questions.

Yaqub also talked to her husband, who told him that he knew their story and was happy for them to meet up. Resham Bee also gave her blessing.

Two weeks later Yaqub took the train to Isobel's hometown, all dressed up in his best and carrying a 'smart black brief-case with gold locks, the executive type'. He had asked Isobel how she would recognise him, and she remembered the 'beauty spot' under his left eye, now hidden by his spectacle rims. The arrangement was clear, but Yaqub was nervous, and he still remembered the snub at Knock station in 1943. Coming off the train he looked around: there was nobody he recognised. He bought some cigarettes to calm his nerves – Rothmans King Size – and then he noticed an anxious woman talking to a railway official. As she walked away, he recognised her back, so he walked after her and caught her hand:

> She looked at my face for my beauty spot. I showed it to her by raising the rim of my glasses. I grabbed hold of her. She dropped her purse on the floor to enforce her grip. She kissed and looked at me, looked and kissed. I held her face in between my hands. She could smile through the tears. I wiped them from her cheeks. But where was her husband? He had picked up the purse from the floor and had been watching a sensational scene of a casualty of war.

They went back to Isobel's house and sat at the table. Yaqub refused to eat any cake until she explained why she hadn't come to see him leave Knock. 'How could I say goodbye to you; Did you want me to cry?' she replied. Yaqub was reassured and happy: the question was answered, the enigma was solved and the wartime scar was healed. He tucked into the cake and they talked of times past. They stayed in touch for many years after that, until Yaqub passed away in 2018.

Another sepoy of humble rank left behind a substantial legacy. This was Nawazish Ali, the poet Quartermaster of 42nd Company, who wrote of the lovers hugging in the streets of Britain. I interviewed his daughter Kalsoom Akhtar at her home near his village of Balesar and was delighted to find that she was a natural storyteller who remembered her late father with enormous affection. She treasured the memories and the material objects that he left behind and was happy to share them with the strange *gora* (white man) with the digital recorder. Towards the end of our time she produced his astrakhan hat, his shoes, photos and then a treasure beyond imagining. This was a book of autobiographical poems, written in Potohari dialect, in Shahmukhi script and mostly in *Si-harfi*, a playful form whereby the poet starts by writing the thirty letters of the Arabic alphabet down the side of the page, and then writes a four-line verse for each letter.[37] Like many Punjabi writers, Nawazish had a *takhallus*, or pen-name. He chose the name Mushtaq, meaning longing or desire, a name that he also gave his son and his shop. The fact that he wrote in Punjabi and Potohari, when he was fluent in Urdu and had some English, indicates that the poems were intended for local consumption. He wanted friends, family and neighbours to read them, he was not interested in a broader South Asian readership, let alone an international one. His five short books of poems are unique as a socio-historical document.

Nawazish clearly had a need to write, perhaps as a way of coping with the boredom and trauma of military life. At one stage, in a light mood, he bemoans the experience of being a soldier far from home, and asks God:

> O Lord! Save us from the Parathas of a foreign land
> and grant us the food of our home.[38]

This is the heartfelt plea of a Punjabi used to good bread, thousands of miles from home. Caught up in a massive conflict, the like of which has never been known before, he responded in verse. Within some of the war-focused verses there is an agony, an anguish that reminds the reader of Wilfred Owen. His fifth book is called *Jangi Safarnama* (War Travel), a harrowing account in couplets of his experience in the Burma campaign of 1944–45, after his return from the UK. Here he describes what he witnessed after a successful attack on the Japanese:

> Dead bodies were in such a bad condition
> I cannot describe the situation.
>
> Some bodies were hanging from the trees
> Some of them had uniforms while some were naked and in pieces.
>
> Some bodies were left like skeletons
> Crows were eating them, it was like Eid for them.

I saw a hole where a bomb had struck
This deep wide hole was filled with corpses.

Allah knows how many dead bodies were there
Maybe a hundred or more.

Dead bodies on top of each other with water as well
They wore uniforms but inside was rotten stinking skin.

There was so much stink that it had no limit
Everyone walked away with a handkerchief on their mouth.

All these dead were Japanese
I saw no dead from my army.[39]

The writer is dumbfounded by the scene, but he finds the ability to write about it, not in great detail, only the surface of the horror. As a human, he is filled with revulsion, but he is also glad that there are no Indian or other Commonwealth dead. Birds feast on the bodies as if it were Eid, the holy festival of sacrifice, and the awful smell has no limit. This scene must have haunted the jemadar for years afterwards, and perhaps writing it down was a way to control the memories. There is an honesty and rawness here in this earthy, personal and passionate account of the life of one sepoy, rare to the point of uniqueness.

As for Abuzar, 'permanent danger to security' and 'traitor' of the Indian Legion, nothing is known of what happened to him after the war. As a relatively young man, in the prime of his life, we can assume that he lived into the second half of the twentieth century. He may have returned to his home village in Jhelum or his cousin's house in Sialkot. Whatever lay behind his decisions may never be known, but it appears he was a smart, capable young soldier, ambitious to get on. On two occasions he was on the horns of a dilemma and chose to switch sides. He rose rapidly up the ranks of 950 Regiment and got further than he probably would have done in the RIASC. According to any traditional view of loyalty, his defection would make him a traitor to the British, but it may also have made him a hero to the nationalists. Perhaps his family and friends in post-war Pakistan saw him in that way, or perhaps he never told the full story. The knowledge has gone from the world, and we can only indulge in guesswork and speculation.

All of which leaves us with the question of loyalty and treachery. Who among these soldiers was the real traitor? In resisting the Germans and remaining loyal to the Crown, were the bulk of the 22nd Company POWs being disloyal to their country that was yet to be? Surely, logically, fighting for the British meant fighting for their enemy? And yet these soldiers had given their oath of allegiance, and however hard the conditions were, this was something not to be broken lightly. This was precisely Anis' predicament, and he found a way through it that was right for him at the time. Yet history makes different judgements. Those who made the choice to fight for the Japanese and the Germans (including a handful of men from Force K6) are remembered in some circles as heroes. Their leader Subhas Chandra Bose is enshrined at the centre of Indian official memory. In the National Archives of India is a large painting that depicts Mother India surrounded by four heroes who helped liberate her: Gandhi, Nehru, Ambedkar and Bose. There are no statues or memorials to those who fought on the side of the British Empire.

* * * * *

In a green field in Bavaria, with a view of *Braunvieh* cattle and the German Alps, I stood by the graves of five sepoys of Force K6 who were laid to rest in 1949. Among the British, Canadian and New Zealander RAF crew, close to black South Africans, Jewish men of the Pioneer Corps and a single Norwegian lieutenant, these five found their final resting place. Their names were typical Punjabi Muslim names: Abdul Aziz, Alif Din, Lall, Sultan Muhammad and Muhammad Zaman. Along with thirty-four other Indian corpses, they were exhumed in 1949 from nearby Bad Tolz and reburied at the Commonwealth War Graves Cemetery just north of Durnbach.[40] The message of this cemetery is the same as that of countless others like it across Europe, Africa, Asia and the Middle East. This is a special place, a place of memory and of commemoration. A place to visit, to sit quietly and to contemplate the meaning of the word 'sacrifice'. These young men were heroes: from across the Commonwealth they came, they answered the call, they fought for our freedom. We should respect them and do them honour, for 'we will remember them'. They are laid out with headstones of identical shape and size in neat parallel rows, and at the centre of the cemetery is a tall cross with the phrase 'their name liveth for ever more'. And they will lie there in perpetuity.[41] That is the discourse of the Durnbach Cemetery.

But these men weren't all young, they weren't all heroes, they didn't all choose to be there. The word 'sacrifice' implies a choice, and some of these men had very little choice. What unifies them, what unites them is something simpler. At some stage they were on the side of the Allies, and they died during the war. The Commonwealth War Graves Commission gives them a common blanket, a way to cover their bodies and a way to see them all, in some way, as the same. This is an honourable pursuit. It becomes all the more poignant at Durnbach as some of those gravestones stand for men who fought for the Germans. Among the list of thirty-nine to be exhumed, three are marked 'Indian Legion'.[42] If this list is correct, then by accident or design, there are some 'traitors' buried there among the 'loyalists'. Thus at Durnbach the traitors and the heroes are buried together: equal in death, equal in commemoration, equally honoured. Because ultimately there were no heroes or traitors, only men and women doing their job, sometimes in pain and anguish, sometimes without having any choice. Ordinary folk in extraordinary times, not wholly bad nor good, but human like you and me.

The best way to remember the men of Force K6 is like that: ordinary men, warts and all, who travelled 7,000 miles to help the Empire and lived alongside Europeans for several years, in a rare and usually happy transnational encounter. A new way of looking at the Second World War is needed: a twenty-first century view. Such a view would transcend nationalism and ideas of 'you were wrong and we were right' and move beyond blame to understanding and true learning. It would acknowledge all contributions, not just those of white men, and it would encompass the full breadth and depth of the conflict. The war was wider than any one of us knows, bigger and stranger and more multifaceted, stretching from the Aleutian Islands to the River Plate, from Mongolia to Morocco. Only a handful of countries were neutral, and all countries were affected. A deeper and wider understanding of the war will benefit all citizens of the world, for this would be more than just a reclamation of colonial contributions, this would be reclaiming all our history.

White Britons will also benefit from an extended view of what the war was like, and step away from 'the tabloid version of the Second World War the world has accepted'.[43] In these days of the 'clash of civilisations' and widespread Islamophobia, we need to be reminded that the King and Queen left the camp at Ashbourne to the shout of '*Allahu Akbar*', that Major Wainwright ordered a copy of the Qur'an and promised to 'treasure it greatly', and that schoolchildren took delight in observing Muslims at prayer. Within a multicultural Britain troubled by racism, the memories of sharing sultanas and playing pranks, of friendships like those between Uncle Gian and the Fosters, can help us see past differences. Paritosh Shapland embodies within him a mixture of Europe and Asia, Cornwall and Punjab, and is happy to be that person, comfortable in his skin. We can all learn from him and his extraordinary story.

The K6 stories have been scattered like shards of a broken pot across British culture – in the office at Waterloo Station, in the *Abergavenny Chronicle* and the *Northern Times*, in the Pathé film archive and the Imperial War Museum, buried in fifty-eight graves. They have waited like smudges of brown on a background of white clay, unrecognised, unconnected, to be identified as pieces of the same pot, and the pot reconstructed. These stories can help to counteract a tendency identified by Raghu Karnad: 'People have two deaths: the first at the end of their lives, when they go away, and the second at the end of the memory of their lives, when all who remember them are gone. Then a person quits the world completely.'[44]

Recent years have seen a correction to the collective memory of the Great War, including a large body of work on the role of the South Asian forces. A similar adjustment for the Second World War is underway. The danger is one of instrumentalisation, that their memory is co-opted for current political use in Britain or South Asia, that their stories are abused. The key to avoiding that trap is to ensure that the complexity and the individuality of these experiences are remembered and honoured. If we can learn to listen carefully to the stories so long ignored, we can restore the voices of men like Yaqub Mirza and Nawazish Ali, who write movingly of their lives. These men were not powerless pawns, neither were the women like Gladys Shapland and Isobel who loved them, or those who helped escapers like Bashir Ud-din Ahmed and Buland Khan. The men of Force K6 – Ashraf, Anis, Akbar, Aurangzeb and all their comrades – have lain without epitaphs until now. The aim of this book is to stand as an epitaph for those 4,227 men, that their stories shall not be forgotten and that their memory shall remain in this world.

Notes

Prologue

1 Yasmin Alibhai, 'Lest We Forget', *New Statesman and Society*, 21 June 1991.
2 Mohammed Akbar Khan, *History of the Army Service Corps Volume III: Royal Indian Army Service Corps* (Karachi: Islamic Military Science Association, 1971), p. 137.
3 'BEF Men Come Home in Thousands: Most May Get Away', *Lincolnshire Echo*, 31 May 1940.

1. Seven thousand miles to help

1 Philip J. Ivanhoe, *The Daodejing of Laozi* (Cambridge, MA: Hackett, 2002), p. 67.
2 Interview with Abdul Mateen, Mohd Akram, Mohd Yunus and Mohd Rafique, 2018.
3 'War Diary, Indian General Hospital, 1939–1943', The National Archives, Kew, London, WO 177/2262.
4 In a telegram to Polish musician and politician Paderewksi on 8 September he wrote 'My whole heart is with the Poles'. M.K. Gandhi, *The Collected Works of Mahatma Gandhi*, Rev. ed. (New Delhi: Ministry of Information and Broadcasting, Publications Division, 2000), vol. 76, p. 314.
5 Gandhi, vol. 76, pp. 433–36.
6 Yasmin Khan, *The Raj at War: A People's History of India's Second World War* (London: Bodley Head, 2015), pp. 221, 38; Tai Yong Tan, *The Garrison State: The Military, Government and Society in Colonial Punjab, 1849–1947* (New Delhi: Sage, 2005), p. 283.
7 Martin S. Alexander, 'Colonial Minds Confounded: French Colonial Troops in the Battle of France 1940', in *The French Colonial Mind: Volume 2: Violence, Military Encounters and Colonialism*, ed. by Martin Thomas (Lincoln, NE: University of Nebraska Press, 2011), pp. 248–82 (p. 256).
8 Quoted in Martin Van Creveld, *Supplying War: Logistics from Wallenstein to Patton*, 2nd edition (Cambridge: Cambridge University Press, 2004), p. 200.

9 Reid Mitchell, 'The GI in Europe and the American Military Tradition', in *Time to Kill: The Soldier's Experience of War in the West*, ed. by Paul Addison and Angus Calder (London: Pimlico, 1997), p. 307.

10 A possible exception to the 'unknown supply troops' might be the 'Red Ball Express' of the US Army in northern France in the summer of 1944, which featured 'a loop system of one-way highways reserved exclusively for the supply service over which thousands of trucks rumbled night and day'. 75 per cent of the drivers were African-American. Van Creveld, p. 220. Another exception is Brecht's *Mother Courage*.

11 J.R.M. Butler, *History of the Second World War, Grand Strategy Volume II September 1939–June 1941* (London: HMSO, 1957), p. 151.

12 Institute of the Royal Army Service Corps, *The Story of the RASC 1939–1945* (London: G. Bell and Sons, 1955), p. 543.

13 Institute of the Royal Army Service Corps, p. 542.

14 Van Creveld, p. 144.

15 Van Creveld, p. 178.

16 André Maurois, *The Battle of France* (London: Bodley Head, 1940), p. 93.

17 'Pack Mules for BEF', 1939, India Office Records at the British Library, IOR/L/WS/1/32.

18 Institute of the Royal Army Service Corps, p. 542.

19 The precise derivation of the title 'K6' is unclear. There was also 'Force K2', 1939, India Office Records at the British Library, IOR/L/WS/1/132; and 'Force K4', 1939, India Office Records at the British Library, IOR/L/WS/1/24. There was also Force K7 – two companies of men from Cyprus, who used Indian mules.

20 'War Diary, 25 Animal Transport Company, Jan–June 1940', p. 25, The National Archives, Kew, London, WO 167/1438.

21 'War Diary, 22 Animal Transport Company, 1940', The National Archives, Kew, London, WO 167/1437; 'War Diary, Reinforcement Unit, Jan–June 1940', The National Archives, Kew, London, WO 167/1435.

22 *RIASC Training Vol III: Transport* (Delhi: Government of India, 1938), p. 127.

23 This information comes from *RIASC Training Vol III: Transport*, also 'War Diary, 22 Animal Transport Company, 1940'; 'War Diary, 25 Animal Transport Company, Jan–June 1940'.

24 Yasmin Khan, *The Raj at War*, p. 18.

25 Yaqub Mirza, *An Autumn Leaf* (Nottingham: Nottinghamshire County Council, 1994), p. 64.

26 Rudyard Kipling, *Barrack-Room Ballads: And Other Verses* (London: Methuen, 1892), p. 23; George Stevens, *Gunga Din* (RKO, 1939).

27 All numbers are from Commanding Officer, 'War Diary, 22 Animal Transport Company', 1940, The National Archives, Kew, London, WO 167/1437; translations from Ian Sumner, *The Indian Army 1914–47* (Oxford: Osprey, 2001), p. 53.

28 Film, 'Interviews on Return, 1944', Imperial War Museum, London, MWY92.

29 R.W.W. Hills (Commanding Officer), 'War Diary, HQ Force K6, 1941', The National Archives, Kew, London, WO 179/5880.

30 Robin Sharp, *The Life of an ECO in India* (Edinburgh: Pentland Press, 1994), p. 23.

31 'Unedited Footage from France' (British Paramount Films, 1940), Imperial War Museum, London, BAY23 1940-01-09.

32 '32 Mule Company RIASC Daily Orders Part II DGIMS', 1941, National Archives of India, DGIMS 8/9/7/1941.

33 Mulk Raj Anand, *Untouchable* (Gurgaon: Penguin, 2001), p. 48.

34 'War Diary, HQ Force K6, 1942', The National Archives, Kew, London, WO 179/5881.

35 'Records of Service of Officers: RWW Hills', 1944, India Office Records at the British Library, IOR/L/MIL/14/19294.

36 'Grant of Permission to Major R.W.W. Hills M.C., I.A.S.C., to Visit Syria and Turkey', 1934, National Archives of India, 335/N.

37 'Force K6 Documents', 1942, India Office Records at the British Library, London, IOR/L/WS/1/355.

38 'AT Companies for France: Force K6', 1942, India Office Records at the British Library, London, IOR/L/WS/1/131.

39 'War Diary, HQ Force K6, Jan–June 1940', The National Archives, Kew, London, WO 167/1433.

40 'War Diary, 32 Animal Transport Company, Jan–June 1940', The National Archives, Kew, London, WO 167/1440.

41 'War Diary, Indian General Hospital, 1939–1943'.

42 'Force K6 Documents', 1942, India Office Records at the British Library, IOR/L/WS/1/355; this story is also found in V.J. Moharir, *History of the Army Service Corps (1939–1946)* (New Delhi: Sterling, 1979), p. 159.

43 'War Diary, 32 Animal Transport Company, Jan–June 1940'.

44 *German Capital Ships and Raiders in World War II. Volume 1: From Graf Spee to Bismarck, 1939–1941* (London: Frank Cass, 2002), p. 17.

45 'War Diary, Indian General Hospital, 1939–1943'.

46 'Papers of Major James English', Imperial War Museum, 18798.

47 'Indian Troops' Trip to France: Account of Voyage', unidentified Indian newspaper, January 1940, Imperial War Museum, 18798.

48 Sepoy Mohd Ashraf in Ilyas Khan, 'A Compilation of Memoirs and Accounts of Service by Native Indian Officers and Ranks in Middle East and North Africa, During World War II (*c* 1941–44)', Sophia Research Institute, Abbottabad, Pakistan.

49 'War Diary, 25 Animal Transport Company, Jan–June 1940'.

50 'War Diary, Reinforcement Unit, Jan–June 1940'.

51 'Indian Troops' Trip to France: Account of Voyage'.

52 'Indian Troops' Trip to France: Account of Voyage'.

53 'War Diary, 47 Supply Depot Section, Jan–June 1940', The National Archives, Kew, London, WO 167/1436.

54 'Indian Troops' Trip to France: Account of Voyage'.

55 'War Diary, Indian General Hospital, 1939–1943'.

56 Raghu Karnad, *Farthest Field: An Indian Story of the Second World War* (Noida, Uttar Pradesh: William Collins, 2015), p. 98.

57 'War Diary, Reinforcement Unit, Jan–June 1940'.

58 'War Diary, Indian General Hospital, 1939–1943'.

59 Mulk Raj Anand, *Across the Black Waters* (New Delhi: Orient, 2008), p. 9.

2. From the Five Rivers

1 A *mahiya* (Punjabi folk poem) from A.B. Rajput, *Social Customs and Practices in Pakistan* (Islamabad: R.C.D. Publications, 1977), p. 45.

2 Roger A. Freeman, *The Mighty Eighth: A History of the Units, Men and Machines of the US 8th Air Force* (London: Cassell, 2000), p. 297.

3 'Report on Operation 350: Mulhouse, Epinal, Belfort and Chaumont Marshalling Yards and Orleans/Bricy Airfield, 11 May (Am)', The National Archives, Kew, London, AIR 40/625.

4 Freeman, p. 140.

5 'Compte Rendu Bombardements', 1944, Archives Départmentales des Vosges, Epinal, 16 W 17.

6 'Bombardement d'Épinal en Mai 44: Liste des Tués et Blessés', Archives Départmentales des Vosges, Epinal, 5 W 1.

7 'Operation 350'.

8 'Frontstalag 315 Epinal', 1944, The National Archives, Kew, London, WO 224/61.

9 'Commonwealth War Graves Commission' <https://www.cwgc.org/> [accessed 8 October 2019].

10 Interview with Nazar Hussain, Abdul Ghafour, Ghulam Rasul, Allah Yar Hussain and Ghulam Abbas Mumtaz, 2018; *Imperial Gazetteer of India:*

Provincial Series: Punjab 1908 (Lahore: Government of Pakistan, 1998), p. 168.

11 Bapsi Sidhwa, *Ice-Candy-Man* (Delhi: Penguin, 1988), p. 108.

12 The information for this section comes from Balwant Singh Saini, *The Social and Economic History of the Punjab 1901–1939: (Including Haryana and Himachal Pradesh)* (Delhi: Ess Ess Publications, 1975); Bernard S. Cohn, *India: The Social Anthropology of a Civilisation* (Englewood Cliffs, NJ: Prentice-Hall, 1971); Government of Punjab, *Rawalpindi District Gazetteer 1907* (Lahore: Government of Punjab, 1907); Rajput; *Imperial Gazetteer*.

13 Rajit K. Mazumder, *The Indian Army and the Making of Punjab* (Delhi: Orient Blackswan, 2003), p. 27.

14 *Imperial Gazetteer*, p. 70.

15 Rajput, p. 61.

16 Cohn, p. 120.

17 Waris Shah, *The Adventures of Hir and Ranjha* (Karachi: Lion Art Press, 1966), p. 37.

18 Mulk Raj Anand, *Folk Tales of Punjab* (Delhi: Sterling, 1989), p. 6.

19 Mirza, p. 21.

20 Drawing on a documentary film about Pindi, *An Eastern Market* (British Instructional Films, 1928), British Film Institute <https://www.youtube.com/watch?v=6aLDcOPTLjw> [accessed 24 February 2020].

21 Rajput, p. 14.

22 Rajput, p. 43.

23 Saini, p. 18.

24 Tan.

25 David E. Omissi, *The Sepoy and the Raj: The Indian Army, 1860–1940* (Basingstoke: Macmillan, 1998), p. xviii.

26 George Morton-Jack, *The Indian Empire at War: From Jihad to Victory, the Untold Story of the Indian Army in the First World War* (London: Little, Brown, 2018), pp. 3, 517.

27 John Keay, *India: A History* (London: Harper Perennial, 2000), p. 476.

28 Omissi, p. 59.

29 Omissi, pp. 53–59.

30 Srinath Raghavan, *India's War: The Making of Modern South Asia, 1939–1945* (London: Penguin, 2016), p. 1.

31 Raghavan, p. 37; Ashley Jackson, *The British Empire and the Second World War* (London: Bloomsbury, 2006), p. 363.

32 Winston Churchill, *The Second World War. Volume IV: The Hinge of Fate* (London: Weidenfeld and Nicolson, 2015), p. 175.

33 Markus Daechsel, 'Military Islamisation in Pakistan and the Spectre of Colonial Perceptions', *Contemporary South Asia*, 6.2 (1997), 141–60 (p. 146).
34 Karnad, p. 259.
35 Philip Mason, *A Matter of Honour: An Account of the Indian Army, its Officers and Men* (London: Jonathan Cape, 1974), p. 349.
36 George MacMunn, *The Martial Races of India* (London: Sampson Low, Marston, 1932), p. 1.
37 Interview with Syed Ali Hamid, 2018.
38 Mason, p. 512; Omissi, p. 43.
39 Interview with Hussain, Ghafour, Rasul, Hussain and Mumtaz.
40 Rajput, p. 49.
41 Jackson, p. 363.
42 Mason, p. 319.
43 Interview with Hussain, Ghafour, Rasul, Hussain and Mumtaz.
44 'Nominees from UK to Enter Training School at Indore', 1919, India Office Records at the British Library, IOR/L/MIL/7/19036.
45 Gautam Sharma, *Nationalisation of the Indian Army, 1885–1947* (India: Allied, 1996), p. 215; 'Temporary Indian Army Commissions; Selection of Candidates for Training at Indore', 1919, India Office Records at the British Library, IOR/L/MIL/7/19014.
46 'Indore Cadets 1918–19', India Office Records at the British Library, IOR/L/MIL/7/19018.
47 'RAMS Cadets Ledger', 1917, Royal Military Academy Sandhurst, WO 151 Volume 9.
48 Interview with Zeenut Ziad, 2018.
49 Alan Shepperd, *Sandhurst: The Royal Military Academy* (London: Country Life, 1980), p. 141.
50 *No 5 Company at Royal Military College Sandhurst*, 1923, Royal Military Academy Sandhurst, 77/806.
51 John Masters, *Bugles and a Tiger* (London: Michael Joseph, 1956), p. 55.
52 Mohammed Ayub Khan, *Friends Not Masters: A Political Autobiography* (London: Oxford University Press, 1967), p. 10.
53 Masters, p. 42.
54 'Indian Contingent. Includes Material Relating to Lovat Scouts', 1943, The National Archives, Kew, London, WO 199/917.
55 Yasmin Khan, *The Raj at War*, p. 72.
56 G.J. Douds, 'The Men Who Never Were: Indian POWs in the Second World War', *South Asia: Journal of South Asian Studies*, 27.2 (2004), 183–216 (p. 199).

57 Kaushik Roy, 'Military Loyalty in the Colonial Context: A Case Study of the Indian Army during World War II', *Journal of Military History*, 73.2 (2009), 497–529 (p. 511), quoting Kusum Nair.

58 Letter from Billcliffe to Darling in 'Indian Talks', 1943, BBC Written Archives Caversham, Reading, R51/257/1.

3. Fony Vaar

1 André Maurois, *Les Silences du Colonel Bramble* (Paris: Bernard Gresset, 1921), p. 49.

2 'Ek Jang-Azmuda Afsar', *Wilayati Akhbar Haftawar* (London, 18 May 1940), p. 2, Imperial War Museum, E6705.

3 Interview with Abdul Jalil, 2018.

4 'War Diary, HQ Force K6, Jan–June 1940'.

5 'Force K6 Documents'.

6 Mason, p. 412.

7 *Film: Indian Troops in France* (Pathé, 1940) <http://www.britishpathe.com/video/indian-troops-in-france-1> [accessed 24 February 2020].

8 'Force K6 Documents'.

9 'War Diary, Advanced Remount Depot Jan–June 1940', The National Archives, Kew, London, WO 167/1434.

10 'Papers of Major James English'.

11 'War Diary, Reinforcement Unit, Jan–June 1940'.

12 Commanding Officer, 'War Diary, 25 Animal Transport Company', 1940, The National Archives, Kew, London, WO 167/1438.

13 'War Diary, Reinforcement Unit, Jan–June 1940'.

14 Commanding Officer, 'War Diary, 25 Animal Transport Company, June–Dec 1940', 1940, The National Archives, Kew, London, WO 179/5906.

15 'War Diary, 47 Supply Depot Section, Jan–June 1940'.

16 Omer Tarin, 'Fony Vaar', 20 March 2018.

17 'An Unexpected Answer', *Fauji Akhbar*, 10 February 1940, Imperial War Museum.

18 S.W. Roskill, *The Navy at War* (London: Collins, 1960), pp. 53–56.

19 Basil Liddell Hart, *A History of the Second World War* (Basingstoke: Pan Macmillan, 1970), p. 41.

20 John Prendergast, *Prender's Progress: A Soldier in India, 1931–1947* (London: Cassell, 1979), p. 114.

21 'Force K6 Documents'.

22 'War Diary, HQ Force K6, Jan–June 1940'.

23 'War Diary, 29 Animal Transport Company, Jan–June 1940', The National Archives, Kew, London, WO 167/1439.

24 'War Diary, 32 Animal Transport Company, Jan–June 1940'.

25 'War Diary, HQ Force K6, Jan–June 1940'.

26 Interview with Zubair Mohammed, 2015.

27 Kessell, *A Contingent of Indian Soldiers Who Were Quartered in Huts Somewhere in France*, 1940, Imperial War Museum, F2345-F2352.

28 'Cartoon: "Je Fais un Pullover pour ma Femme, Elle a Pas le Temps … Elle Fait les Obus"', *Echo du Nord* (Lille, 8 February 1940), Archives Départmentales du Nord, Lille.

29 Nicholas Harman, *Dunkirk: The Necessary Myth* (London: Hodder & Stoughton, 1980), p. 71.

30 Mohammed Akbar Khan, *The History of the Army Service Corps*, pp. 133–35.

31 Puttnam, *Gas Masks*, 1940, Imperial War Museum, London, F2672. Len Puttnam photographed K6 many times, and went on to cover El Alamein. His son David became a film producer, most famously for *Chariots of Fire*.

32 'Une Visite au Premier Contingent de Troupes Hindoues Arrivé en France', *Echo du Nord* (Lille, 13 January 1940), p. 2, Archives Départmentales du Nord, Lille.

33 'War Diary, 22 Animal Transport Company, 1940'.

34 'War Diary, Indian General Hospital, 1939–1943'.

35 'Force K6 Documents', p. 6.

36 'War Diary, HQ Force K6, Jan–June 1940'.

37 'War Diary, HQ Force K6, Jan–June 1940'.

38 *Mr Oliver Stanley, Secretary of State for War, With BEF in France*, 1940, Imperial War Museum, BDY 31/3; Puttnam and Davies, *Visit of the Secretary of State War to BEF*, 1940, Imperial War Museum, F2613-2621.

39 Moharir, p. 161.

40 'Took Indian Unit to France', *Burnley Express & News*, 2 March 1940.

41 Philip Gibbs, 'Splendid Work of Indian Contingent', *Times of India*, 20 February 1940.

42 'War Diary, HQ Force K6, Jan–June 1940'.

43 Moharir, p. 162.

44 André Maurois, *Call No Man Happy* (London: Jonathan Cape, 1950), p. 116.

45 'François Michel de Champeaux', Service Historique de la Défense, Vincennes, GR 8YE 140204.

46 'Possibilités de Cantonnement des Troupes Françaises et Anglaises (Avant L'invasion 1940)', Archives Départmentales du Nord, Lille, 1 W 1100.

47 Mohammed Akbar Khan, *History of the Army Service Corps*, p. 152.

48 'The Indian Troops in France', *Illustrated London News*, January 1940; Kenneth Hord, 'Nothing Can Shake the Loyalty of Our Indian Troops', *Daily Mirror*, 28 July 1941.

49 Government of India, *Scales of Rations and Supplies Issued by the R.I.A.S.C.* (Delhi: Government of India, 1941), p. 81.

50 'Une Visite au Premier Contingent de Troupes Hindoues Arrivé en France'.

51 Major Finlay reported in December 1940 that twenty live sheep were enough for six days for 180 men, in 'War Diary, HQ Force K6, June–December 1940', The National Archives, Kew, London, WO 179/5879.

52 E.M. Collingham, *The Taste of War: World War Two and the Battle for Food* (London: Penguin, 2012), p. 366.

53 The origin of many common English-language military words lies in India, showing the important role that India played within the British military. 'Khaki' means soil or soil-coloured. 'Puttee' is derived from the Sanskrit word for a strip of cloth. David Crystal, *The Cambridge Encyclopaedia of the English Language*, 2nd edition (Cambridge: Cambridge University Press, 2003), p. 126.

54 Waris Shah, *Hir and Ranjha*, p. 56.

55 This tradition of military peacocks continues in both the Pakistan and Indian armies, and there is a daily display of their aggression and beauty on the Radcliffe Line that splits Punjab, at the Wagah border crossing. *The Longest Road* (BBC2, 2009) <https://www.youtube.com/watch?v=LZ0ue-XGl9c> [accessed 24 February 2020].

56 Commanding Officer, 'War Diary, 25 Animal Transport Company, Jan–June 1940

57 D.S. Virk, *Indian Army Post Offices in the Second World War* (New Delhi: Army Postal Service Association, 1982), p. 195.

58 Interview with Najm us Saqib and Ghulam Nabi, 2018.

59 Letter from Hills to Ikbal Ali Shah, January 1940, in 'War Diary, HQ Force K6, Jan–June 1940'.

60 'Sirdar Ikbal Ali Shah', Open University Making Britain <http://www.open.ac.uk/researchprojects/makingbritain/content/sirdar-ikbal-ali-shah> [accessed 18 October 2019]. His son was the famous Sufi writer Idries Shah.

61 'War Diary, HQ Force K6, Jan–June 1940'.

62 'The Indian Soldier in the Expeditionary Hospitals …', *Fauji Akhbar*, 2 March 1940.

63 R.W.W. Hills (Commanding Officer), 'War Diary, HQ Force K6'.

64 'Medal Card of Gooneratne, C Corps: Young Men's Christian Association', 1920, The National Archives, Kew, London, WO 372/8/66779.

65 Elizabeth Station, 'Scholar from Afar', *University of Chicago Magazine*, 2013 <https://mag.uchicago.edu/scholarfromafar> [accessed 2 August 2019].

66 Michel Renard, 'Les Débuts de la Présence Musulmane en France et Son Encadrement', in *Histoire de l'Islam et des Musulmans en France du Moyen Âge à Nos Jours*, ed. by Mohammed Arkoun (Paris: Albin Michel, 2006), pp. 712–40 (p. 718).

67 Mohammed Akbar Khan, 'A Letter from France', *Fauji Akhbar*, 6 April 1940, Imperial War Museum.

68 *Who Was Who* (London: A&C Black, 1980), VII, p. 262.

69 Nun Feroz Khan and Michael Lloyd Ferrar, 'Janab High Commissioner Sahib Ka Khat', *Wilayati Akhbar Haftawar* (London, 20 April 1940), p. 2, Imperial War Museum, E6705.

70 'Shahzadi Elizabeth', *Wilayati Akhbar Haftawar* (London, 27 April 1940), p. 1, Imperial War Museum, E6705.

71 Abdul Majid, 'Imam Sahib Woking Ka Maqala', *Wilayati Akhbar Haftawar*, 11 May 1940, Imperial War Museum, E6705.

72 *The Qur'an*, trans. by Alan Jones (Exeter: Gibb Memorial Trust, 2007), p. 319 verse 96.

73 Gajendra Singh, *The Testimonies of Indian Soldiers and the Two World Wars: Between Self and Sepoy* (London: Bloomsbury, 2014), p. 104.

74 Wilhelm Doegen, *Kriegsgefangene Völker* (Berlin: Verlag für Politik and Wirtschaft, 1921).

75 'Rundfunkpolitische Abteilung', trans. by Fiona Schroeder, 1945, Bundes-archiv, Germany, R 901/48007.

76 Mohammed Akbar Khan, 'A Letter from France to Probyn's Horse', *Fauji Akhbar*, 27 April 1940, Imperial War Museum.

77 Mallindine, *Punjabi Dancers. In Their Hands They Carry a Kind of Castanet Consisting of Pieces of Wood with Bells on*, 1940, Imperial War Museum, London, F3923. I am grateful to Professor Jerri Daboo for confirming the exact nature of the dance.

78 Amir Khusrau, *Amir Khusrau: The Man in Riddles*, ed. by Ankit Chadha (Gurgaon: Penguin, 2016), p. 13.

79 'Indian Troops Visit London', *Morning Advertiser* (London, 7 May 1940).

80 'Force K6 Documents'.

81 Unknown, *Akbar and Others Meet a Gentleman and his Dog in St James Park*, 1940, Imran Collection.

82 'Indian Officers Entertained', *Times of India*, 5 October 1940.

4. Blitzkrieg

1 William L. Shirer, *Berlin Diary 1934–1941: The Rise of the Third Reich* (London: Sunburst Books, 1997), p. 152.
2 Shirer, p. 155.
3 Rajput, p. 31.
4 Mohammed Akbar Khan, *History of the Army Service Corps*, p. 162.
5 Harman, p. 110.
6 Shirer, p. 168.
7 'War Diary, 13/18 Royal Hussars, Sept 1939–June 1940', The National Archives, Kew, London, WO 167/453.
8 'Commonwealth War Graves Commission'.
9 Hellmuth Ellgard, 'Der Dritte Is Nach Hause Geflogen!', *Signal*, 10 September 1940, pp. 15–19, Bundesarchiv, Germany.
10 'War Diary, HQ Force K6, Jan–June 1940'.
11 Rob Brown, 'Loyal Soldier's Poignant Visit to War Camp', *Woking News and Mail*, 25 October 2007 <https://www.getsurrey.co.uk/news/local-news/loyal-soldiers-poignant-visit-war-4832562> [accessed 1 February 2020].
12 'War Diary, 25 Animal Transport Company, Jan–June 1940'.
13 'Recommendation for Award for Sher Mohd', 1940, The National Archives, Kew, London, WO 373/89.
14 Brown.
15 'War Diary, HQ Force K6, Jan–June 1940'.
16 Patrick Wintour, 'Ashdown Tells how Father Stood by Indian Troops', *Guardian*, 8 November 2000 <https://www.theguardian.com/uk/2000/nov/08/patrickwintour> [accessed 26 February 2018].
17 '1 AT Driver Trg Regt Jallandhar Cantt', 1941, National Archives of India, Misc/4460/H.
18 'Force K6 Documents'.
19 There are two main sources for the 25th Company story, which do not always agree. The first is Mohammed Akbar Khan, *History of the Army Service Corps* As the war diary was written in the summer of 1940, I have tended to draw the facts from 'War Diary, 25 Animal Transport Company, Jan–June 1940'.
20 'War Diary, 25 Animal Transport Company, Jan–June 1940'.
21 Harman, p. 161.
22 Mohammed Akbar Khan, *History of the Army Service Corps*, p. 179.
23 'War Diary, 25 Animal Transport Company, Jan–June 1940'.

24 This is the address of Nizam Din as given in 'List of K6 Soldiers Addresses', 1940, Betty Cresswell collection. There were two Nizam Dins listed in 25th Company, this could be the address for either, as the rank is not given.

25 'Recommendation for Award for Nizam Din', 1940, The National Archives, Kew, London, WO 373/89/851.

26 E.W.B. Berry, 'Dunkirk – Carrier Platoon, 8th Battalion Worcestershire Regiment' <http://www.worcestershireregiment.com/wr.php?main=inc/h_dunkirk_8thBn_carrierPl> [accessed 24 July 2019].

27 'War Diary, 25 Animal Transport Company, Jan–June 1940'.

28 Mohammed Akbar Khan, *History of the Army Service Corps*, pp. 171, 172.

29 Wainwright was commissioned into the Queen Victoria Corps of Guides in 1916, in 'John Gordon Wainwright, Personal File', India Office Records at the British Library, IOR/L/MIL/14/3057; Roland Noel Pearson Cole had been an officer initially in the Royal Ulster Rifles in 1922, according to *Indian Army Lists, October 1939*, India Office Records at the British Library.

30 'War Diary, 25 Animal Transport Company, Jan–June 1940'.

31 Harman, p. 143.

32 Christopher Nolan, *Dunkirk* (Warner Bros, 2017).

33 W.H.R. Gardner, *The Evacuation from Dunkirk* (London: Frank Cass, 2000), p. 54.

34 Mohammed Akbar Khan, *History of the Army Service Corps*, p. 177.

35 Harman, p. 154.

36 For example John Masefield, *The Nine Days Wonder* (Kingswood: Windmill Press, 1941); Penny Summerfield, 'Dunkirk and the Popular Memory of Britain at War', *Journal of Contemporary History*, 45.4 (2010), 788–811; Joshua Levine, *Forgotten Voices of Dunkirk* (London: Ebury Press, 2010).

37 Christopher Nolan, 'Spitfires, Flotillas of Boats, Rough Seas and 1,000 Extras: Christopher Nolan on the Making of Dunkirk, his Most Challenging Film to Date', *Daily Telegraph*, 8 July 2017 <http://www.telegraph.co.uk/films/2017/07/08/spitfires-flotillas-boats-rough-seas-1000-extras-christopher/> [accessed 24 February 2020].

38 Henri Verneuil, *Weekend at Zuydcoote* (Pathé Consortium Cinéma, 20th Century Fox, 1964).

39 Hugh Sebag-Montefiore, *Dunkirk: Fight to the Last Man* (London: Penguin, 2007), p. 483.

40 Arthur Bryant, *The Turn of the Tide 1939–1943: A Study Based on the Diaries and Autobiographical Notes of Field Marshal the Viscount Alanbrooke* (London: Grafton, 1986), p. 172.

41 'War Diary, Indian General Hospital, 1939–1943'.

42 Except where noted, all this information is from 'War Diary, 47 Supply Depot Section, Jan–June 1940'.

43 'Service Record for John Finlay', India Office Records at the British Library, IOR/L/MIL/14/1112.

44 'War Diary, HQ Force K6, Jan–June 1940'.

45 'War Diary, 47 Supply Depot Section, Jan–June 1940'.

46 'War Diary, 47 Supply Depot Section, Jan–June 1940'.

47 Reuben Goossens, 'RMS Strathaird' <https://ssmaritime.com/strathaird. htm> [accessed 24 October 2019].

48 Yasmin Khan, *The Raj at War*, pp. 47–49.

49 Rozina Visram, *Asians in Britain: 400 Years of History* (London: Pluto, 2002), p. 225.

50 'War Diary, 47 Supply Depot Section, Jan–June 1940'.

51 Goossens.

52 'War Diary, 47 Supply Depot Section, Jan–June 1940'.

53 Information for the march comes from 'War Diary, Reinforcement Unit, Jan–June 1940'; 'War Diary, HQ Force K6, Jan–June 1940'; 'War Diary, 29 Animal Transport Company, Jan–June 1940'; 'War Diary, Advanced Remount Depot Jan–June 1940'.

54 Marc Bloch, *Strange Defeat* (USA: Important, 2013), p. 43.

55 'War Diary, 29 Animal Transport Company, Jan–June 1940'.

56 'War Diary, HQ Force K6, 1942'.

57 Sebag-Montefiore, p. 496.

58 Max Arthur, *Forgotten Voices of the Second World War* (London: Index, 2008), p. 71.

59 'HMT Cambridgeshire in Rescue of Survivors from SS Lancastria during Evacuation from France', The National Archives, Kew, London, ADM 1/12264.

60 Philip Malins, 'The First to Take the Field', *Army Service Corps Journal* (1995), p. 3.

61 Alan Francis Brooke Alanbrooke, *War Diaries, 1939–1945*, ed. by Alex Danchev and Daniel Todman (London: Weidenfeld and Nicolson, 2001), p. 108.

62 David Low, *Very Well, Alone!*, British Cartoon Archive, LSE2791 <https:// archive.cartoons.ac.uk/record.aspx?src=CalmView.Catalog&id=LSE2791> [accessed 20 March 2018].

63 Kenneth Bird aka Fougasse, *So Our Poor Old Empire Is Alone in the World*, 1940, Punch online <https://punch.photoshelter.com/image/ I00004lS91fhaQno> [accessed 20 March 2018].

5. Mules by the Maginot and the march up the Moselle

1 Decimus Magnus Ausonius, *Moselle, Epigrams, and Other Poems*, trans. by Deborah Warren (London: Routledge, Taylor and Francis Group, 2017), p. 28.
2 '950 Regiment (Free Indian Legion) of the Wehrmacht: History and Interrogation of Former Members', 1945, The National Archives, Kew, London, WO 106/5881.
3 Interview with Colin Hexley, Shirley Sutherland, John Melville and Robert Beaton, 2016.
4 'Individual Service Record for TWP Hexley', India Office Records at the British Library/Private Collection, IOR/L/MIL/14/4661.
5 Hexley, 'T.W.P. Hexley Photo Album', Hexley collection.
6 'Individual Service Record for TWP Hexley'.
7 Hexley, 'Photo Album'.
8 'War Diary, 22 Animal Transport Company, 1940'.
9 Liddell Hart, p. 306.
10 Alfred Cobban, *A History of Modern France. Volume 3: 1871–1962* (Harmondsworth: Penguin, 1965), p. 175.
11 Saul David, *Churchill's Sacrifice of the Highland Division* (London: Brassey's, 1994), p. 13.
12 Patrick Delaforce, *Monty's Highlanders: 51st Highland Division in the Second World War* (Barnsley: Pen and Sword, 2006).
13 David, p. 12.
14 'General Headquarters: Senior Veterinary Officer, Dec 39–June 1940', The National Archives, Kew, London, WO 167/49.
15 'Force K6 Documents'.
16 Jack Sherratt, 'Letter from J.R. Sherratt of Stoke on Trent', 7 May 2002, private collection of Paritosh Shapland.
17 David, p. 26.
18 T.W.P. Hexley, 'Movements of No 22 Animal Transport Company (M) from Approximately 20th May 1940 to 25th June 1940', p. 1, Hexley collection.
19 'General Headquarters: Senior Veterinary Officer, Dec 39–June 1940'.
20 The only source for the following paragraphs is Hexley's sixty-three-page account. This detailed and fascinating document is well written and always clear, with insights into Indian Army life, as well as the first months after the Fall of France. It contains praise for specific members of 22nd Company, and is an unusual and precious document. It must have been written soon after his return to the UK, in summer 1941, or possibly on board HMS *London*.

I am very grateful for Colin Hexley for presenting me with a copy. T.W.P. Hexley.

21 'Individual Service Record for Lawrence William Hitchcock', 1920, India Office Records at the British Library, IOR/L/MIL/14/1513.

22 T.W.P. Hexley, p. 2.

23 Henry Collier Renny Laslett was the son of a Riga timber merchant. He was Mentioned in Dispatches for his work before the surrender. After the war he worked in the motor trade until he died in a car crash in 1959. 'Recommendation for Award for Henry Laslett', 1940, The National Archives, Kew, London, WO 373/89.

24 Interview with Zeenut Ziad.

25 Butler, *History of the Second World War, Grand Strategy Volume II: September 1939–June 41*, pp. 114, 182.

26 Hansard, *House of Commons Debate*, 18 June 1940, vol. 362, cols 51–64', 1940, p. 18 <https://api.parliament.uk/historic-hansard/commons/1940/jun/18/war-situation> [accessed 24 February 2020].

27 T.W.P. Hexley, p. 10.

28 Laurence William Hitchcock, 'In German Hands', *RIASC Journal*, 14 (1946), 8–17.

29 'Convention (III) Relative to the Treatment of Prisoners of War. Geneva, 12 August 1949', International Committee of the Red Cross <https://ihl-databases.icrc.org/applic/ihl/ihl.nsf/INTRO/375> [accessed 11 June 2019].

30 'Indian Prisoners of War in Germany, Italy and East Africa: With Details of Individual Prisoners', 1941, The National Archives, Kew, London, FO 916/52.

31 'OKW Kriegsgefangene Sammelmitteilungen', 1941, Bundesarchiv, Germany, RW 6/270.

32 Martin Bamber, *For Free India: Indian Soldiers in Germany and Italy during the Second World War*, ed. by Aad Neeven (Oosthuizen: Oskam-Neeven, 2010), p. 40.

33 Raffael Scheck, *Hitler's African Victims: The German Army Massacres of Black French Soldiers in 1940* (Cambridge: Cambridge University Press, 2008), p. 27. A memorial to Captain N'Tchorere was erected after the war.

34 Yves Le Maner, 'L'invasion et les Combats de Mai–Juin 1940 dans le Nord de la France', *MEMOR (Mémoire de l'Occupation et de la Resistance en Zone Interdite) Bulletin D'Information*, 19–20 (1994), 13–30 (p. 26).

35 'Die Ersten Farbfotos von Der Grossen Schlacht Im Westen', *Signal*, 1 July 1940, Bundesarchiv, Germany.

36 David Motadel, *Islam and Nazi Germany's War* (Cambridge, MA: Belknap Press of Harvard University Press, 2014), p. 15.

37 Motadel, p. 219.

38 Heinz Guderian, *Panzer Leader* (Aylesbury: Futura, 1974), p. 134.

39 Hexley album.

6. Back in Blighty

1 Miranda, in *The Tempest*. William Shakespeare, *The New Oxford Shakespeare: The Complete Works* (Oxford: Oxford University Press, 2017), II.

2 'Papers of Major James English'.

3 'Personal Record for James English', 1927, India Office Records at the British Library, IOR/L/MIL/14/4461.

4 The English slang word 'blighty' (meaning home or Britain) actually comes from the Urdu word *wilayati* (abroad) derived from the Arabic *wilaya* meaning 'province'. 'Oxford English Dictionary Online' <https://www.oed.com> [accessed 15 November 2019].

5 Sonya Rose, *Which People's War? National Identity and Citizenship in Britain 1939–1945* (Oxford: Oxford University Press, 2003).

6 It is worth recording that nearly one in five RAF pilots in the Battle of Britain were from the Commonwealth or occupied Europe. Richard Overy, *The Battle of Britain* (London: Penguin, 2000), p. 39. At this stage there were no Indian pilots – twenty-four of them arrived in September, six becoming fighter pilots. Florian Stadtler, 'Britain's Forgotten Volunteers', in *South Asians and the Shaping of Britain, 1870–1950: A Sourcebook*, ed. by Ruvani Ranasinha (Manchester: Manchester University Press, 2013), pp. 81–134 (p. 95).

7 'Indian Army Officers Casualty Returns', 1939, India Office Records at the British Library, IOR/L/MIL/14/1513. Thompson was the son of an artist, graduating from Sandhurst in 1931 and serving initially with the Scinde Horse. In 2006 his cavalry sword was donated to the National Army Museum.

8 'Commonwealth War Graves Commission'.

9 *Speak for Yourself: A Mass-Observation Anthology 1937–1945*, ed. by Angus Calder and Dorothy Sheridan (Oxford: Oxford University Press, 1985), p. 113.

10 Rose, p. 29.

11 Pat Kirkham and David Thoms, eds, *War Culture: Social Change and Changing Experience in World War Two* (London: Lawrence & Wishart, 1995), p. ix.

12 Leo Amery, 'Leopold Amery's Diary for 1940', Churchill Archive, Cambridge, England, AMEL 7/34.

13 K. Humayun Ansari, 'The Woking Mosque: A Case Study of Muslim Engagement with British Society since 1889', *Immigrants & Minorities*, 21.3 (2002), 1–24 (p. 1).

14 Purwez Salamat, *The Woking Shahjahan Mosque* (Chichester: Phillimore, 2008), p. 57.

15 'Indian Muslim Soldiers at the Shah Jehan Mosque, Woking', *Islamic Review* (1940), 362–64. The mosque was named after the ruler of Bhopal, who paid for its construction.

16 Brown.

17 J.G. Wainwright, 'Letter from Major Wainwright', *Islamic Review* (1941), 157.

18 'War Diary, 25 Animal Transport Company, June–December 1940', The National Archives, Kew, London, WO 179/5906.

19 'Force K6 Documents'.

20 John Adam, *A History of Rossington* (Doncaster: Rossington History Group, 2008), p. 84.

21 'War Diary, 29 Animal Transport Company, June–December 1940', The National Archives, Kew, London, WO 179/5910.

22 Adam, p. 84.

23 E.P., 'A Colourful Glimpse of the Orient in Yorkshire: Young and Old Punjabi Warriors Meet a "Great English Sahib"', *Doncaster Chronicle*, 8 August 1940.

24 Interview with Betty Cresswell, 2016.

25 'Question of the Grant of Honours to Certain Members of the Indian Contingent in Europe', 1941, National Archives of India, 18(5) - H/41.

26 'MBE for Gian Kapur', *London Gazette* (London, 6 December 1941), p. 3295.

27 Interview with Betty Cresswell.

28 'Letter from Gian Kapur to Herbert Foster', 13 December 1980, Betty Cresswell collection.

29 'King and Queen with Indian Troops', 1940 <https://www.youtube.com/watch?v=gfVvd9uZHNc> [accessed 24 February 2020]; 'The King and Queen in the Midlands', *The Times*, 8 September 1940; 'Their Majesties the King and Queen …', *Fauji Akhbar*, 3 August 1940, Imperial War Museum.

30 'Papers of Major James English'.

31 Pathé, 'Indian Army Special Newsreel (1940)', 1940 <https://www.youtube.com/watch?v=yq6E1luxLQQ&t=> [accessed 25 May 2017].

32 'Indian Soldiers Aid Fete', *Derby Evening Telegraph*, 22 August 1940.

33 'Indian Camp an Ornamental Wonder', *Ashbourne Telegraph*, September 1940.

34 'AT Companies for France: Force K6', 1942, India Office Records at the British Library, IOR/L/WS/1/131.

35 'Girl Works in Flax amid Singing Indian Soldiers', *Daily Mirror*, 15 October 1940, p. 12.

36 'War Diary, Reinforcement Unit, June–December 1940', The National Archives, Kew, London, WO 179/5883.

37 Rosemary Spencer, personal communication, 2016.

38 Interview with Doreen Allsop, 2016.

39 Gerry Williams to Ghee Bowman 2nd May 2015.

40 'Commonwealth War Graves Commission'; Barbara Hollands, 'Letter from Barbara Hollands of Ashbourne', June 2015.

41 'Force K6 Documents'.

42 'War Diary, HQ Force K6, June–December 1940'.

43 'War Diary, HQ Force K6, June–December 1940'.

44 Mohammed Akbar Khan, 'Stonehenge', trans. by Musarat Asif, *Wilayati Akhbar Haftawar*, 28 March 1941, Imperial War Museum.

45 'War Diary, 29 Animal Transport Company, 1941', The National Archives, Kew, London, WO 179/5911; 'War Diary, 32 Animal Transport Company, 1941', The National Archives, Kew, London, WO 179/5915.

46 'War Diary, HQ Force K6, June–December 1940'.

47 'RIASC Men's Impressions of England', *Fauji Akhbar*, 26 February 1944, p. 20, Imperial War Museum.

48 'War Diary, 25 Animal Transport Company, 1941', The National Archives, Kew, London, WO 179/5907; Mallindine, *A Number of Indian Officers Now in this Country are Seen Inspecting Coast Defences in the Southern Command*, 1940, Imperial War Museum, H5764.

49 'War Diary, 42 Animal Transport Company, 1942', The National Archives, Kew, London, WO 179/5919.

50 'Greatest of Honours', *Western Morning News*, 16 November 1940; 'Far from Home', *Daily Record and Mail*, 7 August 1940.

51 'War Diary, Indian General Hospital, 1939–1943'.

52 'War Diary, 25 Animal Transport Company, 1941'.

53 'Force K6 Documents'.

54 'War Diary, 47 Supply Depot Section, 1941', The National Archives, Kew, London, WO 179/5892.

55 'War Diary, Indian General Hospital, 1939–1943'.

56 'War Diary, Advanced Remount Depot, 1941', The National Archives, Kew, London, WO 179/5888.

57 Guy Walters, *Berlin Games: How Hitler Stole the Olympic Dream* (London: John Murray, 2006), p. 295.

58 Hord, 'Nothing Can Shake the Loyalty of our Indian Troops'.

59 Email from Patrick Caseley to Ghee Bowman, 18 August 2017.

60 Visram, p. 254. There are three sources given by Visram on this page, with widely varying estimates.

61 'Directives June 1943', 1943, Mass-Observation archives at the Keep, Sussex University, SxMOA1/3/68.

62 Wendy Webster, *Mixing It: Diversity in World War Two Britain* (Oxford: Oxford University Press, 2018), p. 120; Shompa Lahiri, 'Divided Loyalties', *History Today*, 57.5 (2007), 55–57.

63 'War Diary, 80 Pioneer Coy, 1942', The National Archives, Kew, London, WO 166/9980.

64 'Suresh Vaidya', 1943, India Office Records at the British Library, IOR L/PJ/12/478.

65 E.H. Rhodes-Wood, *A War History of the Royal Pioneer Corps, 1939–1945* (Aldershot: Gale and Polden, 1960), pp. 61–62.

66 'Pte Jan Salah-Ud-Din', India Office Records at the British Library, IOR L/PJ/7/4678.

67 *Indian Comforts Fund: Progress Report Oct 41–March 42*, 1942, India Office Records at the British Library, IOR/L/MIL/17/5/2327.

68 'War Diary, HQ Force K6, 1941', The National Archives, Kew, London, WO 179/5880.

69 'S. Lall – Deputy High Commissioner', India Office Records at the British Library, IOR/L/I/1/1438.

70 BBC, 'Broadcasts to the Forces: Indian Troops', 1940, BBC Written Archives Caversham, Reading, R34/381.

71 'Policy – Messages from India', 1943, BBC Written Archives Caversham, Reading, R34/465/1.

72 BBC, 'Indian Service', 1940, BBC Written Archives Caversham, Reading, R/46/261/2; 'Hello Punjab', *Fauji Akhbar*, 23 May 1942, Imperial War Museum; Mirza, p. 44.

73 BBC, 'Broadcasts to the Forces: Indian Troops'.

74 'Indian Talks', 1941, BBC Written Archives Caversham, R51/256/1.

75 'New War Burials; 1939 – Indian Graves In UK', 1939, Commonwealth War Graves Commission archives, Maidenhead, A/72/1.

76 J. Martin, 'Letter from J. Martin to Paritosh Shapland'.

77 'Commonwealth War Graves Commission'.

78 'Home Guard Tribute to Dead Indians', *Daily Mirror*, 13 January 1941.

79 Abdul Rashid Gatrad, 'Muslim Customs Surrounding Death, Bereavement, Postmortem Examinations, and Organ Transplants', *British Medical Journal*, 309.6953 (1994), 521–23; 'Burials of Moslems – Method', 1947, Commonwealth War Graves Commission archives, Maidenhead, A/175.

80 Philip Longworth, *The Unending Vigil: The History of the Commonwealth War Graves Commission*, Revised and updated edition (Barnsley: Leo Cooper, 2003), p. 34.

81 'Force K6 Documents'.

82 'War Diary, 25 Animal Transport Company, June–December 1940'.

83 'Force K6 Documents'.

7. We'll keep a welcome

1 The song was written by Mai Jones, a stationmaster's daughter from Newport who went on to be a BBC radio producer, Huw Williams, 'Dictionary of Welsh Biography', 2001 <https://biography.wales/article/s2-JONE-MAI-1899> [accessed 23 April 2019].

2 A.G. Khan, 'Ek Hindustani Jashn Rat', *Wilayati Akhbar Haftawar*, 10 April 1942, Imperial War Museum, E6705.

3 Philip Malins, 'The Royal Indian Army Service Corps in the Second World War', *Royal Corps of Transport Journal* (1980), p. 10.

4 J.R.M. Butler, *History of the Second World War, Grand Strategy Volume III (Part II)* (London: HMSO, 1964), p. 647.

5 Churchill, *The Second World War, Volume IV*, pp. 287–88.

6 Alanbrooke, p. 187.

7 'AT Companies for France: Force K6'.

8 'War Diary, 7 Animal Transport Company, 1941', The National Archives, Kew, London, WO 179/5903.

9 'War Diary, 3 Animal Transport Company, 1941', The National Archives, Kew, London, WO 179/5900.

10 'War Diary, HQ Force K6, 1941'.

11 Mirza, pp. 41–42.

12 Moharir, p. 174.

13 'War Diary, HQ Force K6, 1941'.

14 'War Diary, 3 Animal Transport Company, 1941'.

15 *RIASC Training Vol. III: Transport*, p. 60.

16 'War Diary, HQ Force K6, 1942'.

17 'War Diary, 29 Animal Transport Company, 1942', The National Archives, Kew, London, WO 179/5912.

18 Abdul Latif, *History of the Army Services Corps, Volume II* (Rawalpindi: Pap-Board Printers, 1986), p. 68.

19 *RIASC Training Vol. III: Transport*, p. 147.

20 Nadir Husain, 'Kamp Ki Zindagi Main Ek Jhank', *Wilayati Akhbar Haftawar*, 3 October 1941, p. 4, Imperial War Museum, E6705.

21 'Training Pack Horses for the Second Front'. Jodhpurs are named after a town in Rajasthan, India.

22 'War Diary, 32 Animal Transport Company, 1943', The National Archives, Kew, London, WO 179/5917.

23 'Training Pack Horses for the Second Front', p. 15.

24 *RIASC Training Vol. III: Transport*, pp. 77–85.

25 Philip Malins, Brian Nicholls, and Charles MacFetridge, 'The Indian Army Animal Transport Mule', in *The Military Mule in the British Army and Indian Army: An Anthology* (Solihull: B. Nicholls, 2000), p. 52.

26 'War Diary, 47 Supply Depot Section, 1941'.

27 *RIASC Training Vol. III: Transport*, pp. 84–85; This can be seen in the film '32 ATC in France, 1940', Imperial War Museum, London, BCY35 1940-02-10.

28 Ian Richard Netton, ed., *Encyclopedia of Islamic Civilisation and Religion* (London, New York: Routledge, 2008), p. 169.

29 'War Diary, HQ Force K6, 1942'.

30 Nawazish Ali, 'Chand ek Nasihaten', *Wilayati Akhbar Haftawar*, 27 February 1942, p. 4, Imperial War Museum, E6705.

31 'War Diary, 47 Supply Depot Section, 1941'.

32 Moharir, p. 179.

33 'Gift of Canteen', *Times of India*, 21 April 1941; interview with Abdul Jalil.

34 Hord, 'Nothing Can Shake the Loyalty of Our Indian Troops'.

35 J.H. Morgan, 'With Indian Troops in Wales', unidentified Welsh newspaper, October 1941, Hexley collection.

36 'War Diary, 7 Animal Transport Company, 1941'.

37 'War Diary, HQ Force K6, 1942'.

38 Hord, 'Nothing Can Shake the Loyalty of Our Indian Troops'.

39 'War Diary, 3 Animal Transport Company, 1941'.

40 'War Diary, HQ Force K6, 1941'.

41 'Latifa', *Wilayati Akhbar Haftawar*, 13 February 1942, Imperial War Museum, E6705.

42 'War Diary, HQ Force K6, 1942'.

43 Interview with Edgar Parry Williams, 2001.

44 R.F.L., 'On the Evening Bus', *Abergavenny Chronicle*, 26 December 1941.

45 Raymond Lewis, 'Letter: Indians in the Swimming Pool', *Abergavenny Chronicle*, 5 September 1941, p. 5.

46 One of the swimmers was the enterprising figure of Yaqub Mirza, in Mirza, p. 43.

47 Graham Smith, *When Jim Crow Met John Bull: Black American Soldiers in World War II Britain* (London: Tauris, 1987), p. 109.

48 *Carpenters Sada Khan and Charlie Edwards*, 1941, Crickhowell Archives.

49 'Crickhowell St David's Shop', 1941, Crickhowell Archives, 10/1/27.

50 Nawazish Ali, *Fauji Sipahi (Soldier in the Army)*, trans. by Waqar Seyal (Lahore: Qureshi Book Agency, n.d.).

51 'War Diary, HQ Force K6, 1941'.

52 'War Diary, HQ Force K6, 1941'.

53 'Indian Contingent in England', *Fauji Akhbar*, 26 July 1941, p. 13, Imperial War Museum; 'Indian Troops in England', *Times of India*, 12 July 1941.

54 'War Diary, HQ Force K6, 1942'; See also *Lord Mayors Parade* (British Pathé, 1941), British Pathé <http://www.youtube.com/watch?v=W2svWJ2Iihs> [accessed 24 February 2020].

55 Nizam Din, 'London ko hamara ek khas safar', *Wilayati Akhbar Haftawar*, 19 December 1941, Imperial War Museum, E6705.

56 'War Diary, 3 Animal Transport Company, 1941'.

57 Shaukat Hyat Khan, *The Nation That Lost Its Soul: Memoirs of a Freedom Fighter* (Lahore: Jang, 1999), p. 65.

58 Omer Tarin, 'Shaukat Hayat Khan', 6 January 2020.

59 'War Diary, Indian General Hospital, 1939–1943'.

60 William Stewart Empey, 'The Effect of Change of Environment on the Incidence and Type of Tuberculosis in Indian Troops' (unpublished MD, Queens University Belfast, 1942).

61 'War Diary, HQ Force K6, 1942'.

62 'War Diary, Indian General Hospital, 1939–1943'.

63 E.K.K. Pillai, *Medical Services: The Campaigns in the Western Theatre, Official History of the Indian Armed Forces in the Second World War 1939–45* (Delhi: Combined Inter-Services Historical Section, India & Pakistan, 1958), p. 23.

64 'War Diary, Indian General Hospital, 1939–1943'.

65 'War Diary, HQ Force K6, 1942'.

66 'AT Companies for France: Force K6'.

67 'War Diary, HQ Force K6, 1942'.

68 'War Diary, HQ Force K6, 1942'.

69 Akbar Khan, 'Letter from Major Akbar', *Islamic Review*, 1942, 288.

70 The names of these officers have been gleaned from various archival documents including 'War Diary, HQ Force K6, 1942'. The Muslim officers included A.G. Khan, H.A. Majid, Saifullah Khan, Sher Mohd Mir and Syed Amir-ud-Din Jaffery. The Hindus were Gopal Gopa Kumar, Jagat Singh Powar and Parkash Chandra Khanna. There were three Sikhs: Gurdial Singh, Narain Singh and Rattan Singh.

71 'War Diary, HQ Force K6, 1943', The National Archives, Kew, London, WO 179/5882.

72 Shamus O.D. Wade, 'But Where Did the Mules Come From?', *Durbar*, 17.4 (2000), 122–30.

73 Chepstow Society, *Wartime Memories: The Home Front in Chepstow 1939–1945* (Chepstow: Chepstow Society, 2000), p. 25.

74 'War Diary, HQ Force K6, 1942'.

75 'War Diary, 32 Animal Transport Company, 1943'.

8. Hinges and fringes

1 William Gilpin, *Observations on the River Wye 1782* (Oxford: Woodstock, 1991), p. 1.

2 'War Diary, 32 Animal Transport Company, 1941'.

3 Chepstow Society, p. 24.

4 'War Diary, 25 Animal Transport Company, 1943', The National Archives, Kew, London, WO 179/5909.

5 'War Diary, 42 Animal Transport Company, 1943', The National Archives, Kew, London, WO 179/5920.

6 'War Diary, 32 Animal Transport Company, 1943'.

7 'War Diary, 29 Animal Transport Company, 1941'.

8 Bruce Chatwin, *On the Black Hill* (London: Vintage, 2005), pp. 195–96.

9 'War Diary, Advanced Remount Depot, 1941'.

10 'War Diary, Advanced Remount Depot, 1941'.

11 'War Diary, Advanced Remount Depot, 1941'; Empey, p. 2.

12 'Henry Lamb MC, RA', Imperial War Museum, London, GP/55/33.

13 Interview with Alan Jeffreys at the Imperial War Museum, 2019.

14 'Henry Lamb MC, RA'.

15 'Henry Lamb MC, RA'.

16 'Henry Lamb MC, RA'.

17 'War Artists Exhibition', 1941, National Gallery, London, NG24/1941/6.

18 Suzanne Bosman, *The National Gallery in Wartime* (London: Yale University Press, 2008), p. 73.

19 John Fowles and Kenneth Allsop Memorial Trust, *Steep Holm: A Case History in the Study of Evolution* (Sherborne: Kenneth Allsop Memorial Trust, 1978), p. 120.

20 Fowles and Kenneth Allsop Memorial Trust, p. 118.

21 Stan Rendell and Joan Rendell, *Steep Holm's Pioneers* (Self-published, 2003), p. 131.

22 Fowles and Kenneth Allsop Memorial Trust, p. 119.

23 'War Diary, 32 Animal Transport Company, 1941'.

24 Fowles and Kenneth Allsop Memorial Trust, p. 121.

25 Wade.

26 Fowles and Kenneth Allsop Memorial Trust, p. 122.

27 Wade.

28 'War Diary, 32 Animal Transport Company, 1941'; 'War Diary, 32 Animal Transport Company, 1942', The National Archives, Kew, London, WO 179/5916.

29 'War Diary, Reinforcement Unit, 1942', The National Archives, Kew, London, WO 179/5885.

30 Fowles and Kenneth Allsop Memorial Trust, p. 128.

31 'Shaan: Filming and Production' <https://www.imdb.com/title/tt0081491/locations?ref_=tt_dt_dt> [accessed 12 April 2019].

32 Vishnu Sharma, *Panchatantra* (Bombay: Chandiramani, 1974), pp. 204–6.

33 William Robert Spencer, *Poems by the Late Hon. William R. Spencer* (London, 1835), p. 150.

34 Interview with Giovanna Bloor, 2015. I am very grateful to Giovanna Bloor for the interviews in this section. She was 16 in 1942, the daughter of the Nobel Prize-winning physicist Patrick Blackett, and had been evacuated to Pwllheli nearby.

35 'War Diary, 70 Brigade HQ 1942', The National Archives, Kew, London, WO 166/6586.

36 'War Diary, 70 Brigade HQ 1942'.

37 'War Diary, 70 Brigade HQ 1942'.

38 The division of labour can be seen in Lockeyear, *Men from the Cameronians Prepare and Load Pack Horses Which Also Took Part in the Exercise*, 1942, Imperial War Museum, H21593.

39 'War Diary, 70 Brigade HQ 1942'.

40 'War Diary, 70 Brigade HQ 1942'.

41 'War Diary, 32 Animal Transport Company, 1942'.

42 Indivar Kamtekar, 'The Shiver of 1942', in *War and Society in Colonial India*, ed. by Kaushik Roy (Oxford: Oxford University Press, 2006), pp. 330–57 (p. 332).

43 Kamtekar, p. 335.

44 Mirza, p. 45.

45 'War Diary, HQ Force K6, 1942'.

46 Interview with Edgar Parry Williams.

47 Giovanna Bloor, 'Mule Drivers from Rawalpindi in Llanfrothen and Nantmor', *Vale of Ffestiniog*, 2012 <http://voff-snowdonia.blogspot.co.uk/2012/04/mule-drivers-from-rawalpindi-in.html> [accessed 12 May 2019].

48 Interview with Watkin Evans, 2002.

49 Bloor.

50 'Radio Programme by Carys Richards' (BBC Radio Wales), Giovanna Bloor collection. I am indebted to Gwynfor Rowlinson for help with translation.

51 Interview with Jos Williams, 1999.

52 Interview with Edgar Parry Williams.

53 Interview with Nellie Woods, 1999.

54 Dylan Thomas, *Under Milk Wood* (Cheltenham: Nelson Thornes, 2010), p. 27.

55 Bloor.

56 Interview with Edgar Parry Williams.

57 Interview with Watkin Evans.

58 Interview with Giovanna Bloor.

59 Interview with Jos Williams.

60 'Helen McKie, Artist and Illustrator, Papers 1889-2004', 2005, Victoria & Albert Museum, London, AAD 2005/5.

61 'Waterloo Station – War', 1943, Victoria & Albert Museum, London, AAD 2005/5/16.

62 'War Diary, HQ Force K6, 1941'.

9. Heroes and Traitors

1 Winston Churchill, *Winston Churchill, My Early Life: A Roving Commission* (London: Reprint Society, 1944), p. 273.

2 Report by Major Mackay in 'German and Italian Attempts to Suborn Indian Prisoners of War. Activities of Central Free Indian Bureau in Berlin and Rome', June 42–Aug 45, The National Archives, Kew, London, WO 208/802.

3 Again, the only source for these paragraphs is Hexley's excellent report, which was probably written soon after his return to the UK in summer

1941. His accuracy for names, dates, places and quantities is remarkable, and suggests he may have been keeping a diary in France. T.W.P. Hexley.

4 T.W.P. Hexley, p. 17.
5 T.W.P. Hexley, p. 12.
6 T.W.P. Hexley, p. 25.
7 T.W.P. Hexley, p. 36.
8 *22 Animal Transport Company RIASC on the March*, 1940, Bundesarchiv, Germany, 121-0413.
9 T.W.P. Hexley, p. 40.
10 T.W.P. Hexley. A *Stalag* was a standard German POW camp. An *Oflag* was for officers and a *Frontstalag* was a camp in France.
11 T.W.P. Hexley, p. 60. 'Mohd' was slang for Muslim Indian soldier.
12 'Report on Stalag VIIIB Lamsdorf', 1945, The National Archives, Kew, London, WO 224/27.
13 'Indian POWs in Germany, Italy and East Africa'.
14 Midge Gillies, *The Barbed-Wire University: The Real Lives of Allied Prisoners of War in the Second World War* (London: Aurum, 2011), p. 3.
15 Douds, p. 184.
16 'Convention (III) Relative to the Treatment of Prisoners of War. Geneva, 12 August 1949.'
17 'Indian Prisoners in German Camps', unidentified Indian newpspaper, February 1944, Hexley album.
18 'Stalag VC Malschbach', 1945, The National Archives, Kew, London, WO 224/19A.
19 'Stalag VC Malschbach'.
20 'Stalag VC Malschbach'.
21 'Stalag VC Malschbach'.
22 'Commonwealth War Graves Commission'.
23 Claude Shepherd, *War Record of the Indian Comforts Fund* (London: Indian Comforts Fund, 1946), p. 8.
24 Gillies, p. 31.
25 '950 Regiment'.
26 'Books for Indian Prisoners of War', *Fauji Akhbar*, 17 July 1943, Imperial War Museum.
27 'Force K6 Documents'.
28 'German and Italian Attempts'.
29 'Stalag VC Malschbach'.
30 'Censors Reports for Middle East', 1942, India Office Records at the British Library, IOR/L/PJ/12/654.

31 Virk, p. 197.
32 'Secret Camp History of Oflag 79 (VIIIF) Querum', The National Archives, Kew, London, WO 208/3292.
33 'Pictures from Abroad', *Fauji Akhbar*, 4 October 1943, Imperial War Museum.
34 Gillies, p. 260.
35 'Touchstone Magazine from Oflag VIIB Eicshtaett', Bundesarchiv, Germany, MSG/200/797.
36 'Stalag IIIA: July 43–44', trans. by Fiona Schroeder, 1945, Bundesarchiv, Germany, RH 49/40.
37 'Stalag IIIA'.
38 'German and Italian Attempts'.
39 Milan Hauner, *India in Axis Strategy* (London: German Historical Institute London, 1981), p. 576; Madhur Jaffrey, *Climbing the Mango Trees* (London: Random House, 2005), p. 60.
40 Bose is described as a 'quasi-fascist' in Hugh Purcell, 'Subhas Chandra Bose: The Afterlife of India's Fascist Leader', *History Today*, 60.11 (2010), 45. Bose's book *The Indian Struggle* has been characterised as a counterpart to Hitler's *Mein Kampf*, indeed '*Kampf*' translates as 'struggle'.
41 Rudolf Hartog, *The Sign of the Tiger* (Delhi: Rupa, 2001), p. 9.
42 Girija Mookerjee, *Europe at War* (Meerut: Meenakshi Prakashan, 1968), p. 201.
43 Quoted in Giles MacDonogh, *A Good German: Adam von Trott Zu Solz*, Revised edition (London: Quartet, 1994), p. 187.
44 Hartog, p. 34.
45 '950 Regiment'.
46 'CSDIC Report on Nambiar', 1945, p. 38, India Office Records at the British Library, Mss EUR F275/26.
47 Hartog, p. 45.
48 'German and Italian Attempts'.
49 Raghavan, p. 149.
50 Hartog, p. 56.
51 'Typewritten minute marked "Strictly Personal and Secret" from General Auchinleck', India Office Records at the British Library, Mss Eur F274/95, p.4.
52 Hauner, p. 583; Douds, p. 190.
53 'Statements of Civilians in ZFI Zentrale Freies Indien', 1945, India Office Records at the British Library, Mss EUR F275/24.
54 Hauner, p. 583.

55 Yasmin Khan, *The Raj at War*, p. 188.

56 Adrian Weale, *Renegades: Hitler's Englishmen*, Revised edition (London: Pimlico, 2002).

57 Bamber, p. 39.

58 Douds, p. 190.

59 Bamber, pp. 113–14.

60 Interview with Zeenut Ziad.

61 Interview with Zeenut Ziad.

62 Interview with Zeenut Ziad.

63 'Indian POWs and CSDIC', 1945, India Office Records at the British Library, IOR/L/WS/1/1516.

64 Interview with Zeenut Ziad.

65 'Stalag IIIA Unterlagen Und Schriftwechsel Mit Vorgesetzten Dienststellen April 43–45', 1945, Bundesarchiv, Germany, RH 49/35.

66 T.W.P. Hexley.

67 '950 Regiment'.

68 '950 Regiment'.

69 'Kompanie Einteilung Organisationseinheit, 2./ Ind. Inf.Rgt. 950', 1942, Bundesarchiv, Germany, RS 4/1072.

70 '950 Regiment'.

71 'Indian POWs and CSDIC'; 'German and Italian Attempts'. Names have been omitted.

72 Bamber, p. 231.

73 '950 Regiment'.

74 Lothar Günther, *Von Indien Nach Annaburg: Indische Legion Und Kriegsgefangene in Deutschland* (Berlin: Verlag am Park, 2003), p. 5.

75 MacDonogh, p. 198. Von Trott zu Solz was later hanged by the Nazis for his part in the 20 July plot to assassinate Hitler.

76 Sugata Bose, *A Hundred Horizons: The Indian Ocean in the Age of Global Empire* (Cambridge, MA: Harvard University Press, 2006), p. 33.

77 Hartog, p. 113.

78 Hartog, pp. 114–15.

79 Bamber, p. 186.

80 Hartog, p. 128.

81 Hartog, p. 91.

82 Hartog, p. 134.

83 *Launch of the Provisional Government of India, Berlin*, 1943, Bundesarchiv, Germany, 146-1985-130-130.

84 '950 Regiment'.

10. The great escapes

1 Paul Irma Boulanger, 'Souvenir des Destructions et Bombardements d'Epinal', trans. by Hannah Michel-Bowman (Association des Sinistrés d'Epinal), Archives Départmentales des Vosges, Epinal, BR7525.
2 Guy Hamilton, *The Colditz Story* (British Lion Films, 1955).
3 Earl of Cardigan, *I Walked Alone* (London: Readers Union with Routledge & Kegan Paul, 1952).
4 John Nichol and Tony Rennell, *Home Run: Escape from Nazi Europe* (London: Viking, 2007).
5 Nichol and Rennell, *Home Run*, p. 50.
6 The K6 escapers were not the only Indians to make it to safety. In the six months from December 1943 there were thirty-six who made it to neutral territory, 'Prisoners of War: Indian PoWs and Escapees', 1945, India Office Records at the British Library, IOR/L/WS/1/1536.
7 M.R.D Foot and J.M. Langley, *MI9: Escape and Evasion 1939–1945* (London: Bodley Head, 1979), p. 123.
8 'Escaped POW Report for Jemadar Jehan Dad', 1941, The National Archives, Kew, London, WO 208/3301.
9 T.W.P. Hexley, p. 8.
10 'Caskie Papers: Photos', National Library of Scotland, Acc 8846/11.
11 'Force K6 Documents'.
12 'War Diary, 29 Animal Transport Company, 1942'.
13 'War Diary, HQ Force K6, 1942'.
14 Donald Caskie, *The Tartan Pimpernel* (Oxford: Isis, 2008), p. xii.
15 Nichol and Rennell, *Home Run*, p. 42.
16 'Caskie Letters in Church of Scotland World Missions Board Archive', National Library of Scotland, Acc 7548/G92.
17 'Caskie Letters in Church of Scotland World Missions Board Archive'.
18 Cardigan, p. 95.
19 Ruth Eley, 'Birmingham Officer's Amazing Trek after Escape', *Birmingham Post*, October 1941.
20 Interview with Hexley, Sutherland, Melville and Beaton.
21 'Escaped POW Report for T.W.P. Hexley', 1941, The National Archives, Kew, London, WO 208/3304.
22 Cardigan, p. 165.
23 Interview with Hexley, Sutherland, Melville and Beaton.
24 Hexley, 'Photo Album'.
25 Cardigan, p. 161.

26 Hexley, 'Photo Album'.

27 Eley.

28 Hexley, 'Photo Album'.

29 'Escaped POW Report for T.W.P. Hexley'.

30 Hexley, 'Photo Album'.

31 Leo Amery, 'Leopold Amery's Diary for 1941', Churchill Archive, Cambridge, England, AMEL 7/35.

32 Eley.

33 All this paragraph draws on '1 AT Driver Trg Regt Jallandhar Cantt'.

34 'Escape Report for Buland Khan', 1944, The National Archives, Kew, London, WO 208/3319.

35 T.W.P. Hexley, p. 62.

36 'Escape Report for Buland Khan'.

37 'War Diary, Indian General Hospital, 1939–1943'.

38 'Recommendation for Award for Bashir-Ud-Din Ahmed', 1945, The National Archives, Kew, London, WO 373/64.

39 'Recommendation for Award for Mansab Dar', 1945, The National Archives, Kew, London, WO 373/64.

40 'Recommendation for Award for Mansab Dar'.

41 'Recommendation for Award for Mohd Sarwar', 1945, The National Archives, Kew, London, WO 373/64.

42 'Recommendation for Award for Mohd Ashraf Khan', 1945, The National Archives, Kew, London, WO 373/64.

43 '950 Regiment'.

44 'Prisoners of War: Indian PoWs and Escapees'.

45 'Report on Oflag IXA', The National Archives, Kew, London, FO 916/19.

46 Pillai, p. 19.

47 'War Diary, HQ Force K6, 1943'; 'Indian POWs in Germany, Italy and East Africa'.

48 'Indian Escapees from German Prisoner of War Camps', 1942, The National Archives, Kew, London, WO 208/808.

49 'Frontstalag 315 Epinal'.

50 A. Dewan, 'The Famous Indian Mass Escape from Epinal', *United Service Institution of India Journal*, 75.320 (1945), 318–21 (p. 318).

51 '7000 Broke out of Hun Camp', *Lancashire Daily Post*, 23 May 1944.

52 Dewan, p. 319.

53 'Indian Escapees from German Prisoner of War Camps'; 'Indians Cross Swiss Border', *The Times*, 22 May 1944.

54 'Indians Carried Dead Comrade into Switzerland', *Northern Whig*, 24 May 1944.

55 'Frontstalag 315 Epinal'.

56 'Indian Escapees from German Prisoner of War Camps'.

57 Interview with citizens of Etobon: Marianne Peret-Stuart and her husband Jean, Collette Beltran, Josselyne Jeand'heur, Monsieur Pernon, Jacques Croissant, Claude Demet, M. le Maire, Daniel Philippe Perret, 2017.

58 Jean Louis Pernon, 'Souvenir', trans. by Ghee Bowman, 2017.

59 Jules Perret and Benjamin Valloton, *Ceux d'Etobon*, trans. by Katherine Douglass (Montbeliard: Impr. de Metthez frères, 1949).

60 Perret and Valloton.

61 Interview at Etobon.

62 Perret and Valloton.

63 Mahal Singh, 'Letter to Emile Bonhotal', 28 November 1944, Claude Demet collection.

64 Interview at Etobon.

65 'Proposal for Pakistan Memorial at Epinal', The National Archives, Kew, London, FO 371/69748.

11. Should auld acquaintance be forgot?

1 Caskie, p. 30.

2 H.E. Marshall, *Our Island Story* (London: Nelson, 1905), p. 495.

3 'War Diary, HQ Force K6, 1943'.

4 G.E.L. Smith, 'India's Member of Cabinet Visits Native Troops Now Training in Scotland', *Aberdeen Press and Journal*, 1 October 1942, p. 2.

5 'War Diary, 3 Animal Transport Company, 1941'.

6 Wackett, *The Stretcher Party Arrive at the Field Operating Tent with a 'Casualty'*, 1942, Imperial War Museum, H23159.

7 'War Diary, 3 Animal Transport Company, 1941'.

8 Wackett, *HRH Princess Royal*, 1942, Imperial War Museum, H22715; Lockeyear, *His Highness Shaking Hands*, 1942, Imperial War Museum, H23939.

9 G.E.L. Smith.

10 'War Diary, 32 Animal Transport Company, 1942'.

11 'War Diary, 32 Animal Transport Company, 1942'.

12 R.W.W. Hills (Commanding Officer), 'War Diary, HQ Force K6', 1942, The National Archives, Kew, London, WO 179/5881.

13 Hord, 'Nothing Can Shake the Loyalty of Our Indian Troops'.

14 R.W.W. Hills (Commanding Officer), 'War Diary, HQ Force K6'.

15 Dolly Cameron, 'Display at Aultbea Museum' <https://racmp.co.uk/> [accessed 24 February 2020].

16 Email from Maruf Miah to George Milne regarding Seaman Aftar Miah of SS *City of Keelung*, 9 January 2017.

17 'War Diary, Reinforcement Unit, 1942'.

18 Display board at Aultbea.

19 Display board at Aultbea.

20 Hector MacKenzie, 'Horseshoe Find Lucky for Wester Ross Man!', *Ross-Shire Journal*, 11 March 2012 <https://www.ross-shirejournal.co.uk/news/horseshoe-find-lucky-for-wester-ross-man-122141/> [accessed 14 December 2019].

21 'War Diary, 32 Animal Transport Company, 1942'; 'War Diary, 32 Animal Transport Company, 1943'.

22 Interview with Hexley, Sutherland, Melville and Beaton.

23 'Funeral of the Duchess of Sutherland: Large Concourse of Mourners', *Northern Times*, 2 September 1943, p. 3.

24 Email from Alsadair Will to Ghee Bowman, 28 October 2017.

25 Unknown, *Indian Army Sergeant Based in Dornoch WW2* <http://www.historylinksarchive.org.uk/picture/number11889.asp> [accessed 23 May 2017].

26 Hamish Johnston, 'A Corner of Pakistan in Scotland', *Highland Family History Society* (2012); 'Commonwealth War Graves Commission'.

27 Visram, p. 260; for a Scottish example, see Finlay J. Macdonald, *Crotal and White* (London: Sphere, 1991), p. 61.

28 'High Prices as 15,648 Lambs Sold at Lairg', *Northern Times*, 17 August 2016 <https://www.northern-times.co.uk/news/high-prices-as-15648-lambs-sold-at-lairg-148070/> [accessed 2 August 2019].

29 Interview with Joan Leed, Donny MacDonald and Marlyn Price, 2016.

30 'Lairg WVS Entertain', *Northern Times*, 31 December 1942. 'Dr Fazal' is probably Jemadar Fazal Mohd IMD, originally attached to the IGH.

31 Letter is reproduced *in toto* in 'War Diary, HQ Force K6, 1943'.

32 Interview with Veronica and Eddie Lancaster, 2016.

33 'The Aberdeen Mittwoch Blitz - Wednesday 21st April 1943', The Doric Columns <http://www.mcjazz.f2s.com/Blitzkreig.htm> [accessed 31 July 2019].

34 'Indian Soldiers to Anglers Aid', *Aberdeen Press & Journal*, 23 June 1943.

35 Mirza, p. 48.

36 Interview with Hamish Johnston, 2016.

37 'War Diary, 3 Animal Transport Company, 1941'.

38 'Commonwealth War Graves Commission'. There was also one death of a sweeper, Mangli, who was cremated at Aberdeen, 'War Diary, Indian General Hospital, 1939–1943'.

39 'It Is Time to Remember', *Strathspey and Badenoch Herald*, 22 November 2018.

40 Calum Ross, 'New Year Honours: Recognition for 96-Year-Old Highland Woman who Tended the Graves of Indian Servicemen', *Press and Journal*, 28 December 2019 <https://www.pressandjournal.co.uk/fp/ news/highlands/1921492/new-year-honours-recognition-for-96-year-old-highland-woman-who-tended-the-graves-of-indian-servicemen/> [accessed 24 February 2020].

41 'War Diary, HQ Force K6, 1943'.

42 'For Indian Troops: YMCA Home in Edinburgh: A Mosque Provided', *Scotsman*, 25 November 1942, p. 3.

43 'War Diary, 42 Animal Transport Company, 1942'.

44 'War Diary, HQ Force K6, 1942'.

45 'Murder Charge', *Scotsman*, 1 October 1942, p. 8.

46 Among six mule transport companies in Italy, for example, there were 357 human casualties. Malins, Nicholls and MacFetridge, p. 31.

47 'War Diary, HQ Force K6', 1943; 'War Diary, 3 Animal Transport Company', 1943.

48 'War Diary, 42 Animal Transport Company, 1943'.

49 'War Diary, Reinforcement Unit, 1943', The National Archives, Kew, London, WO 179/5886.

50 'War Diary, Reinforcement Unit, 1943'.

51 Kamtekar.

52 John Keay and Julia Keay, *Collins Encyclopaedia of Scotland* (London: Harper Collins, 1994), p. 581.

53 Email from Arthur Hames to Paritosh Shapland, 25 January 2003.

54 'War Diary, 6 Pack Transport Group, 1943', The National Archives, Kew, London, WO 179/5899. Which Singh is unclear, as is which unit, as is the precise date.

55 Interview with David McDougall, Sheena McDougall and Catriona Spence, 2017.

56 Hugh Cudlipp, *Publish and be Damned: The Astonishing Story of the Daily Mirror* (London: Andrew Dakers, 1953), p. 6.

57 Donald Zec, *Don't Lose It Again! The Life and Wartime Cartoons of Philip Zec* (London: Political Cartoon Society, 2005), p. 118.

58 Mark Bryant, *World War II in Cartoons* (London: Grub Street, 2005), p. 141.

59 *Hansard House of Commons Debate,* 23 September 1943, vol. 392, cols 443–4W.
60 'War Diary, HQ Force K6, 1943'.
61 'War Diary, Reinforcement Unit, 1943'.
62 'War Diary, HQ Force K6, 1943'.
63 Moharir, p. 176.
64 'Battle for Britain Sunday in Dornoch', *Northern Times*, 30 September 1943, p. 4.

12. Doing what comes naturally

1 Waris Shah, *Hir and Ranjha*, p. 27.
2 Alison Smith, David Blayney Brown, and Carol Jacobi, eds, *Artist and Empire: Facing Britain's Imperial Past* (London: Tate, 2015), p. 196.
3 Yasmin Alibhai, 'Lest We Forget', *New Statesman and Society*, 21 June 1991, p. 15.
4 '950 Regiment'.
5 Photo caption in John Costello, *Love, Sex and War: Changing Values 1939–45* (London, 1986), p. 144.
6 This account comes from a chapter called 'Casualty of War' in Mirza, pp. 50–61.
7 Webster, pp. 204, 205.
8 Webster, pp. 17, 200.
9 'Directives June 1943' respondent 1211.
10 Unless noted otherwise, the material in this section comes from Paritosh Jeff Shapland, 'Gladys' (Leicestershire, 2011); interview with Paritosh (Jeff) Shapland, 2016.
11 Ms Kelly in Shapland, 'Gladys', p. 40.
12 Janet, 'Letter to Paritosh Shapland', 16 May 2008.
13 '25 Mule Company RIASC Daily Orders Part II DGIMS', 1941, National Archives of India, DGIMS 8/9/5/41.
14 Shapland, 'Gladys', p. 70.
15 Paritosh Jeff Shapland, 'Notes on Telephone Call', 2001, Shapland collection.
16 Interview with Giovanna Bloor.
17 S.M. Ferguson and H. Fitzgerald, *History of the Second World War: Studies in the Social Services* (London: HMSO, 1954), p. 131; Graham Smith, p. 209.

13. The end of the Indian Contingent

1 Sidhwa, p. 111.

2 'Individual Service Record for TWP Hexley'.

3 Shepherd, p. 14.

4 Shepherd, p. 20.

5 Commanding Officer, 'War Diary, 5 Pack Transport Group', 1943, The National Archives, Kew, London, WO 179/5998.

6 'Return of Indian Contingent', *Times of India*, 17 February 1944, p. 4.

7 Film, 'Interviews on Return'.

8 'Return of Indian Contingent'.

9 'RIASC Men's Impressions of England'.

10 'RIASC Men's Impressions of England'.

11 Moharir, p. 177.

12 '7 Ind AT Coy 1941–47', 1947, National Archives of India, Misc/3137/H.

13 '3 Ind AT Coy 1941–47', 1947, National Archives of India, Misc/3133/H.

14 '3 Ind AT Coy 1941–47', p. 7; '7 Ind AT Coy 1941–47'; '25 Ind AT Coy, RIASC War Diary 1944–45', 1944, National Archives of India, Misc/1734/H; '32 Ind AT Coy, RIASC', 1945, National Archives of India, Misc/1729/H.

15 '32 Ind AT Coy, RIASC'.

16 '950 Regiment'.

17 'CSDIC - 950 Regt', 1945, India Office Records at the British Library, Mss EUR F275/25.

18 'German and Italian Attempts'.

19 Bamber, p. 276.

20 'French Treatment of Indian Ex POWs', 1944, The National Archives, Kew, London, FO 371/49116.

21 Lothar Günther, *Die Indische Legion Und Das Dritte Reich: Das Zentrale Kriegsgefangenenlager Der Inder in Annaburg Und Der Kampf Um Indiens Unabhängigket* (Berlin: Verlag am Park, 2013), p. 140.

22 The details of the shooting are disputed: the date may have been 21 or 22 September, and the number varies between 19 and 30. 'French Treatment of Indian Ex POWs'; Günther, *Die Indische Legion*, p. 141; Johannes H. Voigt, *India in the Second World War* (New Jersey: Humanities Press International, 1988), p. 269; Hartog, p. 140.

23 Hartog, p. 159.

24 'POWs and CSDIC & Civilians', L/WS/1/1516.

25 'Indian POW List', 1945, The National Archives, Kew, London, WO 344/360.

26 Gillies, p. 379.

27 Interview with Zeenut Ziad.

28 John Nichol and Tony Rennell, *The Last Escape: The Untold Story of Allied Prisoners of War in Germany 1944–45* (London: Penguin, 2003), p. 53.

29 Hitchcock, p. 17.

30 'Letter from Anis to his Cousin Shahid Amin from Oflag IVE', 19 March 1943, Syed Ali Hamid collection.

31 Jit Singh Sarna, 'Indian Army History Thread', *Bharat Rakshak*, 2007 <https://forums.bharat-rakshak.com/viewtopic.php?f=3&t=2623&start=40> [accessed 26 July 2019].

32 'Mohammed Dost. German POW Card', 1945, The National Archives, Kew, London, WO 416/100/316.

33 Interview with Zeenut Ziad.

34 Gillies, p. 409.

35 John Hobday, 'Papers of John Hobday', Herefordshire Record Office, BZ29.

36 'German and Italian Attempts'.

37 'Subversive Activity against IA by Germany and Italy', India Office Records at the British Library, IOR/L/WS/1/1363; There was also a brief report in '"Indian Legion" in the German Forces', *The Times*, 24 September 1943.

38 'Comd. Supply Depot "Z" Sec.', The National Archives, Kew, London, WO 179/5889.

39 'War Diary, Indian PW Reception HQ, 1945', The National Archives, Kew, London, WO 179/5930.

40 Shepherd, p. 20.

41 'Indian POW Reception HQ', 1945, India Office Records at the British Library, IOR/L/WS/1/704.

42 Shepherd, p. 20.

43 'War Diary, Indian PW Reception HQ, 1945'.

44 'Ham ne yih Jang kyun lari?', *Wilayati Akhbar Haftawar*, 1 June 1945, pp. 2–3, Imperial War Museum, E6705.

45 'Indian POW Reception HQ Liaison Letters', India Office Records at the British Library, L/WS/1/1396.

46 'Policy towards Those who Joined INA & 950 Regt', 1945, India Office Records at the British Library, IOR/R/3/1/330.

47 'German and Italian Attempts'.

48 '950 Regiment'.

49 'Prisoners of Wars', 1945, National Archives of India, Misc/3830/H.

50 'German and Italian Attempts'.

51 'Prisoners of Wars'.

52 'Prisoners of Wars'.

53 'Indian POW Reception HQ Liaison Letters'.

54 Hartog, p. 171; Bamber, p. 336.

55 Letter from Gandhi to Viceroy dated 25/7/45 in 'Policy towards Those who Joined INA & 950 Regt'.

56 Raghavan, p. 446.

57 Hartog, p. 171.

58 'A Tpt Reinforcement Centre RIASC Jullundur', 1942, National Archives of India, Misc/4457/H.

59 '32 Ind AT Coy, RIASC'.

60 Anand, *Folk Tales of Punjab*, p. 9.

61 '3 Ind AT Coy 1941-47'.

62 '25 Ind AT Coy, RIASC War Diary 1944–45'.

63 '29 Ind AT Coy, RIASC War Service Diaries for 1944–45', 1944, National Archives of India, Misc 1732, Misc/1732/H.

64 '32 Ind AT Coy, RIASC'.

Epilogue

1 Mirza Asadullah Khan Ghālib, *Whispers of the Angel (Nawa-E Sarosh): Selections from 14 English Translations of Ghalib* (Delhi: Ghalib Academy, 1969), p. 10.

2 *The Mrs Merton Show*, 19 March 1998 <https://www.youtube.com/watch?v=TbldMCfjwq4> [accessed 24 February 2020].

3 'Paki' is a highly offensive word in the UK, a racial slur used against anyone of South Asian heritage. See, for example, Coco Khan in *The Good Immigrant*, ed. by Nikesh Shukla (London: Unbound, 2017), p. 126.

4 Key writers on collective memory include Maurice Halbwachs and Lewis A. Coser, *On Collective Memory: The Heritage of Sociology* (Chicago and London: University of Chicago Press, 1992); Paul Ricoeur, *Memory, History, Forgetting* (London: University of Chicago Press, 2004); Aleida Assmann, 'Forms of Forgetting' (unpublished lecture, Royal Dutch Academy of Sciences, 2014) <http://castrumperegrini.org/2014/10/30/forms-of-forgetting/> [accessed 25 March 2018]; Raphael Samuel, *Theatres of Memory*, 3 vols (London: Verso, 1994), I; Pierre Nora, *Realms of Memory* (New York: Columbia University Press, 1996).

5 Samuel, I, p. 26; Astrid Erll, 'The "Indian Mutiny" as a Shared Site of Memory: A Media Culture Perspective on Britain and India', in *Memory, History and Colonialism: Engaging with Pierre Nora in Colonial and Postcolonial Contexts*, German Historical Institute London, Bulletin, Supplement No 1 (London, 2009), pp. 117–48 (p. 140).

6 Lucy Noakes and Juliette Pattinson, eds, *British Cultural Memory and the Second World War* (London: Bloomsbury Academic, 2014), p. 1.

7 Michael Paris, *Warrior Nation: Images of War in British Popular Culture 1850–2000* (London: Reaktion, 2000), p. 209.

8 Jacques Frémeaux, 'Les Contingents Impériaux au Cœur de la Guerre', *Histoire, Economie et Societé*, 23.2 (2004), 215–33 (p. 228).

9 See for example Yasmin Khan, 'Dunkirk, the War and the Amnesia of the Empire', *New York Times*, 2 August 2017 <https://www.nytimes.com/2017/08/02/opinion/dunkirk-indians-world-war.html> [accessed 24 February 2020]; Diya Gupta, 'Christopher Nolan's Dunkirk and the Cultural Memory of a Global War', *News 18*, 21 August 2017 <https://www.news18.com/news/movies/christopher-nolans-dunkirk-and-the-cultural-memory-of-a-global-war-1492435.html> [accessed 24 February 2020]; Robert Fisk, 'When You Watch Dunkirk, Remember That It's a Whitewashed Version which Ignores the Bravery of Blacks and Muslim Soldiers', *Independent*, 3 August 2017; Ghee Bowman, 'What Christopher Nolan Left out: Dunkirk's Indian Soldiers', Imperial and Global Forum, 2018 <https://imperialglobalexeter.com/2018/07/30/what-christopher-nolan-left-out-dunkirks-indian-soldiers/> [accessed 24 February 2020].

10 Joe Wright, *Atonement* (Universal Pictures, 2007).

11 Juliet Gardiner, 'Presenting the Past – How the Media Changes History', 2013 <http://www.bbc.co.uk/programmes/b01mn4v4> [accessed 24 February 2020].

12 Miranda Kaufmann, 'Presenting the Black Past – How History Must Change the Media', 14 November 2015 <http://www.mirandakaufmann.com/3/post/2013/11/presenting-the-black-past-how-history-must-change-the-media.html> [accessed 24 July 2015].

13 Chanya Button, *World on Fire* (ITV, 2019).

14 Interview with Hexley, Sutherland, Melville and Beaton.

15 Yasmin Khan, *The Raj at War*, p. 314.

16 Text message from Brigadier Asim Iqbal to Ghee Bowman, 2 April 2018.

17 'Individual Service Record for Muhammad Akbar Khan', 1946, India Office Records at the British Library, IOR/L/MIL/14/72491.

18 'Amery Letters 1947', Churchill Archive, Cambridge, England, AMEL 2/1/41.

19 Interview with Jang family: Aaliyah, Asad Ullah and Sami Ullah, 2018.

20 'Amery Letters 1947'; Interview with Shahid Hasan Khan, Roohi Hasan Khan, Hasan Akbar, Suraiya Aslam and Fareeda Akbar, 2018.

21 Interview with Amna Maqbool and Maqbool Ahmed, 2018.

22 Interview with Jawad Sawarna, Ahmed Sawarna and Nasira, 2018.

23 'Individual Service Record for Anis Ahmad Khan', India Office Records at the British Library, IOR/L/MIL/14/72487.

24 Z.H. Zaidi, *Jinnah Papers*, First Series (Islamabad: National Archives of Pakistan, 1994), II, p. 285.

25 Interview with Zeenut Ziad.

26 Z.H. Zaidi, *Jinnah Papers*, First Series (Islamabad: National Archives of Pakistan, 1999), IV, p. 381.

27 P.K.D. Kapur, *Footprints and Milestones* (New Delhi: General Supply and Transport Army Headquarters, 1990), p. 36.

28 'First Indian Muslim to be Major-General in Indian Army', *Statesman* (Calcutta, 9 October 1949).

29 Interview with Zeenut Ziad.

30 Douglas Currie, 'Letter from Colonel Douglas Currie to Col Mohd Akbar Khan', 1 July 1946, Abdul Jalil collection.

31 Interview with Abdul Jalil.

32 'Letter from M.A. Haq, Mine Owner Padatchaung, Burma to Mohd Ashraf Khan', 30 March 1946, Abdul Jalil collection.

33 Interview with Abdul Jalil.

34 Interview with Zubair Mohammed.

35 Brown.

36 Mirza.

37 Bullhe Shah, *Sufi Lyrics*, ed. by Christopher Shackle (London: Harvard University Press, 2015), p. xviii.

38 Nawazish Ali, *Mahob Rasul (Prophet's Lover)*, trans. by Waqar Seyal (Lahore: Qureshi Book Agency), p. 5.

39 Nawazish Ali, *Jangi Safarnama (War Safarnama)*, trans. by Waqar Seyal (Lahore: Qureshi Book Agency), p. 6.

40 'Durnbach War Cemetery Germany', 1949, Commonwealth War Graves Commission archives, Maidenhead, RA 43111.

41 Longworth.

42 'Durnbach War Cemetery Germany'.

43 Mihir Bose in Bamber, p. 11.

44 Karnad, p. xix.

Bibliography

Primary source materials

British archives
Arctic Convoy Museum, Aultbea
BBC Written Archives, Caversham
Bill Douglas Centre and Special Collections, University of Exeter
Bodleian Library, Oxford
Churchill Archives, Cambridge: Leo Amery papers
Commonwealth War Graves Commission Archives, Maidenhead
Crickhowell Resource and Information Centre
Devon Record Office, Exeter
Doncaster Library
Dornoch Historylinks Museum
Golspie Heritage Centre
The Imperial War Museum, London
India Office Records, the British Library, London
Kelvingrove Museum, Glasgow
Mass-Observation Archives, the Keep, Sussex University
The National Archives, Kew, London
The National Army Museum, London
National Gallery, London
National Library of Scotland, Edinburgh
National Library of Wales, Aberystwyth
Plymouth Central Library
Royal Military Academy Sandhurst
Surrey Record Office, Woking
Victoria & Albert Museum, London

French archives
Archives Départementales des Vosges, Epinal
Archives Départementales du Nord, Lille
Archives Municipales, Dunkerque

Fortress Hackenberg, Veckring
Service Historique de la Défense, Vincennes

German archives
Bundesarchiv Bild, Koblenz
Bundesarchiv Freiburg
Bundesarchiv Lichtenberg, Berlin
Lautarchiv, Humboldt University, Berlin
Zentrum Moderner Orient, Berlin

Indian archives
Centre for Armed Forces Historical Research at the United Service Institution
    of India, Delhi
National Archives of India, New Delhi
Nehru Memorial Museum & Library, Delhi

Pakistani archives
National Documentation Wing, Islamabad

Newspapers and periodicals

United Kingdom
Aberdeen Evening Telegraph
Abergavenny Chronicle
Ashbourne Telegraph
Birmingham Evening Despatch
Burnley Express & News
Cornish Guardian
Daily Mirror
Daily Record and Mail
Derby Evening Telegraph
Doncaster Chronicle
Illustrated London News
The Listener
London Gazette
Morning Advertiser
Manchester Guardian
Northern Times
Scotsman
The Times

Western Morning News

India
Fauji Akhbar
Statesman
Times of India

Interviews

Conducted by Ghee Bowman
Kalsoom Akhtar, 2018
Doreen Allsop, 2016
Idrees Anwar, Fauzia Anwar, Sameena Anwar, and Tehmeena Anwar, 2018
Mark Ashdown, 2014
Giovanna Bloor, 2015
Citizens of Etobon: Marianne Peret-Stuart and her husband Jean, Collette Beltran, Josselyne Jeand'heur, Monsieur Pernon, Jacques Croissant, Claude Demet, M. le Maire, Daniel Philippe Perret, 2017
Betty Cresswell, 2016
Syed Ali Hamid, 2018
Shahid Hasan Khan, Roohi Hasan Khan, Hasan Akbar, Suraiya Aslam, Fareeda Akbar, 2018
Colin Hexley, Shirley Sutherland, John Melville and Robert Beaton, 2016
Nazar Hussain, Abdul Ghafour, Ghulam Rasul, Allah Yar Hussain and Ghulam Abbas Mumtaz, 2018
Nasir Hussain Shah, Aftab Hussain, Asad Shah and Fida Hussain, 2018
Abdul Jalil, 2018
Aaliyah Jang, Asad Ullah Jang and Sami Ullah Jang, 2018
Alan Jeffreys, 2019
Hamish Johnston, 2016
Omer Salim Khan, 2018
Veronica and Eddie Lancaster, 2016
Joan Leed, Donny MacDonald and Marlyn Price, 2016
Stuart Mackenzie, George Miln and Donald Matheson, 2017
Amna Maqbool and Maqbool Ahmed, 2018
Abdul Mateen, Mohd Akram, Mohd Yunus and Mohd Rafique, 2018
David McDougall, Sheena McDougall and Catriona Spence, 2017
Jo Meacock, 2016
Zubair Mohammed, 2015

Najm us Saqib and Ghulam Nabi, 2018
Nighat, Waqas Ahmed and Robena, 2018
Jawad Sawarna, Ahmed Sawarna and Nasira, 2018
Paritosh (Jeff) Shapland, 2016
Aaliyah Tayyebi, Javeria Vaqar, Zehra Jabeen Shah and Zain Shaikhzadeh,
    (Community Archives of Pakistan staff), 2018
Zeenut Ziad, 2018

Conducted by Giovanna Bloor
Watkin Evans, 2002
Edgar Parry Williams, 2001
Jos Williams, 1999
Nellie Woods, 1999

Conducted by Ilyas Khan
'A Compilation of Memoirs and Accounts of Service by Native Indian Officers
    and Ranks in Middle East and North Africa, During World War II (c. 1941–
    44)', Sophia Research Institute, Abbottabad, Pakistan

Unpublished theses

Empey, William Stewart, 'The Effect of Change of Environment on the Incidence
    and Type of Tuberculosis in Indian Troops' (unpublished MD thesis, Queens
    University Belfast, 1942)

TV and radio broadcasts

Button, Chanya, *World on Fire* (ITV, 2019)
The Longest Road (BBC2, 2009) <https://www.youtube.com/watch?v=LZ0ue-
    XGl9c>
The Mrs Merton Show (BBC, 19 March 1998) <https://www.youtube.com/watch?
    v=TbldMCfjwq4>

Films

'32 ATC in France, 1940', Imperial War Museum, London, BCY35 1940-02-10
Hamilton, Guy, *The Colditz Story* (British Lion Films, 1955)
'Indian Army Special Newsreel (1940)' (Pathé, 1940) <https://www.youtube.
    com/watch?v=yq6E1luxLQQ&t=>
Indian Troops in France (Pathé, 1940) <http://www.britishpathe.com/video/
    indian-troops-in-france-1>

'Interviews on Return, 1944', Imperial War Museum, London, MWY92

Lord Mayors Parade (British Pathé, 1941), British Pathé <http://www.youtube.com/watch?v=W2svWJ2Iihs>

Nolan, Christopher, *Dunkirk* (Warner Bros, 2017)

Stevens, George, *Gunga Din* (RKO, 1939)

Wright, Joe, *Atonement* (Universal Pictures, 2007)

Private collections

Abdul Jalil collection
Betty Cresswell collection
Bowman collection
Hexley collection
Jawad Sawarna collection
Omer Tarin collection
Syed Ali Hamid collection
Shapland collection

Published primary sources

Government of India, *Scales of Rations and Supplies Issued by the R.I.A.S.C.* (Delhi: Government of India, 1941)

Government of Punjab, *Rawalpindi District Gazetteer 1907* (Lahore: Government of Punjab, 1907)

Imperial Gazetteer of India: Provincial Series: Punjab 1908 (Lahore: Government of Pakistan, 1998)

Secondary sources

Adam, John, *A History of Rossington* (Doncaster: Rossington History Group, 2008)

Alanbrooke, Alan Francis Brooke, *War Diaries, 1939–1945*, ed. by Alex Danchev and Daniel Todman (London: Weidenfeld and Nicolson, 2001)

Alexander, Martin S., 'Colonial Minds Confounded: French Colonial Troops in the Battle of France 1940', in *The French Colonial Mind: Volume 2: Violence, Military Encounters and Colonialism*, ed. by Martin Thomas (Lincoln, NE: University of Nebraska Press, 2011), pp. 248–82

Alibhai, Yasmin, 'Lest We Forget', *New Statesman and Society*, 21 June 1991

Anand, Mulk Raj, *Across the Black Waters* (New Delhi: Orient, 2008)

——, *Folk Tales of Punjab* (Delhi: Sterling, 1989)

——, *Untouchable* (Gurgaon: Penguin, 2001)

Ansari, K. Humayun, 'The Woking Mosque: A Case Study of Muslim Engagement with British Society since 1889', *Immigrants and Minorities*, 21.3 (2002), 1–24

Arthur, Max, *Forgotten Voices of the Second World War* (London: Index, 2008)

Ausonius, Decimus Magnus, *Moselle, Epigrams, and Other Poems*, trans. by Deborah Warren (London: Routledge, Taylor and Francis Group, 2017)

Bamber, Martin, *For Free India: Indian Soldiers in Germany and Italy during the Second World War*, ed. by Aad Neeven (Oosthuizen: Oskam-Neeven, 2010)

Barrett, Michele, 'Death and the Afterlife', in *Race, Empire and First World War Writing*, ed. by Santanu Das (Cambridge, 2011), pp. 301–20

Bloch, Marc, *Strange Defeat* (USA: Important, 2013)

Bose, Sugata, *A Hundred Horizons: The Indian Ocean in the Age of Global Empire* (Cambridge, MA: Harvard University Press, 2006)

Bosman, Suzanne, *The National Gallery in Wartime* (London: Yale University Press, 2008)

Bryant, Arthur, *The Turn of the Tide 1939–1943: A Study Based on the Diaries and Autobiographical Notes of Field Marshal the Viscount Alanbrooke* (London: Grafton, 1986)

Bryant, Mark, *World War II in Cartoons* (London: Grub Street, 2005)

Butler, J.R.M., *History of the Second World War, Grand Strategy Volume II: September 1939–June 1941* (London: HMSO, 1957)

——, *History of the Second World War, Grand Strategy Volume III (Part II)* (London: HMSO, 1964)

Calder, Angus, and Dorothy Sheridan, eds, *Speak for Yourself: A Mass-Observation Anthology 1937–1945* (Oxford: Oxford University Press, 1985)

Cardigan, Earl of, *I Walked Alone* (London: Readers Union with Routledge & Kegan Paul, 1952)

Caskie, Donald, *The Tartan Pimpernel* (Oxford: Isis, 2008)

Chatwin, Bruce, *On the Black Hill* (London: Vintage, 2005)

Chepstow Society, *Wartime Memories: The Home Front in Chepstow 1939–1945* (Chepstow: Chepstow Society, 2000)

Churchill, Winston, *My Early Life: A Roving Commission* (London: Reprint Society, 1944)

——, *The Second World War. Volume IV: The Hinge of Fate* (London: Weidenfeld and Nicolson, 2015)

Cobban, Alfred, *A History of Modern France. Volume 3: 1871–1962* (Harmondsworth: Penguin, 1965)

Cohn, Bernard S., *India: The Social Anthropology of a Civilisation* (Englewood Cliffs, NJ: Prentice-Hall, 1971)

Collingham, E.M., *The Taste of War: World War Two and the Battle for Food* (London: Penguin, 2012)

Costello, John, *Love, Sex and War: Changing Values 1939–45* (London: Pan, 1986)

Crystal, David, *The Cambridge Encyclopaedia of the English Language*, 2nd edition (Cambridge: Cambridge University Press, 2003)

Cudlipp, Hugh, *Publish and be Damned: The Astonishing Story of the Daily Mirror* (London: Andrew Dakers, 1953)

Daechsel, Markus, 'Military Islamisation in Pakistan and the Spectre of Colonial Perceptions', *Contemporary South Asia*, 6.2 (1997), 141–60

David, Saul, *Churchill's Sacrifice of the Highland Division* (London: Brassey's, 1994)

Delaforce, Patrick, *Monty's Highlanders: 51st Highland Division in the Second World War* (Barnsley: Pen and Sword, 2006)

Dewan, A., 'The Famous Indian Mass Escape from Epinal', *United Service Institution of India Journal*, 75.320 (1945), 318–21

Doegen, Wilhelm, *Kriegsgefangene Völker* (Berlin: Verlag für Politik and Wirtschaft, 1921)

Douds, G.J., 'The Men Who Never Were: Indian POWs in the Second World War', *South Asia: Journal of South Asian Studies*, 27.2 (2004), 183–216

Erll, Astrid, 'The "Indian Mutiny" as a Shared Site of Memory: A Media Culture Perspective on Britain and India', in *Memory, History and Colonialism: Engaging with Pierre Nora in Colonial and Postcolonial Contexts*, German Historical Institute London, Bulletin, Supplement No. 1 (London, 2009), pp. 117–48

Ferguson, S.M., and H. Fitzgerald, *History of the Second World War: Studies in the Social Services* (London: HMSO, 1954)

Foot, M.R.D., and J.M. Langley, *MI9: Escape and Evasion 1939–1945* (London: Bodley Head, 1979)

Fowles, John, and Kenneth Allsop Memorial Trust, *Steep Holm: A Case History in the Study of Evolution* (Sherborne: Kenneth Allsop Memorial Trust, 1978)

Freeman, Roger A., *The Mighty Eighth: A History of the Units, Men and Machines of the US 8th Air Force* (London: Cassell, 2000)

Frémeaux, Jacques, 'Les Contingents Impériaux au Cœur de La Guerre', *Histoire, Economie et Societé*, 23.2 (2004), 215–33

Gandhi, M.K., *The Collected Works of Mahatma Gandhi*, Revised edition (New Delhi: Ministry of Information and Broadcasting, Publications Division, 2000), vol. 76

Gardner, W.H.R., *The Evacuation from Dunkirk* (London: Frank Cass, 2000)

Gatrad, Abdul Rashid, 'Muslim Customs Surrounding Death, Bereavement, Postmortem Examinations, and Organ Transplants', *British Medical Journal*, 309.6953 (1994), 521–23

German Capital Ships and Raiders in World War II. Volume 1: From Graf Spee to Bismarck, 1939–1941 (London: Frank Cass, 2002)

Ghālib, Mirza Asadullah Khan, *Whispers of the Angel (Nawa-E Sarosh): Selections from 14 English Translations of Ghalib* (Delhi: Ghalib Academy, 1969)

Gillies, Midge, *The Barbed-Wire University: The Real Lives of Allied Prisoners of War in the Second World War* (London: Aurum, 2011)

Gilpin, William, *Observations on the River Wye 1782* (Oxford: Woodstock, 1991)

Guderian, Heinz, *Panzer Leader* (Aylesbury: Futura, 1974)

Günther, Lothar, *Die Indische Legion Und Das Dritte Reich: Das Zentrale Kriegsgefangenenlager Der Inder in Annaburg Und Der Kampf Um Indiens Unabhängigkeit* (Berlin: Verlag am Park, 2013)

——, *Von Indien Nach Annaburg: Indische Legion Und Kriegsgefangene in Deutschland* (Berlin: Verlag am Park, 2003)

Halbwachs, Maurice, and Lewis A. Coser, *On Collective Memory: The Heritage of Sociology* (Chicago and London: University of Chicago Press, 1992)

Hansard House of Commons Debate, 18 June 1940, vol. 362, cols 51–64

Hansard House of Commons Debate, 23 September 1943, vol. 392, cols 443–4W

Harman, Nicholas, *Dunkirk: The Necessary Myth* (London: Hodder & Stoughton, 1980)

Hartog, Rudolf, *The Sign of the Tiger* (Delhi: Rupa, 2001)

Hauner, Milan, *India in Axis Strategy* (London: German Historical Institute London, 1981)

Hitchcock, Laurence William, 'In German Hands', *RIASC Journal*, 14 (1946), 8–17

Institute of the Royal Army Service Corps, *The Story of the RASC 1939–1945* (London: G. Bell and Sons, 1955)

Ivanhoe, Philip J., *The Daodejing of Laozi* (Cambridge, MA: Hackett, 2002)

Jackson, Ashley, *The British Empire and the Second World War* (London: Bloomsbury, 2006)

Jaffrey, Madhur, *Climbing the Mango Trees* (London: Random House, 2005)

Johnston, Hamish, 'A Corner of Pakistan in Scotland', *Highland Family History Society* (May 2012), 1–30

Kamtekar, Indivar, 'The Shiver of 1942', in *War and Society in Colonial India*, ed. by Kaushik Roy (Oxford: Oxford University Press, 2006), pp. 81–102

Kapur, P.K.D., *Footprints and Milestones* (New Delhi: General Supply and Transport Army Headquarters, 1990)

Karnad, Raghu, *Farthest Field: An Indian Story of the Second World War* (Noida, Uttar Pradesh: William Collins, 2015)

Keay, John, *India: A History* (London: Harper Perennial, 2000)

Keay, John, and Julia Keay, *Collins Encyclopaedia of Scotland* (London: Harper Collins, 1994)

Kempton, Chris, *Force K6 The Indian Contingent: RIASC Mule companies in France and UK 1939–1944* (London: Kempton, 2019)

Khan, Mohammed Akbar, *History of the Army Service Corps Volume III: Royal Indian Army Service Corps* (Karachi: Islamic Military Science Association, 1971)

Khan, Mohammed Ayub, *Friends Not Masters: A Political Autobiography* (London: Oxford University Press, 1967)

Khan, Shaukat Hyat, *The Nation That Lost its Soul: Memoirs of a Freedom Fighter* (Lahore: Jang, 1999)

Khan, Yasmin, *The Raj at War: A People's History of India's Second World War* (London: Bodley Head, 2015)

Khusrau, Amir, *Amir Khusrau: The Man in Riddles*, ed. by Ankit Chadha (Gurgaon: Penguin, 2016)

Kipling, Rudyard, *Barrack-Room Ballads: And Other Verses* (London: Methuen, 1892)

Kirkham, Pat, and David Thoms, eds, *War Culture: Social Change and Changing Experience in World War Two* (London: Lawrence & Wishart, 1995)

Lahiri, Shompa, 'Divided Loyalties', *History Today*, 57.5 (2007), 55–57

Latif, Abdul, *History of the Army Services Corps. Volume II* (Rawalpindi: Pap-Board Printers, 1986)

Le Maner, Yves, 'L'invasion et les Combats de Mai–Juin 1940 dans le Nord de la France', *MEMOR (Mémoire de l'Occupation et de la Resistance en Zone Interdite) Bulletin d'Information*, 19–20 (1994), 13–30

Levine, Joshua, *Forgotten Voices of Dunkirk* (London: Ebury Press, 2010)

Liddell Hart, Basil, *A History of the Second World War* (Basingstoke: Pan Macmillan, 1970)

Longworth, Philip, *The Unending Vigil: The History of the Commonwealth War Graves Commission*, Revised and updated edition (Barnsley: Leo Cooper, 2003)

Macdonald, Finlay J., *Crotal and White* (London: Sphere, 1991)

MacDonogh, Giles, *A Good German: Adam von Trott Zu Solz*, Revised edition (London: Quartet, 1994)

MacMunn, George, *The Martial Races of India* (London: Sampson Low, Marston, 1932)

Malins, Philip, 'The First to Take the Field', *Army Service Corps Journal* (1995)

——, 'The Royal Indian Army Service Corps in the Second World War', *Royal Corps of Transport Journal*, 105 (1980), 7–10

Malins, Philip, Brian Nicholls, and Charles MacFetridge, 'The Indian Army Animal Transport Mule', in *The Military Mule in the British Army and Indian Army: An Anthology* (Solihull: B. Nicholls, 2000) 1–76

Marshall, H.E., *Our Island Story* (London: Nelson, 1905)

Masefield, John, *The Nine Days Wonder* (Kingswood: Windmill Press, 1941)

Mason, Philip, *A Matter of Honour: An Account of the Indian Army, its Officers and Men* (London: Jonathan Cape, 1974)

Masters, John, *Bugles and a Tiger* (London: Michael Joseph, 1956)

Maurois, André, *The Battle of France* (London: Bodley Head, 1940)

——, *Call No Man Happy* (London: Jonathan Cape, 1950)

——, *Les Silences du Colonel Bramble* (Paris: Bernard Gresset, 1921)

Mazumder, Rajit K., *The Indian Army and the Making of Punjab* (Delhi: Orient Blackswan, 2003)

Mirza, Yaqub, *An Autumn Leaf* (Nottingham: Nottinghamshire County Council, 1994)

Mitchell, Reid, 'The GI in Europe and the American Military Tradition', in *Time to Kill: The Soldier's Experience of War in the West*, ed. by Paul Addison and Angus Calder (London: Pimlico, 1997)

Moharir, V.J., *History of the Army Service Corps (1939–1946)* (New Delhi: Sterling, 1979)

Mookerjee, Girija, *Europe at War* (Meerut: Meenakshi Prakashan, 1968)

Morton-Jack, George, *The Indian Empire at War: From Jihad to Victory, the Untold Story of the Indian Army in the First World War* (London: Little, Brown, 2018)

Motadel, David, *Islam and Nazi Germany's War* (Cambridge, MA: Belknap Press of Harvard University Press, 2014)

Netton, Ian Richard, ed., *Encyclopedia of Islamic Civilisation and Religion* (London, New York: Routledge, 2008)

Nichol, John, and Tony Rennell, *Home Run: Escape from Nazi Europe* (London: Viking, 2007)

——, *The Last Escape: The Untold Story of Allied Prisoners of War in Germany 1944–45* (London: Penguin, 2003)

Noakes, Lucy, and Juliette Pattinson, eds, *British Cultural Memory and the Second World War* (London: Bloomsbury Academic, 2014)

Nora, Pierre, *Realms of Memory* (New York: Columbia University Press, 1996)

Omissi, David E., *The Sepoy and the Raj: The Indian Army, 1860–1940* (Basingstoke: Macmillan, 1998)

Overy, Richard, *The Battle of Britain* (London: Penguin, 2000)

Paris, Michael, *Warrior Nation: Images of War in British Popular Culture 1850–2000* (London: Reaktion, 2000)

Perret, Jules, and Benjamin Valloton, *Ceux d'Etobon*, trans. by Katherine Douglass (Montbeliard: Impr. de Metthez frères, 1949)

Pillai, E.K.K., *Medical Services: The Campaigns in the Western Theatre, Official History of the Indian Armed Forces in the Second World War 1939–45* (Delhi: Combined Inter-Services Historical Section, India and Pakistan, 1958)

Prendergast, John, *Prender's Progress: A Soldier in India, 1931–1947* (London: Cassell, 1979)

Purcell, Hugh, 'Subhas Chandra Bose: The Afterlife of India's Fascist Leader', *History Today*, 60.11 (2010), 45

The Qur'an, trans. by Alan Jones (Exeter: Gibb Memorial Trust, 2007)

Raghavan, Srinath, *India's War: The Making of Modern South Asia, 1939–1945* (London: Penguin, 2016)

Rajput, A.B., *Social Customs and Practices in Pakistan* (Islamabad: R.C.D. Publications, 1977)

Renard, Michel, 'Les Débuts de la Présence Musulmane en France et Son Encadrement', in *Histoire de l'Islam et des Musulmans en France du Moyen Âge à Nos Jours*, ed. by Mohammed Arkoun (Paris: Albin Michel, 2006), pp. 712–40

Rendell, Stan, and Joan Rendell, *Steep Holm's Pioneers* (Self-published, 2003)

Rhodes-Wood, E.H., *A War History of the Royal Pioneer Corps, 1939–1945* (Aldershot: Gale and Polden, 1960)

RIASC Training Vol. III: Transport (Delhi: Government of India, 1938)

Ricoeur, Paul, *Memory, History, Forgetting* (London: University of Chicago Press, 2004)

Rose, Sonya, *Which People's War? National Identity and Citizenship in Britain 1939–1945* (Oxford: Oxford University Press, 2003)

Roskill, S.W., *The Navy at War* (London: Collins, 1960)

Roy, Kaushik, 'Military Loyalty in the Colonial Context: A Case Study of the Indian Army during World War II', *Journal of Military History*, 73.2 (2009), 497–529

Saini, Balwant Singh, *The Social and Economic History of the Punjab 1901–1939: (Including Haryana and Himachal Pradesh)* (Delhi: Ess Ess Publications, 1975)

Salamat, Purwez, *The Woking Shahjahan Mosque* (Chichester: Phillimore, 2008)

Samuel, Raphael, *Theatres of Memory* (London: Verso, 1994)

Scheck, Raffael, *Hitler's African Victims: The German Army Massacres of Black French Soldiers in 1940* (Cambridge: Cambridge University Press, 2008)

Sebag-Montefiore, Hugh, *Dunkirk: Fight to the Last Man* (London: Penguin, 2007)

Shah, Bullhe, *Sufi Lyrics*, ed. by Christopher Shackle (London: Harvard University Press, 2015)

Shah, Waris, *The Adventures of Hir and Ranjha* (Karachi: Lion Art Press, 1966)

Shakespeare, William, *The New Oxford Shakespeare: The Complete Works* (Oxford: Oxford University Press, 2017)

Sharma, Gautam, *Nationalisation of the Indian Army, 1885–1947* (India: Allied, 1996)

Sharma, Vishnu, *Panchatantra* (Bombay: Chandiramani, 1974)

Sharp, Robin, *The Life of an ECO in India* (Edinburgh: Pentland Press, 1994)

Shepherd, Claude, *War Record of the Indian Comforts Fund* (London: Indian High Commission, 1946)

Shepperd, Alan, *Sandhurst: The Royal Military Academy* (London: Country Life, 1980)

Shirer, William L., *Berlin Diary 1934–1941: The Rise of the Third Reich* (London: Sunburst Books, 1997)

Shukla, Nikesh, ed., *The Good Immigrant* (London: Unbound, 2017)

Sidhwa, Bapsi, *Ice-Candy-Man* (Delhi: Penguin, 1988)

Singh, Gajendra, *The Testimonies of Indian Soldiers and the Two World Wars: Between Self and Sepoy* (London: Bloomsbury, 2014)

Smith, Alison, David Blayney Brown and Carol Jacobi, eds, *Artist and Empire: Facing Britain's Imperial Past* (London: Tate, 2015)

Smith, Graham, *When Jim Crow Met John Bull: Black American Soldiers in World War II Britain* (London: Tauris, 1987)

Spencer, William Robert, *Poems by the Late Hon. William R. Spencer* (London: James Cochrane, 1835)

Stadtler, Florian, 'Britain's Forgotten Volunteers', in *South Asians and the Shaping of Britain, 1870–1950: A Sourcebook*, ed. by Ruvani Ranasinha (Manchester: Manchester University Press, 2013), pp. 81–134

Summerfield, Penny, 'Dunkirk and the Popular Memory of Britain at War', *Journal of Contemporary History*, 45.4 (2010), 788–811

Sumner, Ian, *The Indian Army 1914–47* (Oxford: Osprey, 2001)

Tan, Tai Yong, *The Garrison State: The Military, Government and Society in Colonial Punjab, 1849–1947* (New Delhi: Sage, 2005)

Thomas, Dylan, *Under Milk Wood* (Cheltenham: Nelson Thornes, 2010)

Van Creveld, Martin, *Supplying War: Logistics from Wallenstein to Patton*, 2nd edition (Cambridge: Cambridge University Press, 2004)

Virk, D.S., *Indian Army Post Offices in the Second World War* (New Delhi: Army Postal Service Association, 1982)

Visram, Rozina, *Asians in Britain: 400 Years of History* (London: Pluto, 2002)

Voigt, Johannes H., *India in the Second World War* (New Jersey: Humanities Press International, 1988)

Wade, Shamus O.D., 'But Where Did the Mules Come from?', *Durbar*, 17.4 (2000), 122–30

Walters, Guy, *Berlin Games: How Hitler Stole the Olympic Dream* (London: John Murray, 2006)

Weale, Adrian, *Renegades: Hitler's Englishmen*, Revised edition (London: Pimlico, 2002)

Webster, Wendy, *Mixing It: Diversity in World War Two Britain* (Oxford: Oxford University Press, 2018)

Who Was Who (London: A&C Black, 1980)

Zaidi, Z.H., *Jinnah Papers*, First Series (Islamabad: National Archives of Pakistan, 1994)

Zec, Donald, *Don't Lose it Again! The Life and Wartime Cartoons of Philip Zec* (London: Political Cartoon Society, 2005)

Websites

Assmann, Aleida, 'Forms of Forgetting' (unpublished lecture, Royal Dutch Academy of Sciences, 2014) <http://castrumperegrini.org/2014/10/30/forms-of-forgetting/>

Berry, E.W.B., 'Dunkirk – Carrier Platoon, 8th Battalion Worcestershire Regiment' <http://www.worcestershireregiment.com/wr.php?main=inc/h_dunkirk_8thBn_carrierPl>

Bird, aka Fougasse, Kenneth, 'So Our Poor Old Empire is Alone in the World', 1940, Punch online <https://punch.photoshelter.com/image/I00004lS91fhaQno>

Bloor, Giovanna, 'Mule Drivers from Rawalpindi in Llanfrothen and Nantmor', Vale of Ffestiniog, 2012 <http://voff-snowdonia.blogspot.co.uk/2012/04/mule-drivers-from-rawalpindi-in.html>

Bowman, Ghee, 'What Christopher Nolan Left Out: Dunkirk's Indian Soldiers', Imperial and Global Forum, 2018 <https://imperialglobalexeter.com/2018/07/30/what-christopher-nolan-left-out-dunkirks-indian-soldiers/>

Cameron, Dolly, 'Display at Aultbea Museum' https://racmp.co.uk/<http://www.russianarcticconvoymuseum.org/>

Commonwealth War Graves Commission <https://www.cwgc.org/>

'Convention (III) Relative to the Treatment of Prisoners of War. Geneva, 12 August 1949', International Committee of the Red Cross <https://ihl-databases.icrc.org/applic/ihl/ihl.nsf/INTRO/375>

Gardiner, Juliet, *Presenting the Past – How the Media Changes History*, BBC, 2013 <http://www.bbc.co.uk/programmes/b01mn4v4>

Gupta, Diya, 'Christopher Nolan's Dunkirk and the Cultural Memory of a Global War', *News 18*, 21 August 2017 <https://www.news18.com/news/movies/christopher-nolans-dunkirk-and-the-cultural-memory-of-a-global-war-1492435.html>

Kaufmann, Miranda, 'Presenting the Black Past – How History Must Change the Media', 14 November 2013 <http://www.mirandakaufmann.com/3/post/2013/11/presenting-the-black-past-how-history-must-change-the-media.html>

Khan, Yasmin, 'Dunkirk, the War and the Amnesia of the Empire', *New York Times*, 2 August 2017 <https://www.nytimes.com/2017/08/02/opinion/dunkirk-indians-world-war.html>

Low, David, 'Very Well, Alone!', cartoon, British Cartoon Archive, LSE2791 <https://archive.cartoons.ac.uk/record.aspx?src=CalmView.Catalog&id=LSE2791>

Nolan, Christopher, 'Spitfires, Flotillas of Boats, Rough Seas and 1,000 Extras: Christopher Nolan on the Making of Dunkirk, his Most Challenging Film to Date', *Daily Telegraph*, 8 July 2017 <http://www.telegraph.co.uk/films/2017/07/08/spitfires-flotillas-boats-rough-seas-1000-extras-christopher/>

Ross, Calum, 'New Year Honours: Recognition for 96-Year-Old Highland Woman who Tended the Graves of Indian Servicemen', *Press and Journal*, 28 December 2019 <https://www.pressandjournal.co.uk/fp/news/highlands/1921492/new-year-honours-recognition-for-96-year-old-highland-woman-who-tended-the-graves-of-indian-servicemen/>

Sarna, Jit Singh, 'Indian Army History Thread', *Bharat Rakshak*, 2007 <https://forums.bharat-rakshak.com/viewtopic.php?f=3&t=2623&start=40>

Station, Elizabeth, 'Scholar from Afar', *University of Chicago Magazine*, 2013 <https://mag.uchicago.edu/scholarfromafar>

'The Aberdeen Mittwoch Blitz – Wednesday 21st April 1943', The Doric Columns <http://www.mcjazz.f2s.com/Blitzkreig.htm>

Acknowledgements

This book grew from my PhD at Exeter University, so I should first thank the South, West and Wales Doctoral Training Partnership who funded me. My supervisors Gajendra Singh and Padma Anagol gave first-class guidance and advice. Nicola Thomas has been a great encourager. My fellow PhD students have been wonderful: especial mention to Sonia Wigh, Cristina Corti for the maps and Sophy Antrobus for reading my drafts and being a chum. The University Pakistani Society were great for networking and the Digital Humanities Lab helped with digitisation of photos. This book was written on the top floor of the University Library, and all the library staff deserve medals.

I have built this story on the work of archivists and librarians in five countries, who provided access to my bread and butter (original documents) and have been friendly, helpful and supportive. Thanks to all of them, with a special mention to Jo Meacock at the Kelvingrove Museum in Glasgow.

The Indian Military History Society, through its journal *Durbar*, was a great source of contacts, and Chris Kempton provided useful input. The 'Indian Armies of WW2' Facebook group has answered many questions.

Around the UK I have listened to many stories about the boys of K6. Paritosh Shapland's story is in many ways at the centre of this book, and he has been very generous with his time and his resources. Yaqub Mirza's family gave me a great lift right at the end. Betty Cresswell told me of her family's relationship with Uncle Gian, and kindly shared her photo album with me. The late Giovanna Bloor shared everything she knew. I will cherish the memory of a day spent in her cottage under the Cnicht mountain. Paul Watkins, Mark Ashdown, Geoff Sykes and Trilby Shaw helped me along the way. Hamish Johnston drove me around the Highlands and was a great source of information. Colin Hexley was very generous with material about his father, and Shirley Sutherland introduced me to him and others in Golspie. John Barnes and Peter Wilde in Dornoch, Joan Leed, Donny MacDonald and Marlyn Price in Lairg, Marion Smith, Catriona Spence, David & Sheena Macdougall in Kinlochleven, Stewart Mackenzie, George Milne and Donald Matheson in Loch Ewe were all very helpful and welcoming. In Glasgow, Nadeem Bhatti introduced me to the Colourful Heritage project and its staff Saqib Razzaq, Shazia Durrani and Omar Shaikh. In Woking, Mohammad Zubair gave me one of the best interviews ever, Zafar Iqbal aided my networking, the mosque was very welcoming and Rabyah Khan helped get me started. Katherine Douglass introduced me to the lovely people and the extraordinary story of Etobon.

I stand on the shoulders of giants. Rozina Visram is one such – anyone writing on the South Asian presence in Britain is in her debt. I shared beers and laughs with Lloyd Price, and treasure the friendship we developed in India. Many thanks to Yasmin Khan for writing the foreword.

I am a white British man writing a story about South Asians, which throws open many possibilities of cultural misunderstandings and errors. I am grateful to Sandhya Dave, Nazima Khan and colleagues at the Global Centre in Exeter for giving me confidence and helping me learn to step around a thorny area.

My time in Pakistan would have been fruitless without Major General Syed Ali Hamid. He offered warmth, hospitality and boundless contacts. I am forever in his debt. My friend Omer Salim Khan (Omer Tarin) was supremely hospitable and generous during my visit to Abbottabad, and even more so afterwards, commenting on the draft manuscript. Jawad Sawarna drove me round Karachi and introduced me to the wide and warm family of General Akbar, and Imran and his daughter Mahin were particularly generous with time and photos. Zeenut Ziad gave me two interviews, when her parrot would let her. Khizar Jawad was incredibly helpful in Lahore. Brigadier Asim Iqbal of the Army Service Corps gave a late rush of help. Above all, Jenny, Marcel and Luqman ensured I had a safe secure base in Islamabad, Sabur was a wonderful fixer who seemed to know everyone in the Potohari villages, Waheed drove us round those villages and Waqar Seyal was a fantastic translator and interpreter. In India, Shachi and Naveen made me welcome and helped me with my first steps in Hindi/Urdu and Rana Chhina at the United Services Institute in Delhi was extremely helpful.

For permission to use quotes, thanks to Hackett Publishing Company for the quotation from Philip Ivanhoe's translation of *Daodejing of Laozi*, and to HarperCollins India for the two quotations from Raghu Karnad's *Farthest Field*.

I appreciate that I haven't included all the great stories that I heard during my research. If I've missed yours out, apologies. If I haven't heard it yet, please get in touch. All errors in memory or interpretation are entirely mine.

Three people helped and inspired this writing process. My father Bill Bowman showed the way. Clare Grist Taylor believed in me and this story and gave many practical tips. My editor at The History Press, Simon Wright, was always encouraging, constructive but firm.

Three other people made it possible. My daughters Alex and Hannah helped enter hundreds of names in the database, encouraged me and (in Hannah's case) did translations from French. Above all, my thanks and love go to my wife Rebecca. She has supported me and fed me all the way through. A wiser partner would be impossible to find.

Index